THE BATTLE OF FRANCE, 1940

THE BATTLE OF
FRANCE, 1940

10 May – 22 June

PHILIP WARNER

CASSELL&CO

Cassell Military Paperbacks

Cassell & Co
Wellington House, 125 Strand
London WC2R 0BB

British Library Cataloguing-in-Publication Data
A catalogue record for this book is available from the British Library

ISBN 0 304 35644 1

Printed and bound in Great Britain by
Cox & Wyman, Reading, Berks

Contents

Contents

Acknowledgements

Many individuals and establishments have given me generous help in producing this book. The staff of the library at the Royal Military Academy, Sandhurst, have been exceptionally painstaking in tracing sources of information. The Imperial War Museum, as always, has been a tower of strength and provided invaluable advice and documents. So many other libraries and museums all over the country have been helpful that it is impossible to list them all here. Survivors of the battle, British, French and German, have answered my questions fully and patiently. My special thanks go to Lieutenant Colonel Robin Painter, who took enormous trouble to produce, exactly as I wanted them, the detailed sketches from which the maps were drawn.

I am grateful to the following for permission to quote from works published by them:

Batsford Ltd: Anon, *Infantry Officer*
Chatto and Windus Ltd: Captain Sir Basil Bartlett, *My First War*
Harrap Ltd: H. Habe, *A Thousand Shall Fall*
Hodder and Stoughton Ltd: J. Colville, *The Fringes of Power*
Hutchinson & Co. Ltd: C. Gardner, *A.A.S.F.*
Michael Joseph Ltd: H. Guderian, *Panzer Leader*
Methuen Ltd: Anon, *Diary of a Staff Officer*.

Every attempt has been made to trace authors or artists who may own copyrights of any of the works quoted or illustrations used. If any copyright has been inadvertently overlooked, will the owner please contact the author?

Chronology

The following chronology may give the impression that the battle of France consisted of a logical sequence of events. In fact it was a period when confusion – the well-known 'fog of war' – was prevalent at all levels. None of the participants had a clear and accurate idea of what was happening in other areas. This applied both to the Germans and to the Allies, a point brought out in the text.

1939

1 September   Germany invades Poland.

2 September   Poland appeals to Britain and France to begin military action against Germany.
British ultimatum to Germany issued: Germany does not reply.

3 September   Britain and France declare war on Germany.
British Expeditionary Force ordered to France, to be under French command.

6 October   End of Polish resistance to German invasion.

1940

10 January   A German aircraft, carrying documents and maps for Germany's planned attack on Netherlands and

France, makes forced landing in Belgium. Germany therefore changes plans for making main thrust through Belgium to one through Sedan area.

9 April Germany invades Denmark and Norway. Denmark, which has no armed forces, capitulates. Norway tries to fight back.

15 April British forces land in Norway.

10 May Germans invade Low Countries. British advance into hitherto neutral Belgium.

11 May Churchill forms National Government in Britain.
Britain bombs Germany.
Fortress of Eben Emael in Belgium captured by Germans in glider attack.

12 May Guderian's 19th Panzer Corps reaches River Meuse.

13 May Germans cross Meuse by Sedan.

14 May Rotterdam falls.
Surrender of Dutch Army.
RAF sustains heavy losses counter-attacking Germans in Sedan bridgehead.

16 May British begin retreating in Belgium to avoid being cut off and trapped by Panzers coming across from Sedan.
Antwerp falls.
Germans penetrate north-west extension of Maginot Line.

17 May Von Kleist orders Guderian to halt his tanks and consolidate bridgehead around Meuse. After argument with von Kleist Guderian allowed to continue his advance for 24 hours. Guderian obtains permission from German GHQ for fuller reconnaissance and advances 55 miles. Panzers cross River Oise but Hitler very worried about vulnerability of German southern flank, exposed to main French Army; he believes French to be much stronger and better led than they are.

18 May	Germans reach St Quentin.
	Reynaud becomes French Minister of National Defence.
19 May	Gamelin, Allied C-in-C, replaced by Weygand. French remain in superior command of Allied troops, including British. However Gort, British C-in-C, reports to British Cabinet that a retreat to Dunkirk may be inevitable.
20 May	Amiens falls. Germans reach Abbeville.
21 May	British tanks counter-attack at Arras.
22 May	Germans begin attack on Boulogne.
24 May	Von Rundstedt (with Hitler's agreement) halts Panzer columns outside Dunkirk, which is to be left to Luftwaffe. However this does not affect operations against Calais and Boulogne.
25 May	Boulogne falls.
26 May	Hitler and von Rundstedt allow Panzers to advance again.
27 May	Calais falls.
	Evacuation from Dunkirk begins.
28 May	Belgium capitulates.
	Dunkirk evacuation continues.
29 May	Lille, Ostend and Ypres fall.
	Dunkirk evacuation continues.
30 May	Dunkirk evacuation continues.
31 May	Dunkirk evacuation continues.
1 June	Dunkirk evacuation continues.
2 June	Dunkirk evacuation continues.
3 June	Dunkirk evacuation continues.
4 June	End of Dunkirk evacuation.
5 June	Strong French resistance to Germans south of Péronne and Amiens.
8 June	British troops leave Norway.

9 June	51st Highland Division begins its advance towards Le Havre.
10 June	Mussolini declares war on Allies. Germans cross River Seine. 51st Highland Division instructed to divert from Le Havre route and proceed to St-Valéry-en-Caux.
12 June	Bad weather prevents ships evacuating 51st Highland Division from St-Valéry. Still under French command, they are ordered to surrender and do so as there is no hope of evacuation and French have already surrendered. Paris declared an open (undefended) city. Lt Gen. Alan Brooke takes command of a small force and given mission of establishing a second BEF in Cherbourg area. Germans occupy Le Havre. Brooke's force begins its withdrawal.
14 June	Paris surrenders.
15 June	Reynaud resigns and is replaced by Pétain. Pétain asks Germans for an armistice.
22 June	France accepts German surrender terms.
25 June	Hostilities in France end.
1 July	Germans occupy Channel Islands.
3 July	British destroy French naval squadron at Mers-el-Kebir, Algeria, to prevent it being captured by Germans.

At 5.30 a.m. on 10 May 1940 German soldiers invaded Holland, Belgium and Luxembourg. On 14 May they crossed the River Meuse and drove into the heart of France. On 20 May they reached the Channel and Abbeville. The following day British forces attempted a counter-attack at Arras, but it failed and the British Expeditionary Force fell back to Dunkirk. On 24 May von Rundstedt halted the German Panzer forces outside Dunkirk, for reasons which have been controversial ever since. On 25 May Boulogne fell and on the 27th Calais followed. Next day Belgium surrendered. On 29 May Lille, Ostend and Ypres were over-run by the Germans. Between 27 May and 4 June, 338,000 men were evacuated from Dunkirk.

On 12 June British forces surrendered at St Valéry-en-Caux. On 14 June Paris fell, and on 22 June France itself capitulated.

At this time nobody, not even the Germans, could understand how or why all this could have happened. How and why is the theme of this book.

Part I

The
Preliminaries

1 The Seeds of Destruction

L IKE MANY OTHER unexpected and disturbing events, the conquest of France by the Germans in 1940 seemed at first to be a major disaster. But this was not a new experience for the French, and there were precedents to suggest that, although this might well be a lost battle, it was not necessarily a lost war. In 1870–1 France had been overwhelmed by German armies and made to pay huge reparations to its conquerors. Within a few years, however, the French had paid off the debt and become so strong that the Germans were contemplating another invasion in order to forestall a revenge attack. In 1914 the Kaiser's armies had invaded France again, this time using a master plan devised by a deceased general, Count von Schlieffen. The Schlieffen Plan was both ruthless and rigid. By violating Belgian neutrality it brought Britain into the war, but instead of producing victory within weeks it resulted in four years of gruelling trench warfare, culminating in defeat. Then in 1918 the German armies had made an unexpected breakthrough and this time reached a point only fourteen miles from Paris before being turned back. Nevertheless by the end of the year Germany had been totally defeated.

These precedents to the war of 1939–45 helped to create the false impression that Germany had learnt its lesson and, whatever the blusters of Hitler, would not risk another conflict with the Allied armies and their great resources. This opinion was held, not merely by the French and British, but also by many influential Germans including a number of generals. It was, however, an opinion based

3

upon the tactics of the previous war, and was not shared by the young progressives.

When the battle of France ended in June 1940, the belief that Germany would never risk another war with the Allies had been replaced by the view that, like the previous war, this would now settle down to a grinding battle in which the superior resources of the Allies would prove decisive. For the moment Britain was in some danger, with the Germans on the doorstep, but it had an excellent air force, the best navy in the world, and sources of high-quality troops in the British Commonwealth and Empire. The war was seen primarily as a European conflict, although the arrival of the Italians at the end of the battle of France meant that for a while there would be some military activity in North and East Africa while Mussolini's troops were being put to flight.

Although Churchill emphasized that Britain was now in great peril, the public was slow to realize the full extent of the dangers it faced; the air raids would bring that lesson later. The evacuation at Dunkirk which occurred after a series of crushing defeats was somehow transformed in the public mind into a form of victory, instead of one of the most humiliating events in the nation's history. In the course of the next two years Britain would suffer more defeats, in Greece, in Crete and in the Western Desert, before the tide began to turn. Not until mid-1942 did illusion give way to realism.

By that time experience had clarified the minds of the belligerents. The French had learnt that the war which they thought had ended in 1940 was only just getting into its stride and France would once again be a major battlefield; the Russians had accepted the fact that soldiers fight for their homelands more strenuously than they do for political ideology, and had revived patriotic traditions; the British had come to terms with the fact that the tactics and weapons of the First World War were of no value in the Second, and the Germans had realized that their great victory in France had misled them into believing that the world lay at their feet. Instead their Panzers had been checked by Russian distances, Russian guns, Russian tanks, and Russian soldiers, and the expected easy conquest would never materialize. German parachutists, of whom so much had been expected, had taken such heavy losses in the battle for Crete that they would never be used in that role again. Those easy victories in France were now seen to have been a delusion: the battle of France had not been a battle which the Germans had won but a victory which the Allies had presented to them. But the end of illusions in 1942 did not mean the end of the repercussions of the German victory in France in 1940. They are still with us today.

In the realistic climate of the 1990s the illusions which existed prior to the Second World War and for the first three years of fighting may seem difficult to comprehend, but in order to understand the collapse of France in 1940 and the German miscalculations which followed it it is necessary to see how those illusions came into existence and what they were.

As mentioned above, between 1914 and 1918 the Germans had twice been close to overwhelming France, but had eventually failed. When they did so in 1940 the speed and expertise of the campaign made the German Army seem invincible, but in fact the success of the German war machine in France proved to be its own undoing; it gave the impression that they had produced an army which no other country would ever be able to match. The chief victims of this delusion were the Germans themselves: the rapid victory in France convinced the doubters in the Reich that Hitler was right, that he was the man to make Germany the greatest power on earth, and that he was invincible.

Although the Nazi party had been extending and strengthening its grip on Germany for over ten years (before 1929 it had represented no serious threat), there were still many Germans in early 1940 who had misgivings about the sayings and deeds of the bizarre former Austrian corporal, Hitler, who had created a party machine and, through it, risen to the position of supreme ruler of Germany. Many of them were disturbed by the marching, the militarism, the gangster-like tactics in foreign policy, and the unpleasant flamboyance of his close supporters Goebbels, Goering, Himmler and Hess. When Hitler's policies, and his financial wizard, Schacht, had stabilized the German economy, created jobs and organized young people to take part in healthy outdoor activities, there had been approval and relief. But when the persecution of Jews was initiated and the secret police began taking away opponents of Nazism, most of whom were never heard of again, an atmosphere of alarm and impending disaster was discernible.

Other Germans were, however, convinced of their leader's miraculous powers. Abroad, Hitler's record was magnificent. Austria had been forcibly amalgamated with Germany; Czechoslovakia had been dismembered and swallowed; and Poland had been conquered in a swift military operation that no one in the world had been able to prevent, even though the Western democracies, on whom Hitler was always pouring scorn, protested loudly in impotent wrath. Cleverer still had been the astonishing achievement of the Nazi-Soviet pact, by which Hitler had made an agreement with his most dangerous and implacable enemy that they should work together rather than in opposition. Germany needed the grain and oil resources of Russia, and in return was prepared to supply the Russians with arms. The idea that Germany would be arming the country which, until recently, had been her arch-enemy would be ludicrous if it were not actually happening. But, no doubt, Hitler knew what he was doing. The Soviet Army was known to be weak before Stalin's massive purge of all its best officers. Years would need to pass before the Soviet Army could recover, and by that time – well, whatever happened then would long before have been anticipated by Hitler.

Then, into this growing climate of over-confidence came the devastating victories of the German armies in Norway, Denmark, Belgium, Holland and France. England, which in 1914 had sent an expeditionary force that had frustrated German plans for a swift conquest of France by the Schlieffen Plan, had quickly been sent packing this time. It had been lucky to evacuate over 338,000 men from Dunkirk – leaving behind all their arms, of course – and would soon, no doubt, be suing for whatever peace terms Hitler would generously allow.

Even those Germans whose approval of Hitler's past achievements had been muted now began to feel that he was one of the greatest generals the world had ever seen – perhaps the greatest, thought some, a man whose achievements would surpass those of Julius Caesar, Genghiz Khan, Attila and Napoleon. Fanatical Nazis, of course, had no doubts at all: Hitler had divine qualities; he would make the Germans the long-awaited Master Race; he would purify the nation and give it nobility. Finally, the Führer would not make mistakes. They could trust him.

Few of Hitler's ardent admirers knew much history; they were not interested in other people's dreary chronicles, which seemed irrelevant in the new Golden Age that the Führer was creating. Their gods were Nordic heroes; the blinkered Nazi supporters had not heard of Nemesis, the mythical Greek deity who represented the disapproval of the gods at human presumption and the subsequent disaster waiting for the over-confident, or of *hubris*, the arrogance that leads to such a downfall.

The victory in France was not in fact the flawless achievement which most Germans imagined it must have been; it was assisted by considerable luck on their side and massive ineptitude on the part of the Allies. But the perceived ease with which the battle was won created *hubris* in Hitler's Reich, which paved the way for Germany's nemesis long after the guns had ceased firing in 1940. It gave Hitler the confidence to over-rule his generals and to launch his armies into the Soviet Union the following year without the necessary knowledge or equipment. It also set off alarm bells in various other countries. Stalin now realized that Russia would become an early victim of Nazi aggression, and made certain preparations (though not enough of them). It convinced many Americans that, despite their policy to remain neutral, they themselves might eventually be drawn in. It impressed the Japanese, but, knowing that Hitler regarded all Asians as inferior people, eventually to be forced to serve Germany, they made cautious overtures to Russia. Russia, surprised and delighted at this new turn of events, withdrew experienced divisions from the Far East, where they had been waiting for an attack from Japan, and deployed them in Western Russia against the German invaders when they came. And finally the fall of France steeled the resolution of the British and their Commonwealth comrades in Canada, Australia, New Zealand and South Africa to oppose this monstrous, ranting savage with his preposterous, evil doctrine, and once more liberate Europe.

2 Decade of Illusion

T HE GERMAN ARMY had an enormous advantage over the Allies in that it knew exactly what it was required to do, even though it might have preferred to wait a little longer before setting out on its tasks. Britain and France had declared war on 3 September 1939 because Germany had committed an act of naked aggression against Poland. The German armed forces were prepared for conflict and began it at a time when the French Army hoped that it would never have to fight at all, and the British Army was struggling to digest a conscript intake for which no proper facilities were available. The Royal Air Force was still desperately trying to get the maximum number of squadrons combat-ready; while the Royal Navy was deploying its limited resources and wondering if the ship-yards could by some miracle complete the building of craft of various sizes, which all seemed to take an inordinate time to construct.

But the greatest difference was in morale. The German people, whether or not they wholeheartedly approved of Hitler, had become accustomed to seeing him bring off success after success. He had defied the allies, torn up the Versailles Treaty, launched Germany on a huge rearmament programme, forcefully reclaimed the Rhineland as German soil, absorbed Austria, acquired the vast resources of the Skoda arms factory in Czechoslovakia, and finally brought off the incredible coup of the Nazi–Soviet pact. By that last triumph he had removed the inhibiting fear which haunted all German strategic planners – the spectre of having to fight on an eastern and a western front simultaneously. Eighteen days after the declaration of war

8

the German people faced the astonishing fact that Poland too had been conquered – one of the most dramatic victories in the history of warfare – with minimal casualties to the German Army.

Attitudes in France and Britain were very different from those in Hitler's Reich. French morale had been undermined in three ways. First, in the twenty years since the last war had ended France had made only a limited recovery from the devastation caused by the Germans because they had been allowed to escape from paying what the French thought was their fair share of reparations.Secondly, politics in France during this period had been absurdly unstable. France had endured twelve different constitutions in 150 years, and in the 1920s and 1930s had parliaments in which opinions (and thus voting) could change, not merely from day to day but between morning and afternoon. The predominant note was left-wing; there was a deep underlying fear of fascism and the wars which foreign dictators would probably cause. The majority of French people live in close-knit family units and tend to favour any politician who promotes peace, whatever the price, provided it does not upset their domestic lives. These attitudes and fears were cleverly exploited by the press, much of which was either owned or heavily subsidized by foreigners. Thirdly, like all civilized countries France had suffered from the 1929 slump in America, which had subsequently caused economic havoc in Europe.

The only stable factor in French life seemed to be the Maginot Line, a long, intricate fortification on the eastern frontier which was said to be capable of keeping out any potential invader. It was a dangerous delusion: military history contains many examples of fortifications thought by their creators to be invincible but all of which were eventually penetrated.

In fairness, however, it should be remembered that French military morale had never really recovered from the terrible losses of Verdun in 1916 and the costly Nivelle offensives of 1917, which had led to the mutiny of the French Army in May that year. It may therefore be that the reluctance of the French to fight, and their corresponding willingness to bury themselves ostrich-like in a fortification that they had persuaded themselves was impregnable, began not in 1940 but in 1917.

In hindsight it is clear that French morale was brittle rather than intrinsically weak. On paper France's assets were enormous. It had an empire which included Indo-China, part of South America and huge tracts of Africa. It was also an influential figure in the Middle East. Whenever Mussolini trumpeted about the growing power of Italy, the French were quietly confident that their own was vastly superior. France's only misgivings were about the developments in Germany, but against this the French possessed the largest land army in the world, a navy nearly as powerful as Britain's, and what was believed to be a highly efficient air force. It seemed unlikely that anyone would wish to challenge such power.

But within that strong outer crust there were weaknesses. The French were still paying for the last war in every sense of the word. Quite apart from the destruction of northern France, the country had lost a quarter of its manpower in the twenty-to-thirty age group; it also had four million survivors who qualified for disablement pensions of one kind or another. If France was to be involved in another war the French felt it was somebody else's turn to provide the battlefields and pick up the subsequent bills. If not, France would perhaps have to negotiate, which it should be able to do well from its position of strength.

André Maginot was not a professional soldier. Although a former Under-Secretary of War, he had joined the French Army in the First World War as a private and had been wounded and invalided out. After returning to politics he attained ministerial rank in various departments, including that of War, and throughout the 1920s repeatedly pursued his objective of building a defensive line. It was begun in 1929, three years before his death, and completed in 1938.

Although it comprised an ingenious arrangement of strongpoints, connected underground and reinforced in depth, the Maginot Line did not extend to cover the frontier with Belgium. Experience should have told the French that as the Germans had ignored Belgian neutrality in 1914 they were not likely to let it be an obstacle to the plans of a dictator as ruthless as Hitler. But quite apart from its limitations in length, the line had many other deficiencies. The so-called converging fields of fire were badly conceived, and many of the ingenious devices did not work properly; worst of all, the effect of living in an allegedly invulnerable fortification had a disastrous effect on French military morale, encouraging a sense of passive complacency.

When the British first arrived in France in 1939 they noted that the French public were saying '*Il faut en finir*' and translated this to mean

'It is necessary to finish it off.' The implication was that the French had decided to complete the task which had been begun in the First World War. But the French did not mean this. What they meant was that it was necessary to have done with war and all that it betokened. It must stop.

The older generation of French people accepted the fact that at intervals of twenty years or so France had to fight the Germans or go under. The younger generation saw matters differently. They were bored with the whole idea of war. The men had to go away for long periods, often when they were badly needed for the harvest. During the 1920s and 1930s France had been torn apart by strikes, a world slump, unemployment and political instability, and been let down by her allies. The League of Nations was a failure and, although Britain was her most reliable ally, Britain only maintained a tiny army, preferring to keep her own shores safe by spending all her money on a huge navy. The French had no faith that the Belgians or the Dutch would be dependable allies. They suspected that the Dutch would make their own terms with the Germans and would be no help. As for the Belgians, whom the French never really cared for, they would doubtless be over-run in no time and expect the French to rescue them as in the last war. British liaison officers noted these reactions and tried to combat them. But the sense of impending doom was too firmly rooted in French minds for British attempts at morale-raising to have much effect. There was no one on the political scene to rally them as de Gaulle would do decades later. In fact, in the opinion of many France in the spring of 1940 was just waiting to be defeated. *Il faut en finir.*

Captain Sir Basil Bartlett, employed by the Intelligence Corps, was never called upon to confront the Germans with the bayonet or other personal weapon, but his assessment of the strength and weaknesses of both sides would have been valuable if they had been considered carefully by Higher Authority. 'We should do more propaganda in Belgium,' he reported. 'The Germans are going full blast with their propaganda. They have already persuaded large numbers of Belgians that we are responsible for the war.'

In contrast Allied propaganda was pathetic. The French Army was never in the headlines and on account of this its morale suffered. Early British naval victories, such as that at the River Plate in December 1939, when the Germans scuttled their battleship *Graf Spee,* had made the British people proud of their servicemen. But nothing was ever published to make the French feel proud of theirs. Bartlett felt that the war should be treated as a moral crusade. 'Armaments are important. Economics are important. But they are nothing without the crusading spirit. We have behind us all the power of the Churches. There's the Church of Rome with its authority and the Protestant Church with its moral strength and the Jewish Church enveloped in all the dark magic of the Old Testament.' For the first time in history, he noted, all the three great Churches were on the same side.

This lack of spiritual leadership seemed to him to be at the root of France's problems. (There was, of course, little enough moral leadership in Britain at the time.) The key to winning the war, he felt, was to make the French dislike the Germans more than they disliked each other. Too much power was concentrated in too few hands in France: 'It is unfortunate that the French Right has taken advantage of the war to get back all the concessions to the working class it has made during the last ten years.' Nevertheless, when the invasion began Bartlett had more immediate matters to consider than French morale or social injustice. German prisoners whom he interrogated, who were from shot-down aircraft, 'weren't the half-starved lunatics we'd been led to expect. They were rather impressive. They say Hitler is a man of destiny and that everything he does is intuitive and right. What do 100,000 casualties matter so long as he is right?'

The British attitude in 1940 took comfort from the fact that the French Army, the British Expeditionary Force, which had been sent out in September 1939, and twenty-one miles of Channel water stood between England and the German armies; if the French had a Maginot mentality, the British cannot plausibly refute the accusation that they had a Channel one. However, Britain, with its smaller area and concentrated population, was more apprehensive about the effect of bombs than the French appeared to be and set up elaborate civil defence arrangements and contingency plans for the evacuation of civilians. The French government, careless of the perils of bombing, took no such precautions. During the Battle of France the movement of troops would be constantly hampered by streams of terrified, disorganized refugees trying to get away from the fighting.

The British public was particularly anxious about the effects of gas attacks. Alarmists, often scientists of left-wing views such as Professor J. B. S. Haldane, an Old Etonian communist, had predicted that a single bomb could wipe out a town of fifty thousand inhabitants. In

1939 the government ensured that every citizen had a gas mask, an incongruous-looking facepiece that was carried in a container about half the size of a shoe-box. The government warning that the citizen's gas mask should be carried everywhere inevitably meant that they were also left everywhere: cinemas, pubs, railway carriages and buses reaped a steady daily harvest of these articles. A superior version in a canvas haversack was provided for air raid wardens, firemen, rescue workers and the armed services. Although there were rumours that neither type of mask would protect their owners from the type of gas the Germans were most likely to use, arsene, or something even more insidious, their prompt distribution created the impression that the government was protecting the civilian population; and with that fact in mind people began to believe that their lords and masters were equally efficient in other ways of prosecuting the war.

When Chamberlain had gloomily announced on 3 September 1939 that, as Hitler had not replied to his ultimatum, Britain was now at war with Germany, the nation had braced itself for intensive air raids and depressing news of desperate battles along the French frontier. When neither of these occurred, the British people found their nerves tested in a new and unexpected way by a host of minor irritations. In the expectation of thousands of air raid casualties hospital wards were cleared and many ill patients sent home, including large numbers of TB sufferers. Ominously, thousands of cardboard coffins were manufactured. Streets were obstructed with sandbags and surface shelters. Large assemblies of people, such as those for football matches, were banned. Even more infuriating was the fact that a million women and children were evacuated from the cities and billeted on people who, patriotism or not, were as unhappy to be their hosts as the evacuees were to be unwanted guests. Recreation was severely limited, sometimes eliminated, by the fact that hotels and places of entertainment, particularly in spa towns, were closed and reoccupied not merely by government departments or civil defence establishments but by businesses which had obtained leases on them in the preceding months. Widespread dismay occurred when popular local hotels became the offices of large insurance companies.

For the anticipated air raids – which did not in fact begin until after the fall of France when the Luftwaffe could operate from French airfields – a warning of wailing sirens had been devised, a fluctuating howl to chill the stoutest heart. But, as most raids were likely to occur at night, it was necessary that the country as a whole

13

should be blacked out. Street lamps were extinguished, cars restricted to a minimal slit of light, windows curtained with blackout material, and outer doors, in what pubs and cinemas remained open, were cloaked with double curtains to prevent light showing. Enforcing all these regulations was an army of bureaucrats displaying the zeal of modern traffic wardens. In general there was a slight feeling of disappointment among the public when the threatened bombers did not immediately appear. But by the time they did the nation had come to terms with its problems, and the officials had more to do than make themselves a nuisance. Later in the war the wardens earned much respect for their courageous behaviour in air raids; in 1939 and 1940 they were still heartily detested.

The armed forces faced a formidable task. Unlike those in Germany, where military or paramilitary training had been going on briskly for years, at first in secret because it broke the terms of the Versailles Treaty, the British services were trying to absorb and train thousands of potential soldiers, sailors and airmen. Some of them were volunteers, but the services had so many men to cope with from the conscript intake, started in 1939, that even a well-qualified volunteer might have to wait before being enlisted. Large numbers were prevented from being called up by virtue of their being in 'reserved occupations'; some of these categories were patently absurd, such as physicists of twenty-one, and schoolmasters and jobbing gardeners over the age of twenty-five. The Territorial Army was by no means trained for war, although many of its members had to take on the job of instructing conscripts in skills in which they themselves were far from perfect. British service training is regulated by exacting standards and is excellent, and rather than lower those standards large numbers of recruits were kept waiting in time-consuming but futile jobs until properly qualified instructors became available. In order to send the ten divisions of the BEF (a pitifully small number) to France, the British Army had to scrape the barrel and include large numbers of territorials and reservists, who were either half-trained, or trained in skills which had long since become obsolete.

There was also the problem of weapons. The situation was not as bad as in the First World War when thousands of volunteers had had to do their initial training with wooden rifles, but there was a desperate shortage of Bren, anti-tank and sub machine-guns, as well as many other devices which the Germans already possessed in abundance. The worst deficiency was in anti-tank guns. The War

Office had an inexplicable faith in a weapon named the Boys anti-tank rifle; it was extremely unpopular, for it had a kick like a mule, but worse than that it was quite incapable of doing any damage to a tank crew unless fired into one of the observation slits.

In basic training, recruits fired five rounds of .303 ammunition from their Lee-Enfield rifles. Few had had experience of using any other form of weapon, even air guns. Many of them might never be required to fire rifles at all if they were in a service unit, perhaps employed in a workshop far behind the forward area. But one could never be sure. When the Germans had broken through the British line in the spring of 1918 every man who could fire a rifle, whether or not he had ever done so, was pressed into action; cooks, fitters, drivers, clerks and storemen were hastily pushed into the line and acquitted themselves better than might have been expected. The German successes in France in 1940 were to dispel for ever the idea that certain servicemen could ever be non-combatants. However, when confronting a Panzer IV tank that is armed with a 75-mm gun the experience of having fired five rounds of small arms ammunition several months earlier tends to be of limited value.

Most of the problems of 1940 in the British Army were easier to explain than to remedy. To attain even the most rudimentary skill at hitting a target, each recruit would probably have needed to fire at least fifty rounds. Providing, storing, guarding and distributing enough ammunition to give one hundred thousand men even this minimal experience would have been inordinately expensive and time-consuming, quite apart from the inroads it would have made on existing stocks. Some compromise had to be reached: five rounds was, everyone agreed, entirely unsatisfactory, but five rounds it had to be. Fortunately, as it seemed at the time, there were very few automatic weapons, which can blaze away hundreds of rounds of ammunition without appearing to have much effect on the marksmanship of those who are being introduced to them. A year later stocks of everything were improving, but by that time France had fallen and huge quantities of precious war material had been left on the other side of the Channel.

Various irritating catchwords became common currency. Long before a single bomb had fallen on England the standard excuse for incompetence or failure to produce something, such as a piece of timber to repair a fence, was 'Don't you know there's a war on?' There was a more sinister ring to the words 'in short supply', which

15

soon replaced 'scarce'. 'In short supply' would trigger a mild black market, give rise to a little careful food hoarding, cause shopkeepers to have a few goods under the counter – thus creating a shortage – and let them out to more favoured customers.

But there were, of course, many genuine shortages. For years the services had been operating on strict economy budgets. The number of bullets or shells which could be fired in training, and the amount of fuel which could be used by trucks, tanks, aircraft and especially ships, was severely rationed. Some warships cruised around with such small supplies of oil that they could not always respond to an emergency if it was not close by. The British government's assumption during the 1920s and early 1930s was that there would be no war during the next ten years, and this absurd 'Ten Year Rule' enabled the Treasury to keep a tight grip on expenditure by the armed forces, even when it became obvious that war might occur in a much shorter time. Although Germany had had conscription since 1936, there was a naive belief in England and France that the Germans could never rearm effectively because of their shortage of essential raw materials which other countries obtained from their colonies. The belief was a naive one because other countries were unaware of the developments the Germans had made in synthetic substitutes. However, when genuine shortages had become apparent in Germany and some people had voiced their dissatisfaction at the apparently unnecessary state of affairs, they had been silenced by Goering's pronouncement: 'Guns will make us powerful; butter will only make us fat.'

After the initial shock of realizing in 1939 that they were once again at war with Germany the citizens of Britain and France, surprised to find they were still alive, settled down to making the best of it. 'Making the best of it' offered considerable opportunities to large numbers of people to make as much money as they could out of the new circumstances in which they found themselves. Factories were now being changed over from their normal peacetime production to the nearest wartime equivalent. In simple terms this meant changing from making cars to making tanks, from soap to explosives, from machinery to aircraft. One firm which manufactured aircraft, and good ones too, had previously made chicken houses. But it all took time, organization and materials, as well as considerable negotiation with all concerned – not least the trade unions, who did not appear to be motivated by a desire to work for less than they could extract from the government.* But not only factories had to be converted, so too did the people in them. Even in 1939 there were ten thousand parts to a tank and a workforce to produce them had to be trained; designers of all types were at a premium.

In sport there is a saying that you play as well as your opponent allows you to play, and it is equally true that in war you fight as well as your opponent allows you to fight. When Germany attacked France in 1940 it was allowed to fight very well because its opponents had poor equipment and were over-confident and unrealistic. On the other hand Germany had surprise, new tactics, resourceful, well-trained commanders and highly motivated troops. Attacking troops, unless they happen to be unwilling cannon fodder, have an enormous advantage because, if successful, they can see what they are going to gain. In the simplest terms this probably means reputation, material goods and rewards which might include a free hand with the defeated enemy's womenfolk. The defender, on the other hand, has nothing to gain, only something to lose; he is fighting, probably reluctantly, because he must do so in order to preserve what he has. In the initial stages of wars these are vital factors; in the later stages the defender's morale may be much enhanced if he is able to inflict crushing losses on the attackers.

In the nine months between the outbreak of war and the invasion of France the Germans had made the fullest use of their time. In contrast the British and French had been dilatory, training large numbers of troops for a war which they hoped they would never have to fight, and instructing them in tactics which contained no new ideas. The subsequent German victory in France, by contrast, was a victory of tactical doctrine. A highly motivated force smashed its way through Belgium, Holland and Luxembourg, and through British and French forces in France, by using tactics which Britain had pioneered in the previous war and then forgotten. For the main weapons used to such devastating effect were the tanks of Heinz Guderian's Panzer divisions, which he had fought to have introduced into the German Army – the French and British were not alone in suffering diehard reactionaries at the head of their armed forces. There were many who put their faith in the West Wall, or Siegfried Line as it was more popularly called by the Allies. But it was a hastily constructed, badly planned defence; von Mellenthin, another famous Panzer

*See Correlli Barnett, *The Audit of War* for the depressing statistics of strikes and 'go slows'.

leader, commented scathingly on it as having vulnerable positions on forward slopes and being incapable of offering more than token resistance to a determined attack. Fortunately for the Germans, there were no determined attackers on the Allied side to prove him right. In his book *Panzer Leader* Guderian wrote: 'The advance we had made in the organization and employment of tanks was the primary factor on which my belief in our forthcoming success was based. Even in 1940 this belief was shared by scarcely anyone in the German army.' There were plenty of gunners and infantrymen who thought him no more than an imprudent and dangerous dreamer.

The 1930s were in many ways and many countries – and in many senses – the decade of illusion. Unfortunately for the world, some of the most deluded were men who thought they had a clear view of the future.

3 The Armour of War

At THE BATTLE of Cambrai in November 1917, the British Army had produced new and successful tactics. On that occasion the British, who had invented the tank but up till then made scant use of it, decided to launch a full-scale attack using an unprecedented number of these slow, 3½-mile-an-hour monsters. Three hundred and eighty-one tanks lurched forward, without any preliminary artillery bombardment to give warning of impending trouble, and broke a huge hole in the opposing German lines. It was a brilliant but ill-planned venture. After the initial success the tanks came to a halt, uncertain what to do next. The infantry, which should have been available in strength to consolidate the gains, was totally inadequate to do so. The Germans, who were on the point of making a retreat, took stock of the situation and retaliated by a combination of infiltrating infantry and low-level air attacks. The British victory turned into a near disaster.

As a result, the generals on both sides decided that this playing with metal toys was no way to conduct a war. The German never developed a suitable tank force in the First World War, and subsequently were forbidden to have one by the terms of the Versailles Treaty. The British dallied with the idea in the 1920s, but decided that the problems of mechanical warfare outweighed its advantages.

But not everyone agreed – on both sides. The British General 'Boney' Fuller, who as a colonel on the Staff had planned the Cambrai attack, wrote intelligently about the possibilities of that form of warfare in the 1920s. But his words fell on purposely deaf ears – the ultra-conservative thinkers at the War Office looked nostalgically at the past, not imaginatively at the future. The *Times* military correspondent, Basil Liddell-Hart, who had been wounded in 1915 and never reached a higher rank than captain, also wrote articles, pamphlets and books developing the same theme, but his views too were not regarded kindly by the War Office, which felt he was over-presumptuous for a mere captain.

Unfortunately for Britain, these and other writings by progressive British military thinkers, who included General Martel, were eagerly devoured in Germany where Heinz Guderian had reached the – quite erroneous – conclusion that if the Versailles Treaty had forbidden the German Army to have tanks the Allies had decided that they were a decisive weapon. Nevertheless, the fact that he held such views spurred Guderian to try to convince his German Army colleagues that they too must see the tank as the master of the modern battlefield. Although forbidden to possess tanks, the Germans were not prohibited from having mock-ups made of cardboard; secretly enthusiasts also obtained two proper tanks from Sweden in the mid-1920s and practised assiduously with them in remote areas of Germany. They were given training facilities near Moscow by the Russians, who in the 1920s hoped to win favour with the Germans as a prelude to ultimately controlling them. When Hitler came to power in 1933 he abruptly terminated the policy of mutual assistance between Germany and Russia, but by that time Heinz Guderian had become Chief of Staff to General Lutz, head of the Mechanized Troops Inspectorate, and the foundations of the German Panzer armies had been laid. But that all lay in the future; in the 1920s, in the aftermath of the First World War and with Germany suffering the indignities and impossible impositions of the Versailles Treaty, much headway still had to be made to convince those at the top that tanks were the weapon of the future.

In *Panzer Leader* Guderian wrote that his profound studies of the First World War had given him considerable insight into the psychology of the combatants, including those in the German Army. He knew that although in the 1930s the French possessed (on paper) the largest army and the strongest tank force in western Europe they were preoccupied with the idea that the next war would be positional and static, as the last one had been. The British also held much the same view, despite the fact that they had invented the tank and even used it in battle.

However, Guderian realized that there were others who held more original views. He took advantage of these ideas, while their own countrymen remained unconvinced. In *Panzer Leader* he wrote:

It was principally the books and articles of the Englishmen, Fuller, Liddell-Hart and Martel, that excited my interest and gave me food for thought. These far-sighted soldiers were even then trying to make of the tank something more than an infantry support weapon. They envisaged it in relationship to the growing motorisation of our age and thus they became pioneers of a new type of warfare on the largest scale.

He went on to describe how he had learnt from them about the concentration of armour, as employed at the battle of Cambrai. Liddell-Hart had emphasized the importance of armoured units for operating at long range against the enemy's supply columns, and had also put forward the idea of a division consisting of a mixture of armoured and infantry units.

In 1923, when the theories of Liddell-Hart and Fuller were being treated with mild contempt, or totally ignored, by the British War Office, von Brauchitsch, later to be commander-in-chief of the German Army, took the remarkable step of organizing clandestine manoeuvres in Russia to examine the possibilities of using motorized troops in tanks in co-operation with military aeroplanes (this was at the time when the German Army was forbidden to have either). Air and ground armour partnership seems to have been a purely German concept; seventeen years later it was this deadly combination which sliced the Allied armies to pieces in France.

But Guderian was not preoccupied solely with the present or with mechanization. He made a very careful study of Napoleon's campaign of 1806, when Prussia had suffered a resounding defeat by the more mobile French troops. He also studied other battles in military history, even including the use of cavalry tactics in 1914. He did, of course, apply the mobility inherent in cavalry tactics to tank warfare. Those military critics who believe that armies should never consider tactics of the past, but only think of the future, were astonished when Guderian announced how much he had gained from the study of long-past battles. Subsequent military pundits, trying to analyse the factors in the German successes of 1940, have tended to look for more immediate causes than the makeshift planning of the early 1920s. Yet that early planning, when Germany was forbidden to possess the means of waging aggressive war, when the senior members of the German staff were more reactionary even than those in Britain, and when the political leaders were in no way likely to condone, let alone encourage, dreamers of future military victories, was the hard core which eventually set the tone for German Panzer morale. It was an enduring morale, resilient enough to withstand the hardships of enormous losses in Russia and North Africa later. It was forged at a time when Hitler was a mere rabble-rousing trouble-maker, when Germany was falling into the worst economic chaos of her history, and few Germans could look back on the sacrifices and deprivation of the First World War without a feeling of horror.

But even by the 1930s, when Guderian had made his point to the High Command and the future of a German armoured force looked reasonably promising, there was still an enormous amount of work to be done. Clearly much of it would concern tank design and the provision of the right sort of gun. The principal problem any tank designer has to face is whether his tank should be light and fast, carrying small-calibre guns but with a great advantage in manoeuvrability, or be large, heavily protected with thick armour plate, and thus slow – in fact little more than a mobile field gun. The British tanks which had achieved moderate success in the previous war were slow, cumbersome and lightly armed – the worst possible combination. The psychological effect of their presence on the battlefield was considered to be almost as effective as their firepower; and, of course, when ground conditions were stable, they could advance up to a German strongpoint and, firing point-blank, make it untenable.

The Carden-Loyd chassis which the German Army purchased for the basis of their new tanks was a British design. There was nothing remarkable about this: the history of warfare is full of stories of weapons being obtained by theft, purchase or trade from a neighbouring state and then used to defeat the unimaginative seller. The resultant tank was the Panzer I, soon followed by the Panzer II, which carried a 20-mm gun and one machine-gun. Training was carried out with these vehicles, supplemented by new armoured reconnaissance cars. Traditional cavalry regiments, which had previously looked with scorn on these mechanical toys, now began to see their possibilities. At this point Guderian was emphasizing the need to keep things simple; had a deep distrust of elaborate tactics, knowing how easily they can become muddled and lead to disaster.

After Hitler became Chancellor in 1933 German rearmament

steadily gathered momentum. One of Hitler's first acts on achieving this position of supreme power was to abolish the tax on cars and to announce that a new Volkswagen or 'people's car' was to be mass produced. This vehicle would enable the German population to enjoy motoring on the new roads, the Autobahnen, which would now be built. In the event the VW factory was used for producing military vehicles.*

But those days were far ahead. In the 1930s, Guderian realized he could now press on to make the German Army the most innovative and dynamic in the world. Even so, it was not an easy task. Certain senior officers thought that his plans were too optimistic and impractical. At this time he seems to have learnt that when dealing with one's superiors it is best to act first and ask for permission afterwards. If one is successful, everyone takes the credit; if one fails, one may be lucky and escape blame in the general confusion.

Two other decisions which would have long-term effects were taken at this time. The new Panzer units must have adequate guns and armour. In order to penetrate the armour of the French Char 2C tanks, which were likely to be early opponents, the Panzer would need a gun of at least 75-mm calibre; at the same time they must have armour which would provide the crews with adequate defence. A tank is, of course, also packed with ammunition, so if an enemy shell can find its way through into it neither tank nor crew will have a future. The fact that Germany solved these problems in the 1930s, when the British and French seemed hardly aware of them, gave the latter serious trouble later. In particular, some two years after the fall of France British troops in the Western Desert were being asked to fight Panzers equipped with 75-mm guns and case-hardened armour plating; they themselves had two-pounder guns (40-mm) and armour which was quite incapable of stopping 50-mm shell, let alone the 75s and 88s they encountered. When one looks at the development of the Panzers in the 1930s, their devastating victory in 1940 ceases to be surprising: it may not have been inevitable, but it was, at least, highly likely.

All experienced soldiers know the value of training. As early as

---

*After 1945, when it had been heavily bombed, it could have been closed down altogether by the British, in whose occupation zone it lay; instead they preferred to assist its rebuilding, even though its products would compete with British vehicles in the world market for small cars. In 1988 there was a strong possibility that VW would buy up the remains of the Austin Rover group which it had already ousted from its former prominence in world markets.

500 BC the Chinese general Sun-Tzu laid down the importance of training and good tactics. Large numbers of untrained men were but as lambs being led to the slaughter, he affirmed, and he went on to define military requirements such as surprise, the correct use of movement, concentration of force and so on which are just as true today as they were in those days. Guderian believed that the key to victory in a future war would be movement. Skilful manoeuvring would catch the enemy unawares, would make it impossible for him to create adequate defensive positions, and would coax him out of the area he held. Guderian believed that a tank attack did not need a preliminary bombardment to ease the way ahead; if it had sufficient firepower, it could soften up its own targets at will.

In the 1937 German Army manoeuvres he demonstrated the potential of the Panzers. Among the foreign guests invited on that occasion were Field Marshal Sir Cyril Deverell of the British Army, and Mussolini and Marshal Badoglio from Italy. Deverell wondered whether in actual warfare it would be possible to deploy as many tanks as they had seen functioning in manoeuvres. He mentioned that the younger officers in the British Army still adhered to the idea that the tank was primarily an infantry support weapon.

By 1939 Guderian's passionate obsession with the idea of building up a Panzer striking force appeared to have achieved all that could have been expected and more. By that year he had been appointed General of Panzer Troops and Chief of 'Mobile Troops'. He was on good terms with Hitler, who occasionally asked him for advice – although he did not take it. Like Guderian, Hitler thought the officers who constituted the higher command of the German Army were too cautious and lacking in adventurous spirit. Hitler approved of Guderian because the latter's mobile columns had taken a leading part in the occupation of Austria and Czechoslovakia (both without opposition) and had not broken down as often as expected. Guderian, although appreciative of Hitler's support, regarded him warily. When Hitler told the Army to prepare to invade Poland, Guderian and most German officers were apprehensive. If the war were to be limited to Poland, then there was nothing to fear; the Nazi-Soviet pact appeared to have ensured that the Russians would not cause trouble. But of the Western Allies there was no such certainty. Ribbentrop, the ex-champagne salesman whom Hitler had made Ambassador to Britain, said the Allies would not lift a finger to help Poland. Others were not so sure, and memories of the losses of the First World War still lingered. But the Polish campaign was a swift and triumphant success for the German Army. Guderian hoped that the Western powers would accept the *fait accompli* and decide there was no point in continuing the war. But in the moment of triumph he was troubled by the thought that in spite of his successes he had many opponents in the German Army, and the Western powers, so far from deciding to settle for peace, appeared to be preparing a massive counterstroke.

Guderian's pessimistic view of the immediate future was of course wrong, but as regards the long-term prospects he was right. Although he had created a highly motivated, well-balanced strike force, it was outnumbered by the enemy tanks. Furthermore, the German economy was not yet geared to producing the amount of military material required for complete victory: in fact it never would be. Mechanical failure in the Polish campaign had been alarmingly high, and presented a very different picture from the bloodless campaigns in Austria and Czechoslovakia. When information about German problems in Poland began to filter back to the Allies in 1939 and 1940, it reinforced the complacent view they were already taking about the deficiencies of German material. Unfortunately they failed to realize that German tactics and Panzer leadership were light years ahead of their own. The moment of truth would come – on 10 May 1940.

Although in retrospect the Allies' attitude to the German threat seems hopelessly unrealistic, it is easily understandable. In 1918 France and Britain, with a variety of Allies of varying quality, had won a gruelling war of which they themselves had borne the brunt. Germany had been reduced to an army of a hundred thousand with no tanks or military aircraft; the economy was in chaos, the nation war-weary, the fleet at the bottom of the North Sea, and the prospect of an emergent military Germany so fantastic that it was simply ludicrous. In consequence there was no reason for Britain and France to spend more than the bare minimum on their armed forces and, if the worst came to the worst and by some miracle Germany did once again embark on a path of aggression, the methods which had defeated her last time would surely suffice again. Thus the innovative ideas of Fuller, Liddell-Hart and Martel were seen as neither of relevance nor practical.

The French took a slightly gloomier view. Clemenceau, the French Premier who had announced in 1919 that the Allies would squeeze the German orange till the pips squeaked, grew gradually more despondent as he grew older, and even he was pleased to see the Maginot Line started just before he died in 1929. Although France was deluding itself that the Maginot was so formidable that the Germans would never attack, the country also maintained a substantial army and an air force, although the latter left much to be desired. France's belief that she was powerful enough to deter any German aggression was shared by a number of senior German generals. This was not Hitler's view, but when he wished them to attack France immediately after the successful conquest of Poland his generals objected so strongly to the idea of beginning a campaign on the brink of winter that he agreed, reluctantly, to postpone it till January. Nevertheless, even while the Allied generals were under the impression that he was too busy digesting his gains in Poland to wish to take on other commitments, they could very well have been surprised by a brisk German attack on 12 November, and even an invasion of Britain on the same date.

Meanwhile Britain's own version of the Maginot mentality was based on the protection afforded by the Channel, and by the possession of a Navy, which, though weaker than it had been in the past, was nevertheless thought to be more than a match for anything which Germany could produce. It was assumed that not only could the Royal Navy protect Britain from any form of invasion but that it was also capable of blockading the German ports and forcing Hitler to sue for an early peace. The official Whitehall view was that at best Germany had enough supplies for a mere fifteen months.

Those who chose to continue serving in the scaled-down, underequipped British armed forces of the 1920s and 1930s needed to be either so patriotic that they would endure any amount of frustration, or so lacking in talent and initiative that they regarded the services as a safe haven. Most of the officers came from traditional service families, but many of the sailors, soldiers and airmen had joined because the slumps of the inter-war years had taken unemployment figures to previously unknown levels. There were, of course, exceptions to this generalization. Some recruits liked the life in the services, whether it offered a proper living and a future or not. A number of excellent young men – many from Canada, South Africa, Australia and New Zealand as well as Britain – were attracted by the flying and the camaraderie of the Royal Air Force.

In all the services promotion was maddeningly slow, particularly among officers; a man could stay in the same rank for fifteen or twenty years. There were, of course, British officers following a career in the Indian Army, but they were virtually an élite minority. In the circumstances it is remarkable that so many talented officers chose to stay on in their various arms of the service, and positively astonishing that some of them could have generated brilliant plans for the future.

Among the latter were Fuller and Martel. Fuller had joined the Tank Corps in 1916 at the age of thirty-eight, after serving as an infantryman since 1898. His small size, five feet four inches, and weight, eight stone, caused him to be likened to Napoleon and given the nickname 'Boney'.

But there was nothing small about Fuller's intellect or vision or drive, and it is largely due to his efforts that Britain had a tank force at all by the start of the war in 1939. His inability to suffer fools gladly, particularly when they happened to be superior in rank, did not assist his popularity or progress. Giffard Le Q. Martel, slightly younger than Fuller, was a brilliant mathematician who had begun his army life in the Royal Engineers, had fought through the First World War, and knew exactly what armour and armament a tank needed to make it viable.

Another notable Royal Engineer was P. C. S. Hobart, a man of legendary courage and wide experience of warfare. He too was an ardent advocate of mobility, and later in the war would be renowned for his encouragement of what became known as 'the funnies'. 'The funnies' were what the Army disparagingly nicknamed all the enhancements on a normal tank – adaptations which enabled it to beat a path with chains through minefields, to carry bridging equipment and to launch vast containers of explosives in howitzer fashion. Hobart's inventive vision helped to smooth the way of those who landed on D Day in 1944, but he was not able to exercise it early enough to provide a force capable of withstanding Guderian's mercurial thrusts in 1940. Hobart had accurately forecast the course the next war in Europe would take, and eight years later he had the melancholy experience of seeing himself proved right. However, his prickly temperament made him unpopular with fellow officers, particularly his seniors, and his efforts were therefore belittled. Had the trio of Fuller, Martel and Hobart, supported by Liddell-Hart, found a backer equivalent to Hitler in the British government, Guderian's venturesome progress across France in 1940 would –

if it had even been able to begin – doubtless have ended quickly and disastrously.

The fact that makes the German victory almost inconceivable to this day is that the Allied tank force outnumbered the Germans and in many ways was superior. The French had 3000 tanks, and the British 600; the Germans possessed no more than 3400, of which only about 2500 were used in the campaign in the West.* Only 600 or so were the admirable Panzer IIIs and IVs, and approximately half were the old Panzer Is and IIs which were mainly used for training purposes.

Guderian felt that his greatest enemy at this time was not the Allies but the German general staff which, even in 1940, had doubts about the ability of Panzer divisions to conduct long-range operations and, in some quarters, believed that the horsed cavalry should be expanded instead. But before Guderian launched his cherished Panzers into France the German Army was to have other morale-building and reputation-making experiences. The first of these was in the Scandinavian countries, the second in Belgium and Holland; neither campaign was anticipated properly by the Allies.

---

*It is as well to emphasize that few figures of military strength can be treated as being entirely accurate. This is true of vehicles, stocks, numbers of troops involved and, above all, casualties. Sometimes no exact record was kept; at others many of the essential returns are missing. Reports from 'eye-witnesses' should be treated with the utmost caution.

4 The Surprise That Should Never Have Been

For MANY PEOPLE who have subsequently pondered on the events of 1940, the fact that Germany took the Allies by surprise in both Norway and France is difficult to understand. They assume that it must be virtually impossible for a nation to mobilize a huge striking force, with a considerable air element, and launch it on to a victim without the latter having any idea of what is immediately in store for him. But in this Norway and France were not unique in their fate. The following year Germany launched an equally unexpected attack on Russia with forces far greater in size than those involved in the earlier invasions. At the end of 1941 Japan achieved complete surprise when it attacked Pearl Harbor, the Philippines, Malaya and Burma. Subsequent invasions, such as that in North Africa in 1943 and Normandy in 1944, were equally unexpected, although the latter were aided by a variety of deception ploys. Finally, the Japanese had no idea that they were going to have the unwanted distinction of being the first recipients of an atomic bomb.

Today we pride ourselves that, even in the era of missiles and fast aircraft, no nation could take another by surprise in the way which occurred so often in the Second World War. Our satellites, our radar, our agents, we reassure ourselves, would give ample warning. In fact, there might be no warning at all: a future invasion might be made by infiltrators who arrive and position themselves waiting for the order to act. But that is another story.

It is true that the British intelligence services before 1939 were less effective than they might have been, but intelligence, like politics, is

29

the art of the possible; between 1918 and 1939 the art of intelligence was made as difficult as possible by British government parsimony and German security. Nevertheless from the first volume of the official history of British intelligence, published in 1979, it seems that the intelligence agencies and those who were responsible for them may have been dangerously negligent. Having discussed the general organization of intelligence-gathering and assessing, the official history comments: 'Of the departments most involved – the Foreign Office and the three main Service ministries – the Foreign Office, the most important in peacetime, was also the one which displayed the least interest in the problems we have now outlined.' The Foreign Office was not concerned with comparing its conclusions with the analyses of other ministries. It had access to the best sources of information, and it is clear from the official historians' careful phraseology that it combined remarkable arrogance with culpable inefficiency. When the opinions of others conflicted with those of its own mandarins, the dissenting voices were simply ignored. The Secret Service (SIS) had been established in 1919 (under the control of the Foreign Office) and collected information by espionage; this was supplemented by the information that the Foreign Office acquired through diplomatic channels. Although the Foreign Office's main area of interest was political information, the SIS also handled military intelligence under the section known as MI6. Later the names SIS, Secret Service and MI6 were all used to describe the same body.

However, before condemning the Foreign Office too harshly for its high-handed arrogance it should be borne in mind that during the First World War the military establishment had behaved with equal *hauteur*, claiming that it alone knew how the war should be concluded, and whenever possible refused to allow any interference from civilians, even those in the Cabinet. Even the dynamic perseverance of Lloyd George had little effect. Regrettably, these attitudes seem to have continued in diminished form in peacetime; lack of money did nothing to improve matters.

The situation up until 1935 was summarized by the official historians: 'While the Foreign Office was a department without an intelligence branch but with a tendency to regard itself as the fount of all important information, and the final arbiter in the interpretation of it, the Service departments, despite their possession of intelligence branches, had little recognition that intelligence involved more than the collection of factual information.' The writers might have added that even when the commanders in the field received intelligence they were inclined to regard it with suspicion, and sometimes rejected it unless it conformed to their own personal views of the situation. This is not surprising, for fighting men have a long experience of receiving information which may be either exaggerated, or the result of incorrect analysis, clever enemy deception tactics or even of human error. However, between 1935 and 1939 attitudes began to change for the better and an all-round improvement resulted, although it was not enough to produce a clear view of German war plans and their means to implement them.

A very useful source of information which came under the control of the Foreign Office was the Government Code and Cypher School (GCCS), which had been founded in 1919 to advise on the security of British codes and cypher. This became of increasing importance with the development of wireless, and brought in with it Sigint (Signal Intelligence). Sigint obviously depended on the interception of the wireless communications of other countries, a process known as Y. It also involved direction finding (DF), by which the place of origin of signals could be traced, traffic analysis (TA) by which communications networks and techniques could be studied, and finally the decrypting process which eventually became known as Ultra. Between the wars the only service to concern itself with traffic analysis had been the Army. The main problem with intercepting potential enemy signals traffic was not that there was too little of it but that there was too much for the limited British resources to handle.

Aerial photography, later to be known as PR (photographic reconnaissance), was another source of information which had been useful during the First World War but was greatly neglected later. However in 1935 the aggressive behaviour of Mussolini had caused the RAF to take oblique photographs of some of the areas in which he was operating. The French also began experiments with aerial photography at this time, although their efforts were limited to photographing German military targets near the French frontier. More information was clearly needed, so in 1938 SIS engaged an Australian named Sidney Cotton, a former RNAS pilot. He acquired a Lockheed 12a and began operational flights from French bases for joint Anglo-French photographic work. A private company – the Aeronautical Research and Sales Corporation – was formed to provide an explanation of why a foreign aircraft was operating in the air space of another country. At one point Cotton obtained some co-operation from a German photographer, although this necessitated giving the latter occasional flights in the aircraft; but the German had no idea that concealed cameras were photographing military installations. The flights began in March 1939 and, with the Lockheed 12a and a later model of the aircraft, Cotton managed to take many vertical photographs over Germany and the Mediterranean. With the second aircraft, which had extra tanks and better cameras, he could photograph an eleven-mile strip at 20,000 feet.

Unfortunately the interpretation of photographs lagged behind the physical ability to take them, and in any case there was some inter-service friction over who should be in overall charge. Not until after the war had begun was an inter-service unit created for what in future would be seen as one of the most important sources of intelligence. Had it come into existence earlier and been given the resources which such a specialized activity required, Germany might have had more difficulty in taking its victims by surprise in the spring of 1940.

Similarly, inadequate resources for interpretation of economic intelligence led to a serious underestimate of Germany's economic resources, resulting in the comforting but fallacious assumption that Hitler's Reich was so short of vital raw materials that the blockade imposed by the Royal Navy would make it impossible for the Germans to continue the war for longer than fifteen months at the outside. In addition, neither Britain nor France seemed aware of Germany's enormous industrial expansion since Hitler had come to power. Later, both countries would be surprised at their enemy's capacity to provide new ranges of weaponry and also to replace those lost in battle; not until much later in the war would that ability begin to fail.

Normally, one of the best sources of information about another country is one's own embassy or diplomatic mission; this is why governments are reluctant to break off diplomatic relations and withdraw representation if that drastic step can possible be avoided. Everyone in the diplomatic service is aware of the game being played, and knows the rules. The host country knows that the mission would like to obtain as wide a variety of military information as it can by legitimate means, and that it will usually be careful not to use methods of which its host would disapprove. Occasionally these conventions are flouted, leading to expulsions for obvious spying and resultant tit-for-tat gestures. Up until 1939 the British embassy in Moscow had great difficulty in obtaining genuine information about Russia and its intentions, although in that year there were intimations that Germany was making friendly overtures to the Soviets which were not unwelcome. The Nazi-Soviet pact of August 1939 should not therefore have come as quite such a shock.

Although Germany became steadily more unco-operative diplomatically in the 1930s, there were additional sources available, some commercial, some through Germans opposed to Hitler. However, when a democracy is dealing with a dictatorship the former is always at a disadvantage in that the dictators can change their minds and act rapidly without anyone except their immediate circle knowing of their intentions. Sigint was important, but there were distinct limits here too. Governments with sinister intentions do not discuss them through routine signals communications.

In the year before the outbreak of war SIS became the target of much criticism, most of it probably unfair. Both the War Office and the Foreign Office felt that the supply of information coming in was inadequate and not always accurate; on the political side SIS seemed to believe what it was told by Nazi propagandists. SIS did little to enable the government to understand Hitler's state of mind and thus allow it to judge whether he was as belligerent as some of his speeches suggested. Any doubts about the latter point were sharply resolved in the spring of 1939 when he dismembered Czechoslovakia.

In the absence of reliable figures, Germany's military assets were heavily overestimated in the period immediately before the war. It was assumed that the Germans would soon be producing 1500 aircraft a month. They were actually planning for 2000, but even in December 1940 they had only reached a total of less than 800 per month. Similarly the War Office believed that Germany possessed 5000 tanks in September 1939: in fact it had 3000, of which 2700 were light. The total number of U boats was estimated as 66; it was actually 57.

These overestimates were not in themselves crucial, although they may have induced Chamberlain's government to adopt an ultra-cautious policy. What did amount to negligence on a massive scale was the lack of proper reaction to the report that Germany was experimenting with mobile warfare. The worst aspect of this was that the War Office and the Air Ministry did not merely show a lack of interest in this possibility – they actually discouraged their intelligence departments from making any assessments of it. Whether this appalling failure was due to a desire not to contradict the French, who considered such ideas nonsensical (how could they work against the Maginot Line?), or to mental sluggishness which could not stir itself to consider something outside its own experience, is not clear. The most damning indictment of the War Office at this time is that it refused blankly to believe in the existence of the versatile MG 34 machine-gun, and that the Germans could ever use the 88-mm anti-aircraft gun as an anti-tank weapon. In the event, the 88-mm proved one of the most devastating guns in the German armoury and was used in a variety of roles.

Meanwhile the Air Ministry continued to believe that the German Air Force would be used for strategic bombing and not for tactical support of the Army. At that stage Germany lacked suitable bombers to carry out such a mission: if they were to fly to Britain and back they would need to devote most of their carrying capacity to fuel, rather than bombs. Had this deduction been made in 1939, the British Army might have been more aware of the type of threat it would encounter later when the Germans had occupied bases nearer to England. Astonishingly, although Germany used her bombers to support her army in the Polish Blitzkrieg, the War Office did not speculate on the fact that, if Hitler's next move was in the West, he would use the same tactics.

One of the most astonishing intelligence events of the war was the 'Oslo Report', which was sent from an anonymous source to the British naval attaché in Oslo in November 1939. This document contained so many revelations of German scientific and technological progress that it was suspected of being a 'plant' and treated with scepticism. Subsequently, almost every word of it was found to be true.

The report disclosed the fact that Germany had almost completed the building of her first aircraft carrier and that the German Navy was developing remote-controlled gliders; the testing range was at Peenemünde, a name with which the Allies would become very familiar later. It went on to describe new German torpedoes which could be steered or made to home in on a ship; one type, the report said, could be countered by the de-gaussing system used against magnetic mines. There was ominous information about German developments in radar, which to the Allies' general consternation was found to be more advanced in many ways than their version; this was extremely alarming, because many people believed that Britain had a monopoly of this valuable invention. There was information to suggest that the Germans might be experimenting with beam guidance of aircraft, as indeed they were. And, with particular relevance to what would shortly be in store for France and the Low Countries, it was reported that the German aircraft industry was producing large numbers of Junkers 88s. Ju 88s were twin-engined long-range bombers, which could also be used for dive-bombing. The fact that dive-bombers were a tactical weapon which could be used in support or ahead of tanks which had outpaced their own artillery support did not seem to impress the Allied High Command with its importance.

All in all, the Oslo Report seemed too good to be true. It gave astonishing tactical information about how the Germans had defeated the Poles when the latter were firmly entrenched in concrete gun emplacements. As the concrete could withstand normal artillery fire, the Germans obscured them with smoke shells. Blinded by these tactics, the Polish crew withdrew into their bunkers. The Germans then brought up flame-throwers through the smoke-screen and directed them into the apertures of the emplacements. Clearly this was a rehearsal, and a very satisfactory one, for what was planned for the Maginot Line if the Germans were not able to break through elsewhere. Equally clearly, the lesson that the Germans had every intention of attacking France in the near future was also ignored.

Fortunately, in 1939 Allied High Command was in possession of the greatest intelligence asset of the war – the Enigma machine. This encoding device, which resembled an ordinary typewriter, had been invented by a Dutchman twenty years earlier; it had proved a commercial failure, but had been adopted and subsequently modified by the German armed forces. The Poles, who knew that their country was certain to be on Hitler's shopping list for invasion, had built a set of their own, adapted from the commercial version, but in 1939 had found the sophisticated version of the machine developed by the Germans was defeating their efforts to read German codes. However, when Poland was over-run its cryptographers escaped with two machines and began working with a seventy-strong international team at Vignolles, near Paris. This group worked closely with the British GCCS, which was now at Bletchley Park.

Mere possession of the machine did not mean that one could read all German signals without problems. The Enigma machine was designed so that when a letter was struck a different letter would appear in the encoding. As there was an intricate arrangement of wheels and jacks, the resultant enciphering could be based on a million-fold permutation. The setting for the day was indicated by a prefix to the message, and the receiver would then adjust his set for the appropriate decrypting. It seemed that Enigma offered an insoluble problem to an outsider who did not know the setting, but through the team of brilliant decrypters assembled by GCCS at Bletchley certain settings were deduced. But still only a fraction of the messages intercepted could be decoded by the Ultra team, as it was called. The Army settings proved the most difficult, but more success was achieved against the group used by the German Air Force.

Unfortunately nothing intercepted gave any indication of the impending attacks on Norway, Denmark, Belgium, Holland and France. Although GCCS had learnt useful information about the structure of the Luftwaffe, it had obtained no indication that its main function at this stage was to support the Army in the field. The widely held view that the Allies ought to have known all about the plans for the invasion of France from Enigma intercepts is incorrect. There were plenty of reasons for the Allies to anticipate the type of attack Germany was likely to launch on France, but ignoring warnings from Ultra was not among them: there *were* no clear warnings.

There was, however, a very distinct warning from a source code-named A.54. A.54 was an officer named Paul Thummel in the Abwehr, the German military intelligence; he had approached the Czech intelligence service as early as 1936, and from then onwards had supplied not only valuable information about the structure of the German forces but also advance news of the moves by which Hitler acquired control of Czechoslovakia.* A.54 warned the Allies that Hitler was planning to launch an attack on the West on 12 November 1939, and this was confirmed from other sources. He then reported that the attack had been postponed until December 1939. Then it was put back to 17 January. All this time the British and French public, and a number of vociferous American reporters, believed that Hitler had now decided that going to war was a bad idea, that he had twisted the lion's tail once too often, and that peace would soon be arranged. The truth, of course, was very different.

However, the fact that after their success in Poland German morale

---

*There were other sources which were almost as good but unfortunately, even after this length of time, their identities may not be disclosed.

was at its peak would not necessarily have made victory in France certain. Had there not been a chance incident which at first seemed to be a disaster for Germany, but subsequently led to an even greater one for Britain, the famous Blitzkrieg victory might never have occurred and the Germans might once more have become bogged down in northern France.

On 10 January a German major on an airfield in Westphalia took a lift to Cologne in a German aircraft piloted by an old friend. In normal circumstances this would have occasioned no comment, but the unusual feature of this was that the hitch-hiking major was carrying in his briefcase details of the plans for the German attack on Belgium and Holland, which was due to take place exactly a week later. The journey should have been made by train: it was strictly forbidden to carry secret papers in aircraft since they might go off course and be forced down over enemy territory. This was exactly what happened, for after flying through thick cloud the pilot came very low to check his bearings. Being unfamiliar with the Me108 aircraft he was flying, he lost control and crash landed. Neither man was hurt, but to their horror they realized they had landed in Belgium. Belgian frontier guards surrounded the wreckage and took them prisoner. Desperate attempts to destroy the vital papers were promptly foiled.

Although Belgium was guarding her neutrality strictly, King Leopold passed the captured papers to the French. The plans were so detailed and the event so fortuitous that the Allies, particularly the French, were suspicious that it might be a deliberate, though mysterious, hoax. The Commander-in-Chief of Allied Forces in France contented himself with issuing a general alert and then took no further action. Gamelin, who was sixty-seven, was reputed to be suffering from a chronic form of venereal disease and spoke French rapidly, inaudibly and almost incomprehensibly even to his own countrymen, decided that even if the plans did show German intentions of attacking in the immediate future, there was nothing further he could do. More astonishing even than Gamelin's lethargy is that of the Belgian and Dutch governments, which failed to take appropriate action against the dangers they were now clearly facing.

The greatest and most decisive result of the incident was in German strategic planning. Assuming (quite wrongly) that the Belgians and Dutch, backed by the French and British, would now be making herculean efforts to meet an attack through the areas mentioned in the captured plans, the German High Command decided that a totally new approach was essential. There were, of course, few options, a fact decided by the topography of the frontiers. The initial concept had been almost identical with the Schlieffen Plan, with which the Germans had begun the First World War. In 1914 the German armies, pivoting like a door with its hinge at Metz, had swung around in a huge semi-circle, violating the neutrality of Belgium and Holland on the way; but the enormously long lines of communication involved had eventually proved the plan's undoing. Once the initial attack had been checked, both sides settled down to four years of gruelling trench warfare. Even after that experience it did not seem to have occurred to the French that Germany might in future try to adopt a different tactic.

When the Germans found out from their spies that, in spite of their discovery of the original plan in the crashed aircraft, the Allies seemed unaware that Hitler might now seek an alternative to this, the Army decided on a bold gamble. Although the Ardennes was considered unsuitable country for tanks, a successful thrust in that area would take them through to Sedan and Amiens, thus hitting the Allies in the flank along their line of communications. And when the Ardennes was carefully studied by German tank experts posing as tourists, it became clear that though it was not ideal for tanks there were numerous paths through the woods and, provided the German tanks were not strongly opposed in that area, they would have little difficulty in negotiating it. An attack by this route – which Gamelin had assured his generals was impossible for tanks and therefore not worth considering – would have incalculable benefits. Needless to say, Guderian took a prominent part in shaping the opinion of the German High Command in this matter.

Twenty divisions from German Army Group B, which would have made the original drive through Belgium, were accordingly transferred to Army Group A, which would come through the Ardennes and tackle the French forces deployed to defend the River Meuse. In that transfer, seven armoured and three motorized divisions came from the north to the south, thus giving Guderian all the thrust he needed. Reports by French aircraft flying along the border that there were troop movements on the German side did not cause any special apprehension, for bad weather had prevented their observation of the vital move from north to south. Allied forces were warned to be alert, but the possibility that the Germans might be planning to launch an attack towards the Meuse did not seem to have occurred to anyone: the Ardennes were known to be impassable, and there was a full study from the 1914–18 war which proved it. It was assumed that, as Germany had shown no scruples about invading neutral countries in Scandinavia, she might now content herself with occupying Belgium and Holland and then defy the Allies to push her out.

After the fall of France, when the inquest began and excuses were being circulated, it was reported that there *had* been warnings about the Ardennes thrust, and that they had come from intelligence officers and defectors. However, no one had taken them seriously; the Allied High Command was much more concerned with a massive overestimate of German tank strength. The French reckoned this could be as high as 7500, while the British thought of a more exact (though wildly inaccurate) figure of 5800.

Even more serious was the knowledge that the Germans had improved the capabilities of their forces to make a surprise attack. Earlier in the war any attack would have needed a countdown of six days; now one could be launched immediately. But although A.54 notified Allied intelligence on 1 May that an attack would begin on the 10th, and General Oster, second-in-command of the Abwehr – but astonishingly also a member of the burgeoning German resistance – confirmed this on 3 May, the War Office intelligence survey for 8 May said there was no sign of an imminent invasion. Even when a Spitfire reconnaissance of 7 May reported seeing 400 tanks in the Ardennes close to the Luxembourg border, the Air Ministry refused to believe there was an impending emergency.

Nor was this the whole of the sorry story. Most of the records of the Army and RAF headquarters were destroyed by the retreating armies in 1940; rather more surprisingly, there are very few records from Whitehall either. It is clear from what records still exist that the War Office was less concerned with what was happening in central France after the Ardennes breakthrough than it was with the fighting in Belgium and Holland. Enigma was producing less information than usual at the time, but even if the Enigma input had been large it would have had no effect on the fighting in the field when that had begun. Enigma intercepts took time to decrypt, and by the time information was available from them the field situation could have changed dramatically. The only information of real value in a rapidly changing situation came from air reconnaissance, local signal sources and what was known as 'Phantom'.

Phantom was an unorthodox unit which had been created by two highly intelligent officers, one RAF, one Army, to learn what was happening on the ground and transmit the information immediately to GHQ by radio. Vital information was gathered by their French-, Flemish- and Dutch-speaking officers, who used motorcycles to visit units in the forward areas. Phantom sent in a series of reports on the area and size of German penetration; unfortunately the recipient of the information at GHQ seemed too bewildered to organize containing moves or counter-attacks. General Gort's counter-attack at Arras was to be an exception to this. It is easy to criticize the bumblings of headquarters when a fast-moving battle is taking place in the field; it is simpler to send messages, even by carrier pigeon, to large formations whose headquarters are relatively static than to units which are constantly on the move.

French intelligence was based on the findings of the Deuxième Bureau and the Cinquième Bureau, branches of the French secret service. The head of the Deuxième Bureau was Colonel Gauché, a man of great intelligence whose only recreation apart from his work was attending to his pet parrot, to which he was devoted. The Deuxième Bureau considered that military information should not be treated in isolation but taken in the context of economic and political events. Gauché believed that the only occasion when France and Britain could have checked Hitler, and the consequent rise of militaristic Germany, was in 1935 when Hitler finally repudiated the Versailles Treaty and reintroduced conscription. The following year, when German troops marched into the Rhineland, was, in his opinion, too late. This was not a view which many people shared, but it was probably correct.

From then on Gauché issued a series of warnings about the German threat. Although they were broadly true, they struck a depressing note which may have contributed to French defeatism. This was certainly not Gauché's intention: he hoped to stir the French government into taking appropriate action to improve its armed forces, but merely seems to have caused the High Command to shrug its shoulders and hope the Germans would be good enough to wear themselves out by trying to break through the Maginot Line. Gauché, who studied the German campaign in Poland with discernment, advised the French High Command to do likewise, and note the way the Germans used their armour. His advice was ignored. After the outbreak of war changes in the organization of the French

Army, which required that the Deuxième Bureau should be split into two parts, made Gauché's task more difficult. Nevertheless he made an exact prediction of where the main German attack would come in May 1940, and how many divisions would be used.

The German secret service, the Abwehr, was one of several intelligence groups but was the most important and had a very wide range of powers. The word *Abwehr* means defence, and it was said that this title was chosen so that Germany's neighbours would not be alarmed by its existence. In 1935 Admiral Canaris, at that time a naval captain, was appointed its head. Canaris was to grow gradually more disenchanted with Hitler and his Nazis, and in various ways seems to have helped the Allies whenever possible. After being implicated in the 1944 attempt to assassinate Hitler he was executed.

However, the Abwehr contained many highly competent and fanatical Nazis, who succeeded in making a comprehensive assessment of the weaknesses of the French Army. Britain was not regarded as a certain opponent at this stage, so German intelligence concentrated on France. The study was rewarding. Much French equipment was out-of-date and little attempt was being made to remedy deficiences in either the Army or the Air Force. Even more encouraging to the Germans was the knowledge that French strategic doctrine had not changed since the end of the First World War. It was static, rather than mobile; the Germans, French military thinking ran, would be kept out of France by fixed defences (this was even before the Maginot Line was planned), and would be further restrained by France's allies to the east and south of Germany. As those allies were Poland, Czechoslovakia and Romania, France's grand strategy of encirclement had become extremely ragged by 1940.

The Abwehr noted that France still clung to the belief that tanks should be linked to the infantry and have no independent function. The only danger presented by the French, in the opinion of the German High Command, was the stubborn fighting quality of the French soldier. He had demonstrated this at Verdun in the last war in a manner which the Germans were unlikely to forget. When that spirit appeared to have evaporated from whole areas of the French Army in May 1940, no one was more surprised than the Germans.

Hitler was greatly encouraged when France made no attempt to prevent German troops reoccupying the Rhineland in 1936. The venture was a tremendous gamble, undertaken against the advice of his War Minister and Foreign Minister. But Gamelin only mobilized part of his Army and relied on the League of Nations to put pressure on Hitler to remove his occupying troops. Hitler had nothing but scorn for the League, and soon the cries of astonishment at the German coup were replaced by passive bleats from appeasers proclaiming that Hitler had every right to retake the demilitarized Rhineland, that it was legally German territory, and so on. Hitler had now challenged both the Western powers and his own generals, and won on both counts. His successful move in 1936 gave him the confidence to over-ride the advice of his generals in 1939, and at intervals throughout the war. Usually he was right, but in the end his reckless disregard of basic military principles led to disaster.

Although puzzled by the fact that the Maginot Line left both Belgium and Holland unprotected, the German staff made a very careful study of its strength and weaknesses. Every fort and bunker was as well known to the German planning staff as it was to the French occupants; the German war college had built an exact model of it, and not merely staff officers but most of the officers who took part in the 1940 invasion were also well aware of the details of its construction. The German generals also had a good idea of how many divisions the French would mobilize – about a hundred – but just as the French overestimated the number of German tanks, so did the Germans overestimate the French tank strength.

The Germans were pleasantly surprised when the outbreak of war in 1939 appeared to make very little difference to French policy. Instead of urging the Belgians to abandon their optimistic neutrality, the French appear to have calmly acquiesced. They made no effort to penetrate the German lines opposite them, but merely attempted a few ineffective patrol probes. France was fully mobilized by October 1939, but there was so little martial spirit and so little enthusiasm for the war that Hitler decided his attack should take place sooner rather than later. Even so, when he mentioned November as a specific date his staff felt the move was premature. On that occasion Hitler took their advice. As the Germans were able to read all the French cyphers they knew where all the weakest spots lay in the French lines, and did not fail to note that the Ardennes sector was the least defended. They were less well informed about the British dispositions, but they knew that the strength of the BEF was not enough to produce a serious threat.

In spite of his protestations that he had no quarrel with Britain, admired the British Empire and, if allowed to pursue his aims in

Europe without interference, would agree to preserve the integrity of the Empire, Hitler had no doubts that Britain would oppose him initially and then play a waiting game. In Hitler's view, neither Russia nor America would condone Nazi activities for long and sooner or later both would join in the fight. Britain, he considered, was acting with consummate duplicity by playing a passive part until those other two great powers joined in. It was a disturbing prospect, so when his troops won their dazzling victory in France in 1940 he decided that at least one of those powers should be eliminated forthwith. Russia, being the nearer, was obviously the first, and a successful invasion could give the Germans access to enough raw materials, and perhaps conscripted manpower, to challenge the rest of the world. A year later, on 22 June 1941, he launched his attack on Russia, confident of victory.

Had France not fallen so easily in 1940 Hitler would never have dared to bury his armies deep in Russia. It was the first step to making a changed world, and it would not have happened if France and Britain had held firm in the West.

Part II

The
Action

5 Prelude to the French Invasion

HITLER'S TWO CAMPAIGNS of spring 1940, in Scandinavia and the Benelux countries, used different weapons and tactics – the former employed infantry with air support on rough terrain, the latter tanks with air support on flatter ground. Both sides were deceived by the Norwegian affair. Hitler, obsessed with the idea that the Allies would re-invade Europe from there, was determined to occupy that country and therefore tied down troops who would be urgently needed on other fronts later in the war. The British for their part could not conceive that Germany was capable of mounting the Norwegian invasion as an independent operation, and were taken aback when Hitler rapidly followed up his Scandinavian success by attacking the Low Countries.

Although in 1939 Norway, Denmark and Sweden had all been neutral, it seemed doubtful whether they would be able to continue in that happy state if the war in the West came alight. When on 30 November that year Russia had invaded Finland, with no better pretext than that the USSR was protecting its own strategic interests, the Swedes had maintained a strict neutrality which extended to forbidding Allied troops to cross Swedish territory in order to help its smaller neighbour. However, in other aspects Sweden's neutrality was less evident, as she supplied huge quantities of iron ore to the German armaments industry. The ore was shipped from Narvik in northern Norway down through Norwegian territorial waters, where it was immune from Allied naval attack. By April 1940 Britain was no longer prepared to allow this flagrant disregard of the international laws of contraband to continue, and on 8 April laid minefields inside Norwegian waters along the route of the illegal trade. But by then Hitler had already decided that the occupation of Norway was essential to his plans and, on the same date, despatched a naval force to occupy the Norwegian ports.

Churchill aptly described the campaign in Norway as 'ramshackle', but this was no fault of the soldiers, sailors and airmen who tried to fight emergency battles against a well-rehearsed German invasion. Norway was, of course, considered a secondary front to that of France – but if the Norway débâcle had been followed by a spirited defence of French territory the overall record would have looked better. Nevertheless, the fact that the entire Norwegian campaign was a two-month-long military disaster should not be allowed to obscure the heroic efforts which sometimes met with success. This was a classic example of a well-prepared campaign taking place under conditions of maximum favour to the aggressor.

Hitler's decision to invade and capture Norway before launching his attack on the West was a bold enterprise, but did him less good than he had hoped. Although Norwegian airfields were valuable as bases for bombing Britain and the Allies' Atlantic shipping, particularly the convoys to Russia, he was so obsessed with the country's apparent vulnerability to an Allied counter-invasion that he kept three hundred thousand men there to the detriment of his war effort elsewhere.

The German victory also had long-term benefits for the Allies. The Norwegian merchant navy, the fourth largest in the world, escaped to Britain and was of enormous value to the Allied war effort. The course of the campaign showed that British troops, who in future years would once again show themselves equal to, if not better than, any in the world, were at that time wrongly equipped, badly or incompletely trained, and, for the most part, unready for modern war; this last fact led to a drastic overhaul of training when Britain was a besieged island between 1940 and 1944. But the most important of all the gains from the Norwegian fiasco was that Chamberlain, the sadly inept Prime Minister who had thought he understood Hitler, was swept out of office with his equally incompetent advisers. In his place came Churchill, without whose leadership it is doubtful if Britain could have raised herself from the ashes of defeat. Churchill had given the first signs of his grasp of military essentials when, at the outset of the Norwegian campaign, he stated that Hitler had made 'a strategic mistake'. During the remainder of the war he was proved right. Unfortunately, Chamberlain did not resign in time for Churchill to assume power before 10 May, by which time the first moves in the campaign directed against France had been initiated, and nothing Churchill could do at that point could avert the disaster.

At 3 a.m. that day the German government sent a note to the governments of Belgium and Holland, informing them that German forces were about to occupy their countries in order to forestall an Anglo-French action to do exactly the same. The fact that the statement was pure fiction was irrelevant. The purpose of the note was to cause confusion and dismay and, with luck, distract the neutrals' minds from what was actually happening to them at that moment. On previous alerts, such as that in January, the Belgians had deployed troops along the French frontier in case France might want to take preventive action against German aggression. Like other ultimatums in the war, that of 10 May did not reach its addressees until disaster was beginning to overwhelm them.

As soon as dawn broke the whole of the combat strength of the Luftwaffe was launched at airfields, railways, roads, depots and other targets in France, Belgium, Holland and Luxembourg. The entire airborne strength of the German Army, a total of 16,000 men, was dropped on selected targets in Holland and Belgium with the aim of capturing bridges and nodal points before they could be destroyed. It was a brilliantly successful operation, accomplished for a mere handful of casualties.

One battalion of airborne troops was landed around Maastricht where the vital bridge over the Meuse was secured by a clever subterfuge recorded a few days later in *The Diary of a Staff Officer*, published anonymously, since its author was still serving in the British Army, in 1941.

The taking of the Maastricht bridge is a fairy tale, amazing in its daring. A plain clothes man walked over to the sentry on the bridge on the East bank and asked him, as a friend, to allow him across the bridge for a last word with a pal on the West bank. He was allowed to pass, he walked across the bridge and after a few minutes' conversation strolled back towards the sentry with his friend. This second man then, gangster-like, shot the sentry and bolted back to the far bank, where he disconnected the wiring of the mines prepared for the destruction of the bridge. While this

49

was being done, the first man possessed himself of the sentry's rifle and easily prevented any interference. The timing was a work of genius: within a few minutes, parachutists and gliders descended in a cloud on top of the Dutch fortifications, and the Belgian fortifications west of the bridge, which is just in Dutch territory. The Germans ran around pushing hand grenades into loopholes, throwing bombs into gun emplacements and casemates and generally playing hell with the place, literally before anyone realised an attack was about to develop at all. They threw their bombs into open doors, into the turrets of casemates, and within an hour, with the loss of only 300 men, the Maastricht bridge-head was established. It had never been supposed that such an achievement would cost less than 50,000 lives.

This episode, as much as any other, shows how the Germans achieved their surprising and devastating success in 1940. The capture of the Maastricht bridge before the Dutch could destroy it represented the application of all the correct military principles. It had clearly been preceded by careful reconnaissance, with many German 'tourists' photographing all the fortifications in peacetime. The trick by which the gullible sentry was lured out of position before being killed must have been rehearsed elsewhere many times. Once the initial advantage had been gained, it was reinforced with speed. The parachutists all knew their objectives. Deception, surprise, speed, the concentration of force: it was a classic operation.

Von Kleist's armoured columns, with a total of 1500 tanks, were now moving through Luxembourg ready to smash a way through the Ardennes and cut the Allied defences in half, like a wasp which has been chopped by a knife. The Belgians and Dutch, who had been firmly convinced that their salvation lay in a policy of strict neutrality, were having desperate second thoughts. They hastily stood to arms and endeavoured to fight back, and appealed to Britain and France to come to their aid. The Dutch also tried the traditional method which they had always used to keep out invaders: they opened the dykes and flooded their precious farmlands. But it was too late.

The Germans had all the advantages which go with a well-prepared, well-rehearsed and completely unexpected attack. The Belgian troops along the Meuse were so surprised by the arrival of the German gliders that at first they thought they were aircraft in difficulties; their first reaction was to help what they imagined were airmen in trouble. The Germans on all fronts knew exactly where they were going and what they should do *en route* and on arrival. Among their unfortunate victims confusion reigned. Nobody knew where to counter-attack or where efforts to resist should best be made. In theory a mass of tanks moving in the open makes a superb bombing target and, given warning, all sorts of unpleasant surprises can be provided for the spearhead. But for that you need spotter aircraft and some idea of where the columns are heading. The French Air Force could neither tell the direction of the attack nor impede it, because the German fighter cover was far superior to anything they could muster for offensive counter-attack.

At dawn that morning 135 German divisions were moving steadily and purposefully in the direction of France. Ten of these were armoured and they included 1st, 2nd and 10th Panzer in Guderian's 19th Armoured Corps. From north to south there were three main groups. Extending from the sea to Aachen was Army Group B under von Bock. It included 18th Army, which incorporated 9th Panzer Division; and 6th Army, and 6th Armoured Corps, which in turn included 3rd and 4th Panzer Divisions. Not least of the auxiliaries of Army Group B were two airborne groups. In the centre, which initially stretched from Aachen to Trier, was Army Group A, brought down from the north to form the main attack. Army Group A, which was commanded by von Rundstedt, comprised 4th Army, which included 5th and 7th Panzer Divisions (General Rommel was commanding 7th Panzer); 41st Panzer Group, made up of 6th and 8th Panzer Divisions; 19th Armoured Corps (General Heinz Guderian), comprising 1st, 2nd and 10th Panzer; General von Wietersheim's Motorized Corps (three divisions and air support), 12th Army (General List), a conventional division and 16th Army. Although the two latter had no Panzer division, they held a considerable air element. In the southern sector, which faced the Maginot Line and extended to the Swiss frontier, was Army Group C (von Leeb), comprised of 1st Army and 7th Army: neither included any Panzers, but both had an air element.

The broad strategy was simple. Holland and Belgium were to be over-run, the Meuse would be crossed and the Panzer divisions would then force their way across France until they reached the Channel. The southern armies would test the Maginot defences and ensure the French kept large forces immobilized there.

Opposing this mass of metal and manpower were three Allied

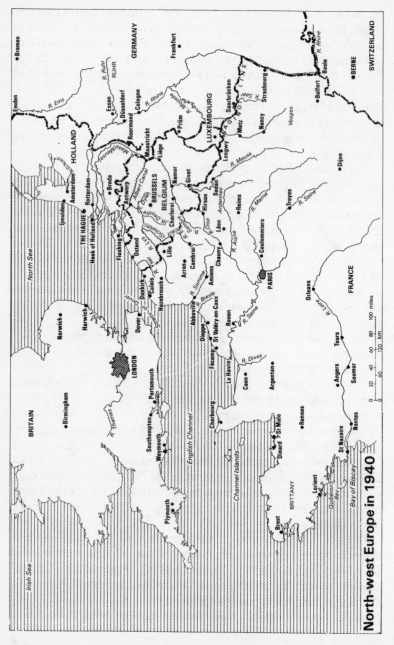

North-west Europe in 1940

groups, deployed from the Channel to the Swiss frontier. In the north, from the sea to Longwy, was 1 Group. Nearest to the coast was the French 2nd Army under General Giraud. As in the previous war, the French Higher Command preferred to have the British inland, although this was remarkably inconvenient for the British and greatly added to their supply problems. Next to Giraud came the BEF under Viscount Gort; it was mainly in the Lille area. After that came the French 1st Army, facing Belgium, the French 9th Army, facing the Ardennes, and the French 2nd Army, approximately facing Luxembourg.

The second Allied Army Group consisted of three French armies (3rd, 4th and 5th) and covered the area from Metz to Strasbourg. The third group, consisting of 8th and 6th French armies, covered the area from Sélestat to the Belfort Gap, in case the Germans decided to violate Swiss neutrality as well and come in through that way too. However, when these dispositions were made Gamelin had not anticipated the weight of the blow which would fall on Holland and Belgium, and still less what was going to happen to his sketchy defences along the Meuse. Total Allied strength was 146 divisions, as opposed to 126 German, but Allied armour was $3\frac{2}{3}$ against 10 German.

There were three main options for the Allies; unfortunately they chose the wrong one and played right into the German hands. Those options were:

1. To let the Germans come forward and then counter-attack when they had come to the end of their initial thrust.

2. To advance into Belgium to the line of the River Escaut (Scheldt) which ran from Antwerp to Ghent, although this would mean abandoning Brussels.

3. To advance to the Dyle Line, Antwerp to the Meuse, approximately following the course of the River Dyle, and thereby support the Belgians who were deployed along the Albert Canal further forward (east). This would also enable support to be given to the Dutch.

Gamelin decided on the third and worst of these options. At best it would take five days for French and British troops to reach their positions along the Dyle Line and dig themselves in. That would take place after the Belgians and Dutch had given their agreement to the proposal, presumably after an exchange of ultimatums and with clear knowledge of an impending German attack. In the event

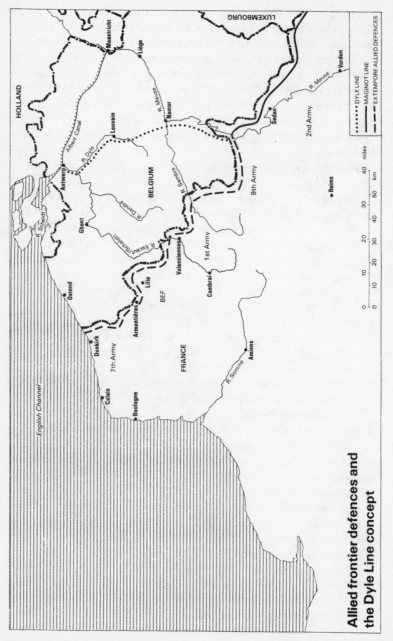

Allied frontier defences and the Dyle Line concept

it took much less than five days, but after the headlong rush forward the rapid movement of events in the central sector would lead to an even more headlong rush back in order to avoid being cut off.

On being given the news of the German attack, Gamelin promptly ordered his troops forward. The time was 6.30 a.m. An hour later, thirty-three Allied divisions were over the Belgian frontier and heading for a line which they believed to be fortified. Before leaving, many of them gazed ruefully on their own lines where they had been digging fortifications for the last eight months, but consoled themselves with the thought that when they reached their destination they would find equally good positions, prepared by somebody else.

Alas for hopes. When they reached their new positions they found there was next to nothing. Certainly nothing to hold up a tank for a moment. Owing to Belgium's policy of neutrality, the Allies had never been allowed to see the area before.

The brightest point in the Belgian defence was a supposedly impregnable fortress at Eben Emael which commanded the bridges on the Albert Canal and the Meuse. It represented the last word in military sophistication, and was perfectly sited for it also guarded Liège. Completed a mere five years earlier, it was 800 yards square, though not a perfect rectangle, and armed with 120-mm and 75-mm guns and a variety of lighter, automatic weapons; it housed a battalion. Rather surprisingly, the fortress carried no anti-aircraft guns, but this was because it was thought to be an unlikely bombing target, being inconspicuous and difficult to approach. But an identical model existed in German airborne headquarters, and its characteristics were as well known as any other part of the Allied defences – probably better. In the early hours of 10 May eleven gliders had left Cologne towed by Ju 52s, the workhorses of the German airborne forces. They carried a total of eighty men – an élite force, carefully selected and meticulously trained.

Two of the gliders slipped their cables *en route*, but the remaining nine reached Aachen at 8000 feet and cast off; they landed with copy-book precision on top of the fort. As they had arrived silently and apparently unobserved by a garrison which did not realize it was already at war, nothing was done to impede the airborne German demolition experts until it was too late. The heavier guns were all destroyed before nearby Belgian forces could take counter-measures against the Germans who were swarming round the exterior. Whatever happened now made little difference, for the main function of

the fort had been neutralized. Inside, 800 Belgian soldiers were trying to get at the invaders and eject them, but neither they nor some
external infantry could dislodge the tenacious airborne troops from
the vantage points they occupied; these had been chosen in advance
from a careful study of the model.

Nevertheless the Germans were relieved in more senses then one
when forward troops from Army Group B arrived on the scene. Now
it was the turn of the Belgians inside the fort to be on the defensive,
and they made a good fight of it against overwhelming odds. When
they realized the position was hopeless they surrendered; they had
sustained 82 casualties, the Germans 21.

This was a crushing blow against the Allies and it had occurred at
the very outset of the campaign. Whenever an 'impregnable' fort
falls it is a serious blow to morale, and occupants of other forts –
such as those in the Maginot Line – began to wonder whether they
might now suffer a similar fate. Clearly the Germans had used very
powerful, though portable, explosives. What were they, and what
other applications might they have?* The whole Allied strategy of
defending the line of the Albert Canal was now in tatters; however,

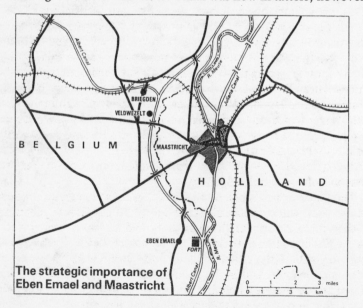

The strategic importance of
Eben Emael and Maastricht

*Hollow charge shot – an explosive that could blow holes through steel and concrete.

they could still defend the Dyle Line from Antwerp to Louvain, and this they prepared to do. Fortunately, as it seemed, the Germans were too busy with their forward attack to pay much attention to the reinforcements rushing up to Belgium, which remained surprisingly unharassed by the Luftwaffe. No ugly thoughts that the Germans wanted the Allies to pack as many men into Belgium as they could crossed anyone's mind.

The Germans could well feel pleased with their first day's work; they had also captured the bridges at Dordrecht, Moerdijk and Rotterdam. In Holland some of their airborne troops had arrived wearing Dutch uniforms. International law frowns on men who wear the uniform of their enemy, and usually they are shot as spies, if captured. These troops were not captured, but their appearance meant that from now on the Allies could never be quite sure whether that handful of men in what appeared to be Dutch, French, Belgian or even British uniform were all that they looked. Doubts of this nature were fanned by German propaganda so that during the remainder of the campaign, and during the subsequent battle of Britain, there was deep suspicion that policemen, nuns, soldiers, almost anyone in a distinctive uniform could be a disguised German parachutist.

The fighting in Holland was brisk enough to suggest that this was the main German attack, and that their strategy was a revival of the old Schlieffen Plan. Rotterdam was clearly going to be isolated and then captured, giving the Germans a vital port and denying it to the Allies. Giraud's 7th Army rushed up to relieve the city before it could be surrounded, but his ill-equipped army was intercepted by 9th Panzer which had come racing across Holland to make just such a move. As the forces engaged, the Luftwaffe hammered Giraud's soldiers relentlessly. It was clear that Rotterdam was not going to be relieved now. However, no one on the Allied side suspected the fate in store for that unfortunate city.

The German aim seemed to be to bring intense pressure to bear at the point where the Belgian and Dutch Armies joined. Junctures such as this are traditionally weak spots, and it proved to be so here, as the Germans forced their way through towards Liège. They were able to outflank the defences along the Albert Canal and threaten those on the Dyle. Unless they could be checked, or at least slowed down before they reached that point, French reinforcements would not arrive in time to add their weight to the defence.

Already on the second day of the battle it was becoming

unpleasantly clear to the Higher Command that the Allies were inferior not only in tactical concepts but also, and even more so, in material. This was particularly true of anti-tank guns: four-fifths of their stocks were the light 25-mm, but only the 47-mm had any effect on the Panzers. Even worse was the French Air Force, which was not merely numerically inferior but was hopelessly outclassed in combat. Its efforts to bomb the bridges which the Germans had captured intact were easily driven off by the Luftwaffe. There was now nothing to stop German troops pouring into the gaps in the already overstretched Allied defences. The only man who seemed unaware of the gravity of the situation was the Commander-in-Chief, General Gamelin. But there was worse to come.

While the eyes of the Allies were fixed upon the disasters which were overwhelming Belgium and Holland, von Kleist's Panzers, which had crossed the Belgian frontier on the night of the 10th, had brushed aside the opposition provided by two cavalry divisions and were heading in the direction of Sedan; the leading division was commanded by Rommel. The thrust which would prove mortal to France was already being launched.

By the third day, 12 May, Giraud decided he was badly exposed on his right flank and should withdraw or risk being cut off altogether. This meant the end of support for the Dutch Army, which from now on would have to fend for itself. Considering that it had been taken completely by surprise, it had rallied and was putting up a much better fight than expected. The outlook for Belgium looked little better and King Leopold ungrudgingly agreed that the Belgian Army should now be treated as part of the Allied force, instead of continuing to fight independently.

The Germans now decided to tighten the screw. So far their assets had been speed and surprise; to these they now added terror. On 14 May Rotterdam suffered the first great blitz raid of the war. The whole German campaign had now received the name 'Blitzkrieg' (lightning war), but the word 'blitz' later came to mean devastating air attacks on cities. Rotterdam was undoubtedly a military target, but with the impending Dutch surrender the Luftwaffe had decided to call off their planned raid. Unfortunately for Rotterdam, the message to postpone or cancel the raid went astray and 57 Heinkels dropped 97 tons of high explosive into the centre of the city. Most of the houses were of wood and blazed fiercely; there was no adequate fire-fighting apparatus such as would be seen elsewhere, as in

London later in the war. The number of casualties was at first given as forty thousand, although later that figure was drastically reduced. In fact nobody knows the real death toll. The Germans pointed out that British raids had already pounded some of their cities, but in view of their later policies of Baedeker raids – raids on historic towns and cities – few were prepared to listen to their excuses.

The Dutch Army, which now finally surrendered, had fought well, sustaining heavy casualties. The government and Queen Wilhelmina escaped to England in a British destroyer. But though Holland was out of the war, its colonies were not, and they continued to be a valuable asset for the Allies until Japan over-ran those in the East Indies.

The principal tool of terror tactics was the dive-bomber. They roared down from the sky, creating fear far beyond the material damage they inflicted, but as their targets were often refugees trying to hurry to safety along already blocked roads they succeeded in hampering Allied movements all along the front and behind it. Among the Luftwaffe's assets was the 'screaming bomb', which had a fluted tail that produced a terrfying shriek; a 'screamer' gave the impression that death was imminent and that all resistance would be useless.

But for anyone foolish enough to believe that, there was a rallying voice to say differently. The new British Prime Minister, Winston Churchill, gave a speech in the House of Commons outlining the military position and promising that Britain would prosecute the war whatever the cost. But, well aware that there was worse news to come, he added, 'I have nothing to offer but blood, toil, tears, and sweat.' Curiously enough, it was a heartening message. Here at last was a realist.

6 The Masterstroke

ALL THROUGH 13 and 14 May the Germans kept up their relentless pressure and war of nerves, never letting the Allies know where their next thrust would come. Rommel crossed the Meuse at Huy, Reinhardt's 41st Panzer went over at Monthermé, and Guderian's 19th Panzer had now reached the outskirts of Sedan. The RAF made a gallant attempt to stop the rot there, sending 109 aircraft to attack the German troop concentration in the area. It was a costly venture, for they were outnumbered by the Luftwaffe and lost 45 planes. The British airmen were attacking under the worst possible conditions, but a loss of this magnitude could not possibly be repeated or there would soon be no viable RAF left.

Although the French were making a vigorous effort to stem the German tide, their morale was not being improved by having to fall back in one area after another. The determination and resourcefulness of the oncoming German troops was even more intimidating than their superior firepower. The Meuse, in which so much British confidence had reposed, was treated by the Germans with almost contemptuous disdain. They crossed it in rowing boats, dinghies or improvised straw rafts. Some of the Germans soldiers were observed to be swimming across it. Guderian himself had crossed the Meuse in a dinghy.

Confronted with so many targets strung along a broad front, the French defenders began to feel that their task was impossible. The minefields which they had hoped would check any invader had somehow been crossed. The gun emplacements in which they had

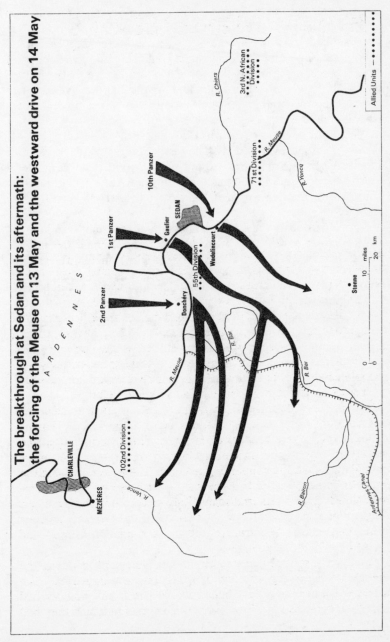

The breakthrough at Sedan and its aftermath: the forcing of the Meuse on 13 May and the westward drive on 14 May

housed their heavier artillery had been hammered into uselessness by a combination of German anti-tank fire and dive-bombers. The dive-bombers had also helped to neutralize French artillery positions behind the lines. The French gunners could stand up to bombing – even if it were continuous there was an even chance that many of the bombs would miss their appointed targets; but the dive-bomber gave the impression that the whole aircraft was coming to obliterate what lay underneath.

When they could raise their heads the French defenders searched the sky for their own aircraft. They looked in vain. Wherever the French Air Force was, it was certainly not here where it was needed. Finally it appeared, in conjunction with the RAF, but like the British force mentioned earlier it had little but losses to show for its trouble.

German troops were now past Sedan and had built a bridge at Gaulier, over which tanks were now pouring. Behind the ragged French line the roads were already clogged with refugees. The French artillery, which relied on horse transport, was now immobilized because most of the horses had been killed by low-flying Luftwaffe machine-gunners.

Gamelin's headquarters staff heard reports of these disasters with growing dismay. In theory the Germans should have been checked on the Meuse – if they reached that far – and decimated by heavy casualties. Instead they had swept past this natural obstacle, on which the French defence relied heavily, and now had formidable troop concentrations to the west of it. Nobody knew exactly where the Germans were, and how far their probing tanks had reached. There were ominous rumours – proved later to be true – that French soldiers, stunned by the totally unexpected weight and ferocity of the air bombardment, had abandoned their positions and run for it. Already an incredible thought was beginning to dawn: the Germans were invincible.

In fact, this was far from true. They had been able to land on each side of Sedan, leaving that famous frontier town with its Vauban fortifications virtually unmolested. But their two bridgeheads consisted only of infantry and if the French had been able to mount a vigorous counter-attack, using armour, the Germans would have been trapped in a nightmare position – without tanks or anti-tank guns, in unfamiliar, forested country, with their backs to the river and completely exposed to frontal and flank attacks. Tactically it was an extremely hazardous move by the Germans and the French should have been able to neutralize them while the French Air Force pounded the Gaulier bridge and prevented tanks from crossing it.

Every hour which passed was vital to the success or failure of the attack. The order to counter-attack had been issued by the French 10th Corps Commander, General Grandsard, but the two infantry regiments and two tank battalions allotted to the task decided to wait until night before they moved and thus avoid the attentions of the German dive-bombers. It was a fatal decision, for when they did move their progress was hampered by a disorganized mixture of retreating soldiers from the front and the first tide of refugees. Thus they lost vital time, all of which was being employed by the Germans to bring over their tanks and heavier weapons.

Morale was already being seriously affected. It had not been high at the beginning, and now the sight of panic-stricken troops, stumbling back with horrific stories of dive-bombing, depressed it further. In such situations ruthless but realistic commanders have been known to shoot a few of the panic-stricken stragglers as an example, and to turn the others round and make them go forward at the point of a gun; however, the French had no commanders with the requisite experience.

Not all French morale was bad; there were certain pockets of resistance which would have been notable even in the finest days of French armies. But German propaganda had done its work well, and was continuing to do so. When the fighting began, the Germans dropped leaflets over the interior of France. In the Second World War, when there were many fewer civilian radios than there are today and almost no television, the simplest means of communicating with people in remote areas was by dropping leaflets from aircraft. Britain had scattered propaganda leaflets widely in Germany since the start of the war. They advised the Germans not to co-operate with Hitler and finished with the words: 'This might have been a bomb.' The leaflets can have had no effect at all. Later in the war the Japanese would use crude leaflets to try to persuade American and British troops in the Far East that, while they were in danger of being killed, troops at home were seducing their wives. These mostly caused amusement.

But the leaflets in France had rather more effect. They reminded the recipients that in the previous war many French people had been trapped in German-held territory and their lives had not been pleasant. The thought that this might occur again caused many families in eastern France to take to the roads and to try to find a new home further west. It was a disastrous decision in every way. France does not possess the network of minor roads which exist in Britain, and the refugees, as they were soon called, moved on to the excellent trunk roads, blocking them completely. When German aircraft came over and bombed and machine-gunned them, the chaos was indescribable. The worst effect was on military transport, which found itself unable to move guns and other materials to places where they were desperately needed. The first refugees set off in cars, usually with a mattress and bedding strapped on top and with the family packed inside. Then followed the bicycles and the pedestrians, all carrying as much as they could. They left behind farms on which cows were left unmilked, and all animals unfed and untended.

Among the refugees were French soldiers who had thrown away their arms, saying that the struggle was hopeless. The stories the soldiers told did little for morale. They spoke of German troops advancing shoulder to shoulder. French field guns and machine-guns opened fire and blew away the front ranks. But still more came on. Nobody paid any attention to the dead and dying. German soldiers simply marched over them, ignoring their pathetic cries for help, and German tanks drove over them and crushed the living and the dead. German soldiers advanced as if they were subhuman, or perhaps drugged into insensibility. British soldiers, who were now encountering fanatical Nazi stormtroopers in Belgium, were telling the same story.

At first the French families in the rear areas tried to do what they could for the refugees, but when the numbers grew too great the task became impossible and was abandoned. The civilian and military authorities tried to get them off the roads, and to clear the path for military traffic. Perhaps the most tragic aspect of it all was that the refugees did not know where they were going or what they planned to do when they stopped. Their worst moment came when they realized that fleeing from the invading armies in eastern France was eventually taking them into the path of the Germans advancing from the north. When that happened they began to retrace their steps, but most of them would not see their homes again for many months. When they did, there would be little trace of the stocks they had built up with years of frugal living and hard work. Often they would find someone else in possession. Families who had become separated, perhaps lost a child or even a wife or husband in that wild trek across country, might never be reunited.

For the advancing German army the fact that the whole of northern France was in turmoil, and that nearly all the major roads were so clogged that vital traffic could not move, was a valuable asset. It was not a benefit the Germans had expected, but when it came it was quickly appreciated as being far more effective than anything that saboteurs could have done by blowing up bridges or mining roads. France was caught in a totally unexpected and disastrous situation. The British had expected the large-scale destruction of their cities by bombs and had made provisions accordingly; but the French had never subscribed to the idea that the Germans would try to defeat them by strategic bombing and had therefore not contemplated extensive evacuation, still less an army of refugees.

Wild rumours passing as fact were not confined to refugees. They existed in the High Command too. While Gamelin was being informed that the Germans at Sedan had been contained and were being counter-attacked, the French 7th Armoured Battalion was being destroyed by German Panzers which had crossed the Gaulier bridge. The 213th Infantry Regiment was swept aside with equal ease. Had those units moved forward twelve hours earlier, all the advantages would have been with them and the battle of France could have taken a different turn. If the Germans had been checked in this area, they would not have been able to get in behind the troops moving up to Belgium; a stable line could have been established. The morale of the German generals, which was known to be brittle, would have been badly affected and the more conservative of them would have taken the opportunity to restrain those wild and dangerous thrusts by insubordinate and over-confident tank commanders.

But the situation was already worse for the French than anyone on either side imagined. In the northern sector of the Sedan area the 55th Division, having lost one armoured and one infantry regiment in an abortive counter-attack, now disintegrated. In the southern sector the 71st Division, which should also have been putting in a counter-attack, decided on its own initiative to withdraw. In the ensuing chaos local commanders, lacking any proper picture of the battle, issued orders they thought were appropriate. The soldiers, feeling that their officers were as bewildered as they were themselves, obeyed the orders telling them to withdraw and ignored those telling them to stand and fight.

Unaware of the undisciplined chaos ahead of them, other troops of the French 2nd Army were now moving forward. The commander, General Huntziger, told them their task was first to hold the German invaders, then to drive them back in a counter-attack; the latter would be put in 'regardless of loss'. This order echoed the spirit which had infused the French soldiers in the desperate battles of the previous war. It was the last chance to stop the Panzers before they broke out, and it could also have turned the battle round completely. Guderian was now at his most vulnerable point. Having reached farther into the French defences than he had hoped for in his most optimistic expectations, he now decided to put into effect the battle tactics he had often worked out on paper and in manoeuvres. He swung 1st and 2nd Panzer Divisions to the right, knowing that, if successful, this would give them a chance to break right through the French forward defences and rampage at will in the rear areas. But it was a risky manoeuvre. If the tanks of the French 2nd Army could come in behind them, they could create a gap in the German column before 3rd Panzer could reach it and close it. The speed of the forward Panzers had left the German infantry behind, and 3rd Panzer was also well to the rear.

The French had resources well capable of exploiting this opportunity. It would not be quite as easy as the earlier opportunity that they had missed, but it could ultimately have been even more effective. Second Army had four excellent tank regiments, good artillery and plenty of motorized infantry. While Guderian was forging ahead with 1st and 2nd Panzer, 2nd Army could prepare an adequate reception for 3rd Panzer which was equipped with the earliest, oldest and least efficient of the German tanks.

Once again the French were slow in setting off, but not so slow that they could not reach their objective if they made all possible speed once they were on the road. But on the late afternoon of 14 May, when the French regiments allotted to this task were eager to go and were licking their lips at what looked like being a crushing victory over the Boche, they received a counter-order. Instead of driving forward as an armoured spearhead, they were to take up defensive positions on a twelve-mile front south-east of the German breakthrough. They were told to disperse and to use their tanks to make a series of small strongpoints. If Guderian had been praying at that moment, this is exactly what he would have asked for. The French orders were completed on the night of the 14th.

But on the same day General Georges, who had been deputed by Gamelin to take overall charge of this sector of the line, and whose vacillations were largely responsible for the state of chaos, now decided that the counter-attack should be put in after all. However it would not be headed by the armour, but be an infantry operation, using tanks but keeping them in close contact with the infantry and not employing them as a wedge, as the Germans were doing. Its worst feature was that, as now organized, it could not possibly reach the Meuse; at best it could pinch the German lines and harass them. But it was better than doing nothing.

Unfortunately for any success this new attack might have had, its first requirement was that the tanks which had been dispersed should be assembled again. That lost precious time. The attack was timed for midday, but the failure of the tanks to return quickly enough from their dispersal points caused it to be postponed until late afternoon. At 5 p.m. so few tanks were available that it was postponed once more – until dawn the following day. This was 15 May: the invasion was five days old, and the ineptitude of the French Higher Command was so great that it seemed that it could only be explained by treachery. The Russians would have shot most of the generals in similar circumstances. But there was worse to come, and the French would not be the only ones to make disastrous mistakes.

Already two French divisions on this front had disintegrated and melted away. The average number of soldiers in a division at that time was fifteen thousand; therefore thirty thousand stragglers were now in the rear area. Their effect on morale may be imagined. Infiltrated among them were French-speaking Germans whose task was to spread alarm and despondency. Their task was not difficult, for at intervals German aircraft flew down the roads bombing and machine-gunning the long lines of helpless refugees. If there was one thing calculated to confirm the refugees' view that they were wise to flee from the merciless Boche, the bombing and strafing of helpless, unarmed civilians supplied it.

In spite of the previous hesitation and vacillation, 15 May began well for the French. Gross-Deutschland, a crack SS regiment, had seized the town of Stonne the previous day. On the 15th it was pushed back out again by the French 2nd Army troops. The Germans tried to recapture it but failed. During that day and the next the front stabilized, and by 17 May Guderian had become very worried by the fact that both the bridgeheads were now surrounded by superior numbers of French troops who had also brought up their artillery. As the German casualties mounted, confidence began to return to the French. Their colonial troops, Algerians, Moroccans and Senegalese, were more than a match for the Germans. Guderian realized that he must make a quick and successful move if he was to regain the initiative. If it failed, his whole strategy would fail with it. He could not afford to let the French keep Stonne, for the high ground around it dominated the battlefield.

While Guderian was visiting the headquarters of Gross-Deutschland he received orders from von Kleist that the present bridgeheads must not be extended and there must be no further advance anywhere. He was furious at being thus frustrated in his plans. Having failed to persuade the Panzer Group Chief of Staff to make von Kleist change his mind, he spoke to him himself. Von Kleist was not pleased. However, after a heated telephone discussion in which Guderian paid little deference to von Kleist's rank, the latter grudgingly agreed to allow the advance to be continued for another twenty-four hours.

This was enough for Guderian. He knew that if he was not given a firm order to stop he could continue his attack in whatever direction he pleased, if necessary giving the advanced thrust the name of 'reconnaissance probes'. The Panzer crews, who had been on the road since 9 May, were now very tired, and ammunition was running low. However, when Guderian captured an order which he believed originated from Gamelin, and which said: 'The torrent of German tanks must finally be stopped', he deduced that the French Army was on the point of giving way completely, and resolved that whatever the state of his own troops the Panzer attacks must be continued.

When the order was given to continue the advance, tiredness was forgotten. Guderian had been right in interpreting Gamelin's message as a cry of despair. Once the Panzers had broken through the French 2nd Army there was nothing to stop them. They were in open country. By the end of the day they had reached Marle and Dercy, fifty-five miles from Sedan.

But on the morning of 17 May, to Guderian's astonishment, he was told that his advance must be halted immediately. Furthermore he was told that von Kleist was coming to see him personally. The ensuing interview would have brought great joy to the Allies if they had known of it, but it brought none to Guderian. Without even greeting him with a 'Good morning', von Kleist launched into a tirade about

Guderian's insubordination in disobeying orders. Guderian listened in silence, but at the end he asked to be relieved of his command. Although surprised, von Kleist gave his instant agreement. The interview was over and Guderian returned to 19th Corps headquarters; from there he sent a radio message to von Rundstedt saying that he had now handed over his command and would be flying to GHQ to make a report.

Before he could move, however, a reply came from von Rundstedt ordering him to remain where he was. Soon General List arrived; he told Guderian he would not be allowed to hand over his command but the order to stop the advance must be obeyed, as it had come from the Army High Command. Guderian would, however, be allowed to continue his 'reconnaissance in force'. Even while he was pondering this order he heard that, before the order to stop had reached them, 1st and 10th Panzer had covered another twenty miles, crossed the Oise and established a bridgehead on the far side. The masterstroke had worked.

7 Rumour and Reality

THE TRUTH of what had happened in these critical days would not be established until years later, but when it eventually emerged it would show that, in spite of certain sectors of the French Army collapsing after putting up little resistance, others had fought with stubborn gallantry. In the fighting before Guderian made his first breakthrough German losses had been so high on several occasions that the validity of their whole strategy was called into question. But during most of the campaign almost all the information available consisted of out-of-date reports on long-changed situations, and wild rumours.

All crises produce rumours, but military crises produce rumours which exceed all others. In May 1940 there was little else to go on. As virtually no information was available from French official sources, British headquarters filled in the gap with highly imaginative versions which bore little relation to reality. On 10 May most staff officers had been taken completely by surprise when the BBC announced that the invasion of Belgium and Holland had taken place. The BBC, of course, knew nothing of what was in store for Sedan.

Within hours there were stories of the bombing of Brussels, Antwerp and Amsterdam. These had probably come from German radio, but were true. More encouraging news said that all the bridges over the Meuse had been demolished by French troops. German parachutists who had landed in Holland were said to have all been rounded up and captured. Reports came in that the Dutch Army was resisting well and had retaken all the airfields they had recently lost to German parachutists. News that British troops were now advancing rapidly into Belgium was regarded with mixed feelings. All through the winter months British soldiers had been preparing defensive positions on the Belgian frontier. Now these were to be abandoned. Was this wise? Meanwhile the Luftwaffe seemed to be ranging through Allied air space at will. Not for the last time would the question be asked: 'Where are our fighters?' The RAF was credited with a miraculous ability to intercept and shoot down any German aircraft which ventured into the skies above France. The bridge at Maastricht was reported to have been destroyed; then came another message to say that unfortunately it had not been and German troops were now pouring across it.

Staff officers were expected to know what was going on, and if they remained tight-lipped the assumption was that they were obeying orders, rather than ignorant of the general situation. No one could doubt the importance of a staff officer in the early days of the war. Usually he wore a broad, distinctive armband with a large G (for Operations), A (for Personnel) or Q (for Supply) on it. Outsiders entering a headquarters usually received a frosty welcome – if in fact they managed to penetrate that far. Headquarters were easily identifiable from large notices with the words 'This entrance for Brigadiers and above only'.

At home the war seemed even more remote. Brian Horrocks, then a colonel but later to be a lieutenant-general, was senior instructor at the Staff College Camberley on 10 May 1940. His first information that the war had started came from his batman, who brought him a cup of tea at 7.30 a.m. As Horrocks gulped it down, he could scarcely have imagined that in three weeks' time he would be standing up to his knees in the sea off Dunkirk trying to shepherd the remnants of a brigade on to the flotilla of rescue ships. The Germans had planned to take the Allies by surprise and had certainly done so, but one effect of their shock tactics was that they were nearly as surprised as the Allies, and almost as far out of touch with the course of events.

Once the French civilians had recovered from the initial surprise at being at war they responded briskly until they were over-run or became refugees. Almost every aircraft in the sky, whether German or not, seemed to trigger off an air raid alarm, given by sirens supported by church bells. The alarm was rang by sonorous peals, and the all clear by the more cheery notes usually heard when a newly married couple leave the church.

71

As the British official history of the war (*Grand Strategy*, Vol. II, by J. R. M. Butler) succinctly puts it: 'Until the night of the 13th the situation in the land battles did not appear particularly alarming. The British Expeditionary Force had reached their appointed position on the Dyle more or less unmolested, the bulk of the Luftwaffe being engaged elsewhere, and the French First Army were in place on their right. Little was known of what was happening on the far side of the Meuse. . . .'

By 16 May a very different picture had emerged. On the 14th the news of the German breakthrough at Sedan had been reported and in consequence the French 1st Army had decided to withdraw from the position it was holding on the right of the British line. The Dutch were known to have surrendered. In London the Cabinet, which had already been alarmed by the use of German parachutists in Poland, Norway and Holland, ordered that Civil Defence should be fully alerted. The first steps towards setting up the Home Guard, the Local Defence Volunteers, were taken, although unfortunately there were so few arms for them that they had to rely on private shotguns and what could be borrowed from museums. The French Prime Minister's appeal for more British fighter planes to be sent to France was debated but considered too risky, as the British government felt that this would reduce the United Kingdom's own fighter strength to a figure below the safe minimum. Relations between Britain and France were not improved by the fact that Britain had authorized a bombing raid on the Ruhr towns on 15 May. It seemed to have done little damage, had no effect on the course of the war, but had been given priority over the obviously more important task of checking the German invasion of France by armoured divisions. However, the RAF in France was working to the limit of its pilots and aircraft.

The disastrous failure of the French Army at Sedan now had repercussions throughout the entire Allied armies. It was reported that members of the best French regiments wept openly when they heard that the Germans had been able to cross five miles of fortifications with minimal losses. Apparently it had been considered that the defences in this area, combined with the Meuse, made such a formidable barrier that they could be manned by low-grade troops; but when these men were dive-bombed they simply abandoned their posts. Attacking French morale had become a high priority with the Germans. Many of their bombs were fitted with delayed-action fuses, so that no one in a recently bombed area could be sure that the worst was over when the enemy aircraft flew off.

Disillusionment was now widespread. Before hostilities began the French Army was said to have a substantial number of 70-ton tanks, which would be more than a match for anything the Panzers could produce. The 'substantial number', thought to be in the region of a thousand, now turned out to be about twenty, but even these were not in evidence. The famous French 75-mm guns, which could have given the German tanks a warm reception at every bend in the road, were nowhere to be seen. The terrible poverty of Gamelin's strategy was now revealed: he had no strategic reserve. Once again the French Prime Minister, Monsieur Reynaud, appealed for more fighters to be sent from Britain. Churchill and the British Cabinet were reluctant to comply, even though the French told them the road to Paris was open to the marauding Panzers.

Churchill could not easily grasp a situation in which a small number of German tanks, which by now must be low on fuel and ammunition as well as being in need of urgent maintenance, could be treated with such awe by the French. However, when the French pleaded that they had now lost all their best artillery (much of it was in the territory the Germans had over-run), and that they only had 150 fighter aircraft left, Churchill and the Cabinet reluctantly agreed to allot six more squadrons to France. This left thirty for the defence of Britain. However, as Britain had already sent twenty squadrons to France, there was no room on the French airfields for the additional six, which had to be based on airfields in Kent and work over France. It was hoped that this generous gesture would provide a much-needed boost to French morale and at the same time enable the French Army to assemble a strategic reserve.

Churchill was convinced that the Panzers had made themselves so vulnerable by their deep incursions that spirited counter-attacks cutting them off from their bases could not fail to be successful. No doubt if he had realized that at that moment the German High Command, the French Army and the BEF all shared a common view in wishing to stop the further progress of Guderian's Panzers, he would have taken an ironic pleasure in the coincidence. It was said that Churchill did not understand how desperate the French position was, and how low French morale had sunk, until he flew over to Paris for a brief conference with Reynaud on the 16th. As he stood in the conference room, he could see French foreign ministry files being burnt in the gardens outside. Within a week of the beginning of the German attack the French were preparing for their enemies to be in control of the capital of France.

However, in spite of the collapse of French morale the war was by no means lost – yet. It was nevertheless clear that the main danger was not that the Germans would reach Paris before they could be stopped, but that they would reach the Channel ports. In doing so they would cut across France behind the British Expeditionary Force, which had unwisely abandoned its position and dashed forward into Belgium. That last tactical move had been based on various misconceptions. It had been assumed that the Belgians would be able to hold the German attack; no one had dreamt of such lightning blows as that at Eben Emael. The French troops which had entered Belgium in company with the British were of vastly superior quality to those in the Meuse area, but when both advancing and withdrawing they were badly hampered in their movements by the flood of refugees. Swift and orderly progress became impossible.

From the outbreak of war liaison between the British and French commands had not been as close as it should have been. There were several reasons for this. Gamelin, the French Commander-in-Chief, was a legendary figure in French eyes and considered himself omniscient. In numbers the French forces greatly exceeded the British, and as they were in separate sectors there seemed little reason for co-ordination of plans, apart from the broad general strategy. The British accepted the French view that the Maginot Line was impregnable, and in view of the vastly greater size of the French contribution scarcely dared criticize the overall strategy. Subsequently it transpired that at no point had Britain really understood the implications of Gamelin's concepts – that the Maginot Line was impregnable and that no strategic reserve was therefore necessary. When the realization had sunk in on 19 May – after the breakthrough – Sir John Dill, one of the shrewdest British generals of the war, who had now become Vice-Chief of the General Staff, was despatched to make a lengthy stay in General Georges' HQ. While there he had to explain as tactfully as possible what steps Britain might have to take if the French did not manage to stabilize the position in their own sectors.

Dill was not, of course, suggesting that it was a *sauve qui peut* situation. His aim was to boost French morale and ensure that the French remained intact as a fighting force (even though they had been badly battered), but at the same time to make clear that British tactics might, in the long run, be beneficial to all. He did not, however, point out that if the general situation continued to deteriorate as fast as it had been doing the British Expeditionary Force might have to fall back on the Channel ports and see what resistance could be maintained from there. That thought was in his mind, and no doubt in the minds of the French, who took it a stage further and considered that the British at any moment might scuttle to the sea, where the Royal Navy would rescue them, and leave France to its fate. Dill was aware that, although the British point of view was that the French had created the present chaos by allowing the Germans to penetrate the Sedan sector so easily, the French view could well be that if the British contribution of land forces had been two or three times larger it would have made an admirable strategic reserve. He knew that German propaganda was trying to split the Allies by circulating the old jibe that England would always fight to the last Frenchman, but he also wished to see whether the French still believed they could make a miraculous recovery at the last minute.

When the Germans had first made their breakthrough, many French soldiers were consoling themselves with the fact that something very similar had occurred in 1914. On that occasion also, the French had been taken by surprise when the Germans smashed through Belgium (violating its neutrality) and came close to Paris before being checked. In their hour of extremity France had rushed all available troops to the front, even using taxis. In those days, of course, France had had Foch and Joffre; now they had Gamelin and Georges. Every French soldier knew of the heroic battle of the Marne in which the German Army had not only been checked but even made to fall back. Few realized that France had changed greatly since 1914.

Desperate diseases, it is said, need desperate remedies. Even while the Cabinet was discussing the vital need for the British to show by actions as much as by words that they were wholeheartedly supporting the French, a rumour that the British were contemplating withdrawing and leaving France went like wildfire through the French Army. Unfortunately it found plenty of believers in French GHQ. Dill promptly reported the rumour to Churchill and pointed out that its potentially damaging effects must be countered immediately.

Churchill responded at once. Instead of sending a message he sent the Chief of the Imperial General Staff himself, General Sir Edmund

Ironside, to France with the specific instruction that the British Army must now take up a position to the left of the French Army, whatever the circumstances. Ironside promptly delivered this message to Viscount Gort, Commander-in-Chief of the British Expeditionary Force. Gort was a man of outstanding courage who had won the Victoria Cross in the previous war and was of no mean ability as a general, but even he could not do the impossible. The inescapable fact was, as he explained to Ironside, that the area between the BEF and the French was already occupied by German armoured columns. Seven of his own divisions were already locked in conflict with the Germans up on the Scheldt. For the task which Ironside now entrusted to him he had neither the men, the material nor the ammunition. Although Gort did not say so at the time, the thought was already in his mind that unless the British Army could be collected up and withdrawn to the Channel ports there might soon be no British Army to continue the fight.

By this time Guderian had decided that the battle for France was almost won but that the chief obstacle to victory was the German High Command and not the fighting ability of the French and British armies. Realizing that his German superiors were now monitoring his radio messages to make sure that he was obeying their orders, he ordered a radio silence and sent his instructions by telephone. He knew that unless a miracle happened he would soon have reached the Channel ports, and when that occurred his insubordination would be overlooked as everyone else took the credit for his achievement.

8 Battle in the Skies

THE BEF WAS NOW in serious trouble as it tried to cope with its various commitments. Not least of its problems was keeping the Advanced Air Striking Force in viable being. At that time this overworked unit was trying to deal with the problems arising from the long and rapid retreats. As the Germans approached the forward airfields, the AASF had to arrange the movement of essential spares and other vital assets to new sites. As they were short of transport – which in any case had to force its way along congested roads – it often seemed as if the Panzers might catch up with them before they had reached their new position. Fortunately they were able to borrow two hundred trucks from the French Air Force to help with their task.

The AASF, which would have to continue its inconvenient retreats until France finally fell, had had a frustrating nine and a half months' existence, but when required to act did so with great forthrightness and courage. Its early work had been mainly on photographic reconnaissance and for this it had no fighter escorts for its Fairey Battle medium bombers. Losses soon began to mount because the rear gunner in the Battle could not depress his gun to aim at the Messerschmitts when they came from underneath. In consequence pilots had to adopt an unnerving procedure to shake off their attackers. On sighting the Messerschmitts they dived for the ground, knowing that the German fighters would not be able to pull out of their dives if they came after them. However, coming close to the ground in this manoeuvre took them within range of the German machine-guns. Later aircraft which flew with the squadrons included Whitleys and Blenheims, which were better equipped to deal with the Messerschmitts.

The Allied airfields were the targets of continuous German raids after the May invasion. The AASF's own aircraft were paying special attention to the German supply lines but were outnumbered, and often faced superior machines. In consequence, the group lost 60 per cent of its aircraft. The Germans were using Junkers 88 bombers, Dorniers and Messerschmitt 109s and 110s.

The highest peak in the achievements of the AASF was the bombing of the bridges in the Maastricht area on 12 May. These had erroneously been reported as demolished earlier, although one had been captured by a trick and the other by parachutists. They were put to full use by the Germans, who immediately installed batteries of anti-aircraft guns as well as fighter cover.

No. 12 Squadron was allotted the task. It was clearly a near-suicide mission, so the squadron leader, having pointed out the hazards, asked for volunteers. Everyone stepped forward. The names were then put in a hat. Six machines set out in two flights, but one machine had to turn back almost at once because of engine trouble. They had an escort of three fighters; the Germans met them with thirty Messerschmitts. Although the British fighters destroyed several enemy aircraft, they themselves were shot down. As the five planes flew on towards their target, even more enemy aircraft appeared and there was also a heavy anti-aircraft barrage. The three bombers in the leading flight hit one bridge and turned for home, but all three were then shot down by the anti-aircraft guns. The two aircraft in the second flight were also hit, but not before they had destroyed the second bridge. One was shot down but the other managed to land. There were two survivors of the raid. Subsequently two posthumous VCs were awarded to the leaders of the first flight.

For the remainder of the battle of France the AASF was continuously in action. It was always outnumbered, but this never stopped its pilots attacking large formations of Dorniers, Junkers 88s, Heinkels and Messerschmitt 110s. In single combat the Hurricanes were more than a match for their opponents, but such occasions were rare. The pilots on each side soon acquired a marked respect for each other's flying skills. Often the British pilots (and perhaps the Germans too) appeared to have been shot down and killed, but on a number of occasions they survived and, having borrowed some form of transport, or even walked, managed to report back to their astonished comrades who had philosophically accepted the fact that they were dead. Most of them were very young and looked, behaved and spoke like the schoolboys they had been not long before: 'We had a wizard scrap this morning – five of us and only eight of them. We got five – and lost nothing. The other three ran away!' 'Wizard' was a popular all-purpose word; 'prang', which described any form of crash, was equally widely used and was a euphemism designed to mask the sad reality of what was often the death of a comrade.

In the second week the bombers were concentrating on the German lines of communication. This caused considerable disruption, but as the Panzers forced their way deep into France they were able to refuel from captured petrol stations and feed themselves from stocks in the French towns. The most valuable target was ammunition supplies and dumps, for that was something the Panzers could not rely on finding in France. German aircraft losses were estimated at over two thousand, and although the figure may have been pitched optimistically high by the Allies, there is no doubt that the losses in this war of attrition had a considerable effect on later German plans for the invasion of Britain.

Usually it was almost impossible to obtain a detailed account of an aerial combat from a pilot, mainly because he would shrug it off by some vague statement such as: 'It was a piece of cake, really. The Dornier just came in front of me and I gave him all I'd got', but when a pilot had been shot down himself, a more realistic and detailed version might be available. One flying officer gave the following account of his activities:

My squadron is one of those which has been out here in France since the beginning of the war. Until the invasion of Holland and Belgium most of our work had been patrolling, and we had quite a number of fights with German aircraft up and down the frontier. We shot down quite a number and had got lots of trophies for our mess – badges off the side of Dorniers, German machine-guns, airscrews, and things like that. In those days a fight was very much of an event but when the Blitzkrieg started our squadron, like the others out here, had to be at it the whole time. The Germans were sending over very large waves of machines, and their bombers were nearly always escorted by large formations of fighters.

It was our job in the Hurricanes to get through their fighters to the bombers, and also to protect our own airfields and bases. At the same time we had to escort our own bombers, especially on the most important of their trips. In all this we had so many fights that it is difficult to keep track of them, and since I've been out of the squadron now for ten days or so because of a wound I don't know what their score of German machines is. When I was wounded it was already about thirty-five, so by now it must be getting on for eighty.

There are two things I can remember clearly about scraps in which I was involved. In one fight I chased a Messerschmitt 109. We began our fight quite high up, and the German dived for the ground as hard as he could and eventually got right down on to the tree tops and headed for home. But I kept up with him, twisting and turning. He set a course for his home airfield at three hundred miles per hour. I got within range when he flew straight for some high tension cables, obviously hoping I would not see them at all but go slap into them. Luckily I did see them, and flew under them and got a lucky shot which hit him just as he pulled up in front of me. He burst into flames and crashed into the side of a hill.

The other fight I remember well is my last one, because in that one the Germans got *me*. I had been on patrol and was having to come back because of oxygen failure. On the way back I picked up a message addressed to some other Hurricanes, saying there were some German bombers in the district. Naturally I looked round, and just above me I saw some wings with black crosses on them – they were three Dorniers.

I went up to attack them and I had just got on to the tail of one of them when there was a terrible explosion in the cockpit. A Messerschmitt 110, which I had not seen, had come down out of the sun and was pumping cannon-shells and explosive bullets into my aircraft. As the German hit me I pressed my own firing button and was lucky enough to hit the Dornier, causing it to burst into flames and crash. As the Messerschmitt shot me I felt a jar in my leg and in my back and gathered that I had been hit.

But that time my own cockpit was filled with flames and fumes, so I undid my straps and baled out. When I opened my parachute I heard the roar of engines and the noise of machine-guns and I saw tracer bullets passing all round me. The Messerschmitt had followed me down and was trying to shoot me up as I dangled on the end of my parachute. I tried to spill air out of my parachute to increase the rate of my descent and so avoid the bullets but I found I couldn't raise my right arm because of the wounds in my back. But eventually the Messerschmitt joined his formation and left me to float gently to the ground – luckily not having hit me.

During that second week of the invasion it became clear to the AASF that daylight low-flying attacks against heavily defended German positions were beginning to prove unacceptably costly. Night flying was not popular, for there had been many accidents in training and the Fairey Battle bombers were not suitable. However, by 20 May it was obvious that night operations must begin: from then on day casualties were 20 per cent and night casualties 2 per cent. Unfortunately, although many successes were recorded, not without cost, there was no evidence that their harassing tactics were doing anything substantial to check the relentless German advance.

In the final stages of the battle for France the Boulton Paul Defiant was brought into action. Manufactured by an engineering firm at Wolverhampton well known for its chicken houses, it had a mixed reception, being praised by the press but regarded with uncertain feelings by the pilots. Its unusual feature was that it had no guns firing forward; its armament of four guns was concentrated in a power-turret mounted behind the pilot, and none of the guns could fire downwards. Although this two-seater fighter had the same Rolls-Royce Merlin engine as the Hurricane, it was slower because the power-turret caused a certain amount of 'drag'.

Nevertheless these planes were to have their brief moment of glory. On the first day of the Dunkirk evacuation a handful of Defiants and several accompanying Hurricanes cruised along quietly until they encountered a large group of Messerschmitts. As these came into range the Hurricanes flew off and gave the Defiants a clear field of fire. The effect was devastating, for the Messerschmitts had no counter to the deadly burst of firepower which was suddenly unleashed on them. Before the German pilots learnt the lesson that it was certain suicide to approach the Defiants from behind, they had lost thirty-eight aircraft; perhaps even more important was the fact that they had been kept away from Dunkirk for long enough to enable the evacuation to get under way. Once the secret of the Defiants was understood, the German pilots changed their tactics and the Defiants never had such success again.

The AASF was not, of course, the only air arm fighting the Germans in France. As the situation deteriorated, more and more aircraft were sent from Britain to engage the Germans on both sea and land. Eventually this drain on British airpower, which seemed to be to no avail, so alarmed Air Vice Marshal Sir Hugh Dowding, the head of Fighter Command, that he warned Churchill that no more could be sent without seriously endangering the RAF's ability to defend Britain if and when the Luftwaffe crossed the Channel. It was an inevitable decision, but one that was bound to cause much bitterness and recrimination. The average Frenchman believed that his country's Air Force had been sacrificed to hold back the Germans, but now that the British was expected to make the same sacrifice the RAF was to be withdrawn to save Britain. The story was not true. As subsequent evidence proved, French airpower had been totally inadequate and, although individuals had fought bravely, the French Air Force as a whole was sadly deficient.

9 Emergence of a Leader

AT THIS CRITICAL STAGE in the battle, with the French Army virtually defeated, the Allied air forces rapidly running out of aircraft, the Dutch and Belgians out of the war and the British Expeditionary Force in an untenable position, we should perhaps look at the Commander-in-Chief of the BEF, Viscount Gort, on whose view of that unhappy situation the result of the entire war would ultimately depend. Brave as the proverbial lion, indifferent to pain, hardship, hunger and cold, Gort had been brought up in a tradition of defending trenches or other positions to the last man and the last round. From his personal and military record it might have been expected that he would now decide to take on the Germans at the moment of their apparent triumph and, fighting with the desperation of the doomed, attempt to turn the tide in a reckless final counter-attack. If it failed, no one could have done more, and he would undoubtedly die with the men holding some last bloody outpost. But astonishingly, although he tried a counter-attack, he also took the vital decision which saved 338,000 fighting troops and made it possible for Britain to continue to fight in the war; he has never been accorded the proper credit and gratitude he deserves.

General Viscount Gort was a member of an Irish aristocratic family with a distinguished military tradition. He had served in the First World War with the Grenadier Guards and fought at Mons, Ypres and the Somme. John Colville wrote of him: 'Danger he disregarded entirely because, as the troops quickly discovered, fear did not seem to be included among his emotions.' He had won a Victoria Cross for capturing the important Prémy Ridge in the closing stages of the war. While walking about in the open carrying nothing more dangerous than a walking stick he had been hit by shell fragments, which cut through an artery in his arm. He continued to direct the battalion from a stretcher, though greatly weakened from loss of blood.

Between the wars, Gort's career had continued to prosper but he had been unable to impress any of the politicians with whom he came into contact of the need to rearm in the face of increasing danger from Italy and Germany. Although happy with the prospect of seeing further fighting with Germany – 'It will be fun to see those field-grey coats again' – he approved of the Munich agreement because it bought vital time when war was clearly inevitable. However, with memories of 1918 when the French armies had eventually become militarily excellent, it seemed normal and natural for the small British Expeditionary Force to be put under French command. He assumed that Gamelin would be as competent as Foch, whom Gort greatly admired and, when Chief of the Imperial General Staff, he recommended his appointment as Commander-in-Chief of Allied Forces. It was a disastrous decision but in keeping with the general lack of realism at the time. Gamelin was not surprised at finding the British holding this view of his military omniscience, but stipulated that whoever commanded the British Expeditionary Force it must not be General Ironside.

Although Gort had some sympathy with Liddell-Hart's views on the use of tanks in battle, he felt that whatever else happened there should always be a strong defensive element in reserve. This view approximated to that of Gamelin himself, although the latter went much further and believed that the Germans would wear themselves out skirmishing in front of the impregnable Maginot Line. In 1939 Gamelin's personal adviser, Colonel Retibon, had told the British military attaché in Paris that, if the Germans were so foolish as to attack Poland, the Poles must be warned not to be too ambitious and try to reach Berlin in a day. This bizarre miscalculation of German military strength must have come from Gamelin himself, but does not seem to have shaken Gort's confidence in the Supreme Commander, even though the Gamelin fantasy had no support in the British camp.

When war was declared in September 1939 the decision as to who would command the British Expeditionary Force had to be made rapidly. Ironside was ruled out because he would not be approved by Gamelin. Although Generals Alan Brooke and Sir John Dill were both senior to Gort on the Army List, both were passed over in favour of their junior colleague, who was liked by the Army although known to be at daggers drawn with Leslie Hore-Belisha, the Secretary of State for War. Gort's post as CIGS was now taken over by Ironside. Brooke and Dill were both intellectually far superior to Gort, but whether they would have had the military prescience he displayed later seems open to doubt. With the benefit of hindsight it is clear that the German armies were certain to win the battle of France in 1940, but what will never be known is whether anyone but Gort would have had the military sense and courage to take the steps which he did: when the battle was only ten days old he warned the British Cabinet that, as the battle was probably irretrievably lost, plans to withdraw the BEF should be made promptly.

During the winter of 1939–40 Gort had preserved a brisk and cheerful outward appearance, but inwardly felt extremely pessimistic. He soon realized that Gamelin was no Foch and that his idea of strategy was purely defensive. Gamelin's only tactical move was to suggest that when Belgium and Holland were attacked by Germany, as they inevitably would be in spite of their protestations of neutrality, the BEF should advance to the Scheldt. This plan, although subsequently implemented, did not find favour with the BEF, for there was no opportunity to prepare suitable defences. Gamelin, however, was adamant; subsequently it was learnt that he had been less interested in the general strategic situation than in moving the fighting as far away from Lille, Roubaix and Tourcoing as possible. But Gamelin cannot be blamed for miscalculating the briefness of the resistance that the Belgians and Dutch would be able to offer to a German attack.

In retrospect it seems surprising that Gort was capable of making any decisions at all in May 1940. Although he was never likely to have made a friend of Hore-Belisha, Gort would have found him easier to work with if the War Secretary had not constantly upset most of the generals in the British Army. In France, Gort had so many visitors that he never seemed to have a free night. One of them was King George VI. Gort wrote to his daughter: 'In our new house where he will stay, the *chauffage* works dubiously, analysis of the water shows 50% sewage, and the electric pump to get it from the well is already broken.'

Many of the troops which Gort had been promised, and most of the arms, failed to arrive; even worse, he never knew, during the winter of 1939–40, whether the troops he had with him would stay in France or be withdrawn to the United Kingdom for use as a strategic reserve. He had no control over the Advanced Air Strike Force, which remained firmly RAF – although the Army had to provide for its needs, including making and guarding the airfields. Such tanks as he had were inadequate in quantity and quality. Some of the territorial troops sent out to him had had no training at all; they had been used for guard duties or manual labour instead. One division arrived without knives, forks or mugs. However, within a short time of landing many of these troops had learnt their jobs and were highly motivated, making a sharp contrast to the French troops who, having been trained years before, now regarded military life with apathy or positive dislike.

Unfortunately, although the Army under Gort's command seemed to be improving daily the news from the French sector became increasingly depressing. Gamelin and Georges disliked each other intensely and, as each had his own band of supporting officers, there was little harmony in French GHQ. There were additional antipathies, such as those between Roman Catholics and others. In the previous war these divisions and dislikes had been suppressed by the need for total co-operation; during the 'phoney' war they flourished.

Astonishingly, in spite of all his problems and frustrations Gort remained remarkably cheerful, to outward appearances. Knowing he would have little time for personal correspondence in the next few weeks, he wrote a last letter to Lady Marjorie Dalrymple-Hamilton, a lifelong but platonic friend: 'We are now approaching the real test and on that the fate of our democracy and our Europe depends. We shall get through it as we have done in the past but it will be a tough struggle for a while. I have never ceased to warn them at home that this would happen, but nobody seemed particularly interested in it. . . .'

When the British Army advanced into Belgium Gort went well forward with a smaller number of officers to a village near Lille, where he set up his command post. By doing so he hoped to get a better impression of the fighting and not have to work from his former overmanned headquarters at Arras. It was the decision of a man who saw himself primarily as a fighting soldier who needed a small staff but none of the administrative clutter and interruptions of a large headquarters if he was to do his job efficiently. Unfortunately it proved to be a disastrous decision, for although his subordinate commanders knew where GHQ was they did not know how and where to find Gort in an emergency. And there were plenty of emergencies. Many of these were caused by lack of communications. In theory Gort should have been able to make the quick and effective decisions required from a field commander. To his dismay he found that within days he was virtually cut off from GHQ, to which most of the most urgent messages were being sent. GHQ had good links with the Army in the field, but in order to reach Gort's new command post had to rely on the civilian telephone network. As the Germans came closer the civilian operators, first to hear bad news, were often the first to slip away and leave their posts unmanned.

Fortunately for Gort's peace of mind he could regard his deputy commanders with some confidence. The Chief of the General Staff was Lieutenant General H. R. Pownall, and his headquarters staff included the then Colonel Gerald Templer. Major General F. N. Mason-Macfarlane was his head of Intelligence. Commanding divisions were the future field marshals the Hon. Harold Alexander and Bernard Montgomery. One of his brigade commanders was M. C. Dempsey, later to prove himself one of the shrewdest soldiers in the war.

As the situation in Belgium deteriorated, Gort moved further forward so as to be more closely in touch with events; he set up his command post first at Renaix and then, two days later, at a village called Lennik St Quentin, close to Brussels. While at the latter, on 15 May, he learnt that the Germans had crossed the Meuse; in fact they had done more than cross the river. GHQ had more recent information, but by now Gort was virtually out of touch with it; and at GHQ itself, without the steadying presence of the Commander-in-Chief there was considerable confusion and dismay. The French seemed better informed of the disaster which had occurred in the Ardennes sector, and were so distressed that normal working began to drift into chaos. Their dismay was understandable. Everything they had been told about their Army and the impregnability of the Maginot Line was now known to have been false.

Although Gort's personal observations had shown him that the Belgian Army was crumbling fast and the French looked like following suit, he had no scope for initiative as he was still under the French Commander-in-Chief. He waited impatiently for directions to tell him what part the BEF should now play, but he waited in vain.

By 16 May he felt he could delay no longer and sent General Eastwood to confer with General P. Billotte, the Co-ordinator of the Allied Armies. He pointed out to Billotte that the withdrawal of the French 1st Army was leaving the British forces with an open flank; as a result Billotte ordered that the entire Allied line should move back in stages until it finally stood on the Scheldt. There, Gort was given to understand, it would fight. No more ground would be given up.

But, unknown to Gort, events had now passed far beyond the stage of any part of the Allied armies being able to dig in resolutely and fight to the death. Reynaud had sent a signal to London to say that the battle in the southern sector was already lost. Churchill had decided to fly to Paris and judge the situation on the spot. When he saw the French burning their archives, and contemplated the fact that the Dutch were already out of the war, he must have wondered what Gort was making of it all. Gort, alas, was still in ignorance of the full nature of the disaster.

Two days later he had had ample opportunity to judge the situation first-hand. As the BEF had carried out their withdrawal, the Air Component, that part of the RAF in France whose primary responsibility was co-operating with the BEF (thus differing from the AASF whose function was to strike ahead, deep into the German communications), had been literally shot to pieces by the vastly more numerous Luftwaffe. However, they had inflicted such heavy losses on the Germans and been of such enormous assistance to the BEF that Gort requested as many more squadrons as could be spared from Home Command. Three were sent promptly, but instead of being used to protect the BEF they were sent to the French in response to an urgent request. The French Command felt that if their troops could be spared the attentions of the German dive-bombers they would stand and fight. In fact, most of the French armies had been so deeply penetrated and demoralized by the Panzers that the chances of this happening were negligible, but the request could not be refused in the circumstances.

Gort kept his counsel; he was not given to crying over spilt milk. He realized that the French Army of 1940 was very different from the one he had admired in the previous war, and that for all practical purposes the BEF was now on its own. If, however, he could take advantage of what looked like over-confidence on the part of the Germans, there might be a chance of the French rallying for a counter-attack. In the meantime, he must take steps to defend the BEF from attacks on three sides – the front, the right flank and the rear.

In the event the situation was slightly better than expected, for the French 1st Army had not crumbled as much as he had feared. However, at this point he was ordered by General Georges to send a brigade or more to help defend the Canal du Nord. The only part of his force not yet fully committed was 23rd (Northumbrian) Division. This comprised 69th and 70th Brigade, who now found themselves allotted a frontage fifteen miles long. On arrival, 70th Brigade expected to find the French holding the line to the right, but to their surprise discovered there was no trace of any French forces. Gort was only too well aware that in sending these half-trained, inadequately armed territorial units to check the German Panzers he was asking the impossible, but he had no option. He could not refuse the request even though the aircraft, which he had hoped might take some of the pressure off these troops, had been snatched from his grasp. Gort was not a man to disobey orders, but he must have known that, whether he did so or not, he would be blamed for the disaster which now threatened the entire BEF. His principal concern was to try to avoid having flanks 'in the air'. This unhappy situation occurs when a unit takes up a position only to find that the troops to its right or left are not there as had been promised, and that it is therefore in great danger of being bypassed or encircled.

On 18 May the Germans had captured Antwerp and broken through to the coast. On the same day they had reached Amiens and were forcing forty thousand vehicles of all types through the fifty-mile-long gap which had now appeared in the French line.

By this time Gort was losing patience with his French superiors, who were now giving him contradictory orders, and decided that the BEF could only be saved by his personal initiative. He was not concerned with his own reputation, realizing that whatever course he took in this catastrophic situation could undoubtedly be criticized later by some know-all politician or military historian as being the wrong one. In the event, some of the unfair criticism which came his way later was from his Director of Military Intelligence, Major-General Frank Mason-Macfarlane, to whom he now gave an independent command which became known as Macforce.

Comprising 127th Infantry Brigade, two RA field regiments, an anti-tank battery, and elements of Signals, Engineers, RAMC, RASC and Phantom, Macforce performed a useful service in protecting the right flank of the BEF. Both Mason-Macfarlane* and his deputy Gerald Templer, the future field marshal and expert in guerrilla warfare, relished their task. Macforce collected up soldiers who had become detached from their units or whose original purpose had disappeared in the breakdown of the battle plan. There were plenty of the latter; over half the 294,000 British troops first sent to France were administrative and, before the fighting began, had been employed in preparing the ground for the arrival of larger groups of reinforcements. Making preparations for massive inflows of trained troops who in the event never arrived was a feature of the Second World War: it happened in the early days in North Africa, and again in Burma and Malaya. Macforce performed very well during its brief existence, and slowed down the Germans considerably by demolitions and small counter-attacks, but it was essentially an emergency creation.

Not least of Gort's problems was reliable intelligence. There was plenty of information, as there always is in times of disaster, but much of it was unverifiable. Even to this day it has never been established exactly when certain events occurred. Some accounts describe Cambrai as being captured on 18 May; others say this did not occur until the 19th. In a fast-moving, fluid battle the arrival of a few enemy motorcyclists may give the impression that the main body of the enemy is nearer at hand than was thought. There were several occasions when strong German armoured units came up behind Allied forward positions; they had broken through at a weak point further along the line and were in a precarious position, as they themselves doubtless knew. Poorly disciplined troops tend to panic when enemy units appear behind them, but experienced old hands know that the intruder is highly vulnerable. Several Military Crosses were won in France by experienced officers who weighed up such situations quickly and dealt promptly with unwelcome visitors who were trying to come in by the back door rather than the front.

Nevertheless Gort had enough information to decide that the general situation gave little grounds for optimism. Although he had personally witnessed the discouraging sight of Belgian troops who had thrown away their weapons mingling with the refugees who were fleeing from the Germans, he still retained a faint hope that King

---

*After a distinguished military career he became Labour MP for North Paddington in 1945.

Leopold could rally enough of his countrymen to hold the southern part of their coastline. It might also be possible for the Belgian Army to retreat in good order and join up with the BEF and French 1st Army to stabilize the overall position. Time was vital, but if the RAF could upset the long, vulnerable line of German communications, and the BEF could counter-attack the over-extended Panzer columns which by now must surely be running out of fuel and in desperate need of spares and maintenance, some form of military stability might begin to emerge.

Gort, like others, was beginning to wonder if the events of the last few days were only a fantasy. It could not be possible that the whole of the French and Belgian Armies had really collapsed; it must surely be the case that this German breakthrough would now be checked, just as the spearheads of the Schlieffen Plan had been checked by the battle of the Marne in 1914. He recalled the spring offensive and breakthrough by the enemy in 1918, which had eventually led to their armies being pushed back on to German soil. But unfortunately the BEF, which had been retreating hastily from point to point, was itself short of food and ammunition, and the news was that the Germans were not just a few isolated spearheads but a heavy concentration of troops.

In the circumstances the decision he took was partly a compromise. He decided that GHQ must move from Arras to Hazebrouck and that administrative and other specialist troops, who would be useless in the fighting line, should move to Boulogne – from where, if necessary, it would be relatively simple to evacuate them. It was, however, essential to put in a counter-attack against the Germans first and prove to the entire Allied forces that the invaders were not invincible.

On the 19th Churchill decided to fly over to France and talk to Gort personally, but the plan was quickly abandoned. Instead he wrote a speech for broadcasting that evening and sent a telegram to Roosevelt, asking for fighter aircraft. At this time America was not in the war and any supplies which Roosevelt sent to Britain were in defiance of the widespread American view that the USA should remain neutral and not become involved in any foreign war. Fortunately, Roosevelt was a realist and that very week had requested Congress to authorize a massive increase in the defence budget, which would now include financing the production of fifty thousand new aircraft every year.

At this moment Gort would, no doubt, have been glad of some clear guidance from Churchill and his Cabinet, but, as the diaries of John Colville (at that time Personal Assistant to Churchill) reveal, the British government was in no position to give guidance to anyone. He wrote on 19 May: 'Winston dictated a telegram to Reynaud, expressing his distress at the plight of the French Army and insinuating that we had been rather let down. I gather the French Army are in a deplorable state of pessimism and depression.' On the 20th May he noted:

Every morning now at No. 10 there is a time of feverish activity when the PM's box returns. It contains all the work he has done overnight, in fact everything that it has not been possible to thrust under his nose during the previous days – telegrams, letters, Cabinet papers, Chiefs of Staff Reports, etc. Many of them come back untouched and have to be placed in the next night's box: others have illegible instructions scrawled on them in red ink and have to be dealt with immediately.

On the following day the entry ran: 'The situation in France is extraordinary. Owing to the rapid advance of armoured troops, the Germans are in many places behind the Allied lines. Enemy troops have reached Amiens and are thought to be on the way to Abbeville.' In fact, unknown to the British Cabinet the Germans had already reached Abbeville and would soon be at the Channel ports. Colville continued: 'At Admiralty House there was chaos owing to the lack of information being received, because communications have broken down. I have not seen Winston so depressed and while I stood by him, trying to get M. Reynaud on the telephone, he said: "In all the history of war I have not seen such mismanagement."'

Churchill was convinced that the BEF should ignore the roaming Panzer columns and concentrate on attacking the main German forces. He was, of course, baffled by the unexpected collapse of France, and frustrated by the fact that, even as he heard one piece of bad news, another always seemed to be following close behind. And there was worse to come.

10 Pawns Against the Panzers

O N 20 MAY the spearhead of von Rundstedt's Army Group A, a force composed of five armoured divisions, was approaching the Canal du Nord. Immediately behind were two more armoured divisions. The spearhead contained seventeen tank battalions with guns varying between 20-mm and 75-mm, two thousand machine-guns, fifteen battalions of motorized infantry, five motorcycle battalions, twelve field batteries and a number of anti-aircraft and anti-tank guns. This massive, balanced force was confronted by two British infantry divisions, one of which was the 23rd (Northumbrian) mentioned earlier, and the 12th. Both were territorial and both were undertrained, under strength (having about half their normal complement) and without artillery. As they took up their position, seventeen incomplete guns were found from a nearby training school. Neither of the two TA divisions had ever been in action before and they were already weary from lack of sleep and long marches.

Although they did not know it, they were about to take on some of the most experienced and battle-hardened troops of the German Army, troops who had learnt their military lessons in the Polish campaign and applied their knowledge in the present one against the Belgian and French Armies. The TA divisions did not, of course, know the strength of the force they were about to encounter but, even if they had, would not have let it dent their morale. Their view was that if the Germans thought they had an easy task they would soon learn their mistake.

The story of this clash between the full might of von Rundstedt's Panzers and what the official history describes as 'the few British pawns set out on the board' could only have one ending, but before it reached that point produced many examples of great courage and resource against overwhelming odds. Seventieth Brigade were mainly in open formation as a precaution against enemy aircraft, which were extremely active. As they marched to their new positions they picked up a considerable number of men from the Royal Ordnance Corps who, although able to fire a rifle, would not normally have been expected to be called on to do so. Some Auxiliary Military Pioneers, few of whom possessed any arms when they arrived, also joined in to play their part. Seventieth Brigade put up the best defence it could, and one which exceeded anything which could have been expected, but at the end of a day of pitting themselves against German tanks and dive-bombers fourteen officers and 219 other ranks fell back to brigade headquarters; the fate of the rest of three infantry battalions, and some Royal Engineers, a total of some two and a half thousand men, was not known.

They went into action after marching for three days, with little time for rest as they were harassed on the way by enemy aircraft. Near Blairville they met the leading tanks of the German 6th and 8th Panzer Divisions. It was a hopelessly unequal contest for 70th Brigade had none of the heavier weapons which would have knocked out the tanks. However, with their small arms they made the Germans pay dearly for their gains.

Seventh Panzer Division, commanded by Rommel, spent a whole day attacking Arras but without success. Frustrated by this dogged defence, Rommel pressed to the front with his advanced armour, but then turned back to ensure he did not get out of touch with the main body of his division. On the Arras-Cambrai road he found that he was surrounded by French tanks, an experience which lasted for several hours. The French were quite unaware what a useful captive was in their grasp, for they omitted to round up their temporary prisoners. The thought of the course of the war from which Rommel had been removed in 1940 is an intriguing one: that the Germans would have found anyone else with a talent for desert warfare equivalent to Rommel's seems unlikely.

There were probably many other heroic actions which remained unchronicled because the defenders fought to a finish and there

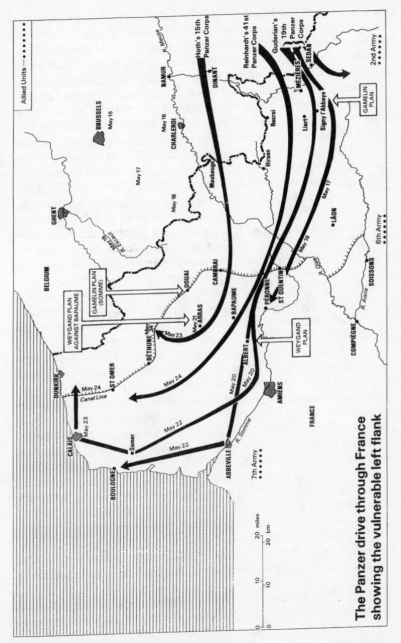

The Panzer drive through France
showing the vulnerable left flank

was no record of them. But the war diaries of the German Army sometimes laconically mention a British unit which gave them considerable trouble before being overwhelmed. Sixth Panzer describes the residue of a battalion of the Buffs (East Kent Regiment) as 'English troops who fought tenaciously' and 'artillery which exhausted all its ammunition before being over-run'; there was mention of the dogged resistance of the Royal West Kent Regiment at Doullens and the 7th Sussex which would not give in, but stood and fought until it was totally destroyed. Others who enhanced the reputation gained by their forebears in former wars were the Black Watch, the Durham Light Infantry and the Queen's.

On the 20 May Arras was surrounded on three sides but was still holding out. At this critical time General Ironside arrived from England at Gort's headquarters, bringing with him the order for Gort to move towards Amiens and take up a position on the left of the French Army. At the same time General Billotte, Commander of 1st Allied Army Group and responsible for co-ordination with the Belgian Army, was to be informed that the best hope for the Belgian Army was to move to points between the British Army and the coast. The unrealistic order to Gort can only be explained by the fact that the War Cabinet was totally out of touch with the position in France. Gort was already fully occupied in trying to hold the Escaut line; to move to Amiens would mean exposing the flanks of his meagre force to the thrust of the German armoured columns. Even if Gort had wished to obey this absurd demand, he would not have been able to do so without the agreement of his immediate French superior – General Georges. Georges, however, was in no state to give orders, let alone to organize bold counter-attacking measures. He was still waiting to hear from the new Commander-in-Chief. Weygand had been flown home from Syria the day before to replace Gamelin. His new title was Chief of the General Staff of National Defence and Commander-in-Chief. Unfortunately he knew no more than Gamelin had about armoured warfare and was already 73 years old. He was a veteran of the 1914–18 war and had a brilliant reputation as a staff officer. What he did not have was an effective tank defence.

The only purpose achieved by Ironside's visit to Gort's headquarters was that he saw how desperate the Allied position was; he was therefore able to take back to the Cabinet the gloomy assessment that France was now virtually lost, and that if the BEF was not to follow suit urgent preparations must be made for its evacuation.

However, in the meantime Gort had decided that a small counterattack in the Arras area was feasible. He did not believe, as he had been informed by the Cabinet, that 'the Germans cannot yet be in any great strength and must be considerably disorganized by demolitions, the distance they have marched and, above all, by air action, with the mechanized forces tired and the main bodies strung out'. This helpful advice from the comfort of the Cabinet Offices had accompanied the request that he should make the move to Amiens; it was sound in theory, if not in practice.

The Arras counter-attack was to be made by Frankforce. Codenames abounded at this stage as hastily assembled units were pushed forward into actions which could be no more than forlorn hopes; Frankforce derived its name from its organizer, Major General H. E. Franklyn. The original intention was that this attack should be made with two divisions, but in the event the numbers were reduced to two battalions plus tanks, in other words to some two thousand instead of fifteen thousand. The chosen battalions were the 6th and 8th of the Durham Light Infantry, and they were accompanied by 74 tanks. The tank strength should have been much greater, but had been reduced by mechanical breakdowns. Furthermore the tanks which did reach the battlefield had been on the road for many days, and every one of them needed an overhaul. There was little about them to create confidence. The 58 Mark Is were heavily armoured but were, in consequence, very slow. Their only offensive power came from a single 7.9-mm machine-gun. They were infantry tanks, designed to make a breakthrough for infantry to support, and were therefore very different from the faster, better-armed Panzers they were likely to encounter. The 16 Mark IIs were also infantry tanks but were bigger and had a two-pounder gun in addition to the 7.9-mm machine-gun.

Frankforce was commanded by Major General Le Q. Martel, one of the early tank enthusiasts. Martel planned his attack in two columns. The right consisted of the 7th Royal Tank Regiment (RTR), the 8th Durham Light Infantry (DLI), two field artillery batteries, an anti-tank platoon and a motorcycle scout platoon. The left contained

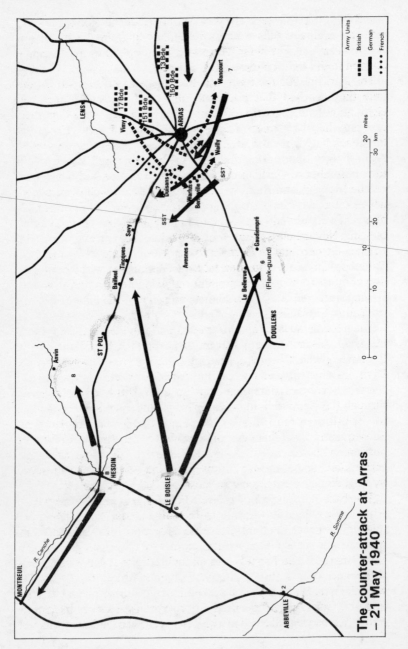

**The counter-attack at Arras
– 21 May 1940**

4th RTR, 6th DLI, two artillery batteries, an anti-tank platoon, and one company plus a motorcycle platoon from the 4th Royal Northumberland Fusiliers, who had also supplied the motorcycle platoon to the right column.

The start line for the force was the Arras-Doullens road. By the time they reached that point the infantry had already marched eight miles and, because of traffic and refugees impeding their progress, had had great difficulty in arriving on time. However, the attack began in early afternoon and went better than expected. Against light opposition, the right column captured Duisans and took a number of German prisoners. This was repeated when they reached Warlus and Berneville. However, each batch of prisoners necessitated detaching troops to guard them and, as Frankforce's numbers were already limited, these successes were not an unmixed blessing. Nevertheless the attack kept rolling forward until it met the advanced troops of the German 7th Infantry Regiment and the SS Totenkopf Division, who checked the British troops with a combination of mortar and machine-gun fire supplemented with an air strike. Having sustained heavy losses, this part of Frankforce then fell back to Warlus and Duisans.

The left column also ran into opposition from the start. It captured Dainville, Achicourt, Agny and Beaurains and reached Wancourt. In the last it ran into heavy opposition from the German 6th Infantry Division, which formed part of 7th Panzer. Six French tanks and two armoured troop carriers then came up to Warlus and forced a way through the German hold on the Warlus-Duisans road. This helped the British troops in Duisans to withdraw under cover of darkness. Subsequently the remainder of Frankforce fell back to its former position with the aid of covering fire from 9th DLI's Bren gun carriers and some anti-tank guns which had been held in reserve by brigade for an emergency such as this.

The bare details do not convey the full flavour of this attack. Although it ended by retiring to the original start line, it had put up a performance in infantry/tank co-operation which showed that, with a few more of either, a different picture of the campaign might have emerged. The Panzers had undoubtedly over-extended themselves and were distinctly nervous. Seventh Panzer reported in its war diary that it had been attacked by five British divisions. Four hundred Germans had been taken prisoner. Frankforce, according to the German war diary, had also destroyed nine medium tanks and several light ones, as well as inflicting 378 casualties. The casualties included some missing, who perhaps turned up as prisoners, but even so the numbers are impressive. When he heard the news, all von Kleist's former doubts were revived. Another attack by the BEF could have caused enough disruption to make the German High Command insist that the Panzers should halt, regroup and undertake overdue repairs.

But there was no other Frankforce, and no possibility of raising one, and the following day the Germans regrouped and set off again. It was a wary advance at first, but it did not have far to go now to reach the Channel ports. In the previous few days they had run into opposition from unexpected sources. Gort's instruction that troops who would not normally have been brought into the fighting line should all take their share had produced some remarkable achievements. A bridge had been held at a critical time by a force composed entirely of padres, who had temporarily become more militant than clerical. Even a mobile bath unit, normally accustomed to confronting no better-armed enemies than lice, had put up a spirited performance. The Belgians were still in the battle, even though General Billotte had sustained injuries in a car accident from which he died two hours later.

Although it was extremely risky for him to do so, Churchill decided that once again he must fly to Paris and obtain a clear view of the situation, if a clear view was to be had at all. Accompanied by Dill, he arrived on the 22nd and immediately went into conference with Reynaud, the French Prime Minister, and Weygand. As a result of this meeting of three minds, each of which was well out of touch with what was actually happening in the field, Gort received yet another directive. It can have done little except exasperate him, for it suggested that the Belgian Army should now retreat to the Yser and there stand firm, that the BEF and French Army should attack in a south-westerly direction towards Bapaume and Cambrai with eight divisions, and that the RAF should operate by day and night.

Churchill's instructions to Gort were followed by a broader directive to the Allied forces from Weygand; it was no less impractical. Among its provisions was one that the German should be prevented from reaching the sea; they had reached it two days earlier. The Somme crossings must be recaptured and the road system with which the Germans were making free must be taken back into Allied hands and fortified with strongpoints. The Panzers 'must be hemmed in within the area into which they have so rashly advanced'.

No one could dispute the necessity of those provisions that were still possible; the only problem was finding the troops to carry them out. There was, of course, the slight difficulty that the German Army might object to being bundled out of the positions they had so easily occupied with their superior forces. Instead of waiting for the Allies to eject them, the Panzers once more went on the offensive. In consequence the 1st Royal West Kent Regiment were heavily engaged, and the 1st/6th Queen's lost four hundred men in two days. The defence works which had been dug in the winter of 1939–40 and which had been reluctantly abandoned for the original move into Belgium were now proving their worth. The Belgians were fighting hard, the French 1st Army was dourly holding on, and Boulogne and Calais, though under siege, had not fallen.

But the situation was precarious in the extreme. Although the German Army was no doubt tired, it was probably less tired than the battered defenders who were obstinately clinging to their positions. The British had more justification for feeling exhausted than anyone on the battlefield. They had been rushed forward into Belgium and then they had had to fight a long rearguard action on the retreat. They had strong German forces attacking them in front and other German forces marauding around behind them. They were outnumbered, their supplies were running low, and they were being hammered by the Luftwaffe flying from nearby bases while their own air protection could only come from England. British air reconnaissance had virtually ceased to exist, so there was no possibility of knowing when the next blow might fall. There was therefore no chance of trying to concentrate forces where they would be most useful.

On 23 May the BEF were put on to half rations. Fortunately, ammunition stocks were better than food stocks and for the moment there was no crisis there. But, unknown to the BEF as they thoughtfully inspected the meagre food in their mess tins, von Rundstedt had that day made a decision which was to save the BEF. He ordered the Panzers to halt.*

Why von Rundstedt took this extraordinary decision has been debated ever since.** It is known that on 22 May Colonel Schmundt,

*'Halting' did not, of course, mean standing still. It allowed for reconnaissance and probing of possible weak points, but no general advance.
**See Chapter XX.

who was responsible for maintaining contact between the German Army and Hitler, telephoned von Rundstedt asking for information about the situation at Arras. He had learnt from 7th Panzer that it had been attacked by 'five British divisions' and that heavy French tanks had inflicted considerable damage on the lighter Panzer reconnaissance tanks. Hitler found this information extremely worrying. The worst fears of the German Higher Command, which he had previously scoffed at, now seemed justified. If the Allies counter-attacked at this point, with the Panzers spread all over northern France in an unco-ordinated manner, the Great German Victory could rapidly become the Great German Disaster, an event which could lead to the collapse of Nazism. For anyone who did not realize how complete the Allied defeat already was, the threat the French Army offered to the long southern flank of the German armies must be taken extremely seriously. By no means averse to telling his generals what to do, even when he himself was hundreds of miles from the operational area, Hitler insisted that precautionary steps must be taken against counter-attack from the south.

Von Rundstedt was not happy about the position either, but estimated the danger as being less than Hitler feared. Every day that passed consolidated the German position in France, as it brought in more infantry troops for a defensive role, and the repulse of the Arras counter-attack indicated that the Allies lacked strength in depth or they would have followed up the first probing attack with a second, much stronger one.

However, there were two facts which could not be ignored. The Panzers had long ago exceeded the period for which they should be kept in the field without maintenance, and unless overhauled within the very near future could develop a series of mechanical faults which could lose them any forthcoming battles. And, with a large part of France still untouched by German forces, there could be tank battles which the Panzers would be physically unable to fight. Von Rundstedt was well aware that the Germans had begun the war with a numerical inferiority in tanks. In the circumstances it seemed logical to tell the Panzers to stop advancing and to attend to overhauls and maintenance instead. It would clearly be folly to allow them to batter their way into Dunkirk, where the resistance might be extreme and where they could even be defeated. While they were locked in combat in Dunkirk or along the northern coast, the French could come up from the south, slice through the German lines of communication and then at leisure pick off the heads of the armoured columns. From a military point of view, halting the Panzers was an eminently sound and sane decision. The German Army had already taken appalling risks; the luck could not possibly hold.

In hindsight, von Rundstedt's decision was a mistaken one. If armoured columns had forced their way into Dunkirk few of those waiting for evacuation would have ever been taken off. For the remainder of the British Army which arrived in Dunkirk was a defeated force, a force which had travelled so far, and fought so hard, that it was incapable of further serious resistance. Subsequently the 338,000 who were rescued were described by an enthusiastic British press as 'the heroes of Dunkirk'. There was, of course, nothing heroic about being rescued from a beleaguered beach, but looking over the entire campaign there were plenty of reasons for applying the term 'heroes'. There had already been numerous examples of heroic conduct during the desperate efforts which were made to check the German onslaught, and there would be many more. Gamelin's generalship had been disastrous and many French units had put up minimal resistance, but against this some French units fought admirably and maintained their morale in the most adverse circumstances. The BEF had been sent on a wild goose chase up into Belgium and then brought back again. Outnumbered, they had fought with enormous courage against superior forces. This is not to say that *all* had been heroic: sad to say there were many cases of low morale and cowardice, but overall it was not unfair to describe the achievements of the BEF as heroic. But on 23 May, although a critical stage had been reached and a momentous decision taken, the battle was far from over.

Gort's immediate concern on that day (for he could not have guessed at von Rundstedt's order even in his most optimistic imaginings) was to hold what was known as the Canal Line between Gravelines and Béthune. This area had a network of rivers and canals which, if defended, could impose a lengthy check on the movement of the German divisions. However, as his original organization had been mauled beyond recognition, Gort could only hold this line by improvising *ad hoc* units such as Frankforce and Macforce. Polforce was already in existence; Woodforce, under Colonel J. M. D. Wood, was now formed to cover Hazebrouck. Although hastily assembled forces of this type were clearly far from ideal, for few of their members had worked together before or even knew each other, they were the best that could be provided in the circumstances. The principal shortage was of trained infantry, but as the defence was working from comparatively static positions ignorance of field tactics was unimportant if the soldiers, from Royal Engineers, Ordnance, Service Corps or any other specialist unit, could fire a rifle.

The first information about von Rundstedt's decision came from a secret intelligence unit which would play an increasingly important part in the war. It was known as the Y Service and drew its operators from the Army (Royal Signals), Navy and RAF. The Y Service spent its time listening to enemy broadcasts with a view to feeding the insatiable appetite of the code-breaking teams of Ultra at Bletchley Park. Its operators, all highly skilled, ranged over the frequencies picking up whatever enemy broadcasts they could find. Apparently one operator, whose name is unknown, picked up a message in clear – not encoded or enciphered – which simply stated that the German attack on the Dunkirk-Hazebrouck line was to be 'discontinued for the present'. Neither the originator nor the intended recipient was known; it was one of those pieces of 'chatter' between field units, in which one passes information to another without reflecting that it is probably top secret; for units in the field it doubtless seemed routine information.

If Gort's GHQ had appreciated the importance of this intercept, it might have caused him to alter his plans; as it was, the information aroused hardly a flutter of interest – probably because, as noted earlier, fighting soldiers are inherently suspicious of information coming from unidentified sources. Up until 22 May there had been a limited, but important, quantity of photographic intelligence, but after the 22nd this was virtually negligible owing to lack of available aircraft. Had Photographic Intelligence been able to continue, that too would have reported that the Panzers were no longer advancing.

Apart from the infantry, and the mixed *ad hoc* units such as Macforce, there were highly creditable actions by other 'arms'. Units of the Royal Artillery took a heavy toll of advancing German forces before they ran out of ammunition and were overwhelmed; often a single gun fired so frequently that German war diaries reported it as more than one. An armoured car squadron from the 12th Lancers, though reduced to only five vehicles, enjoyed itself hugely on a brief reconnaissance in the St Omer region. Among its achievements were escorting a detachment of artillery to the point to which it had been told to withdraw, covering a party of Royal Engineers whose demolition had been hampered by the arrival of enemy tanks, and having a brush with enemy tanks themselves. The 5th Inniskilling Dragoon Guards, supplemented with a squadron from the 15th/19th Hussars, lent their support to the infantry engaged in frustrating the attempts of the Germans to penetrate the Canal Line.

Arras, which had first come under German attack on the 19th, was still holding out on the 23rd. By the evening of that day it was surrounded on three sides with a gap of only five miles separating the enveloping German forces. At that point the Arras garrison received an order from Gort that 'it must be held to the last man and the last round'. Cynics interpreted this as a sign that Arras was about to be evacuated and on this occasion they were right, even though similar orders in other places in the past had been obeyed to the letter. The withdrawal began at midnight and developed into a classic rearguard action, in which many units, notably the Welsh Guards, fought with admirable tenacity. The defenders of Arras had done all that could have been expected of them and more. They had occupied the leading German troops long enough to enable other areas to consolidate their defences and then make an orderly withdrawal; they had defied Rommel, and put the German Army on the defensive in that area for a vital period. Arras had acquitted itself well.

But the worst was yet to come. The Allies now had insufficient forces to stage a successful counter-attack. They would fight on, but when the Germans had built up their strength with units arriving from the rear areas, those must inevitably clinch their victory. Nothing could then save the British Army from the most devastating defeat in its history. No one could have guessed that it would be allowed to disengage, to cross twenty-one miles of water, and then, four years later, return to win a gruelling campaign. But much would have to happen before that occurred, and the most critical period would come in the next few days.

11 View from the Battlefield

ONE OF THE most vivid accounts of an infantryman's war appeared in an anonymous book entitled *Infantry Officer*. It was so anonymous that the word 'anon' did not even appear on the title page when it was published in 1943 by B. T. Batsford, who in 1988 had no record or recollection of the author. However, in a 'publishers' note' to the book, which was printed on the inferior paper necessitated by wartime 'authorized economy standards', the author is revealed as a regular soldier (for he passed out of Sandhurst two months before the outbreak of war) and the recipient of a Military Cross, although he does not mention the matter himself. After Dunkirk he fought in Africa, became a temporary Commando, and, at the time the book was published, was training as a glider pilot. He had been evacuated unscathed from Dunkirk but on arriving home had tripped over a small stone; the result was a damaged cartilage which necessitated an operation. While in hospital he began writing about his experiences in order to pass the time. Subsequently he expanded his notes into a short book and later still it was passed by the censor for publication.

Most of his soldiers were Cockneys and he recalled that 'a Cockney can laugh at a bomb that is screaming down to obliterate him – at least that's what I found. However cold, however bored, however frightened, he can always find an answer – a bawdy joke or a dig at his mate.' He once heard two of his men during 'a frightful bombardment' arguing whether or not the No. 16 bus went along the Charing Cross Road. Soon after arriving in France his regiment was sent up to Belgium and saw minor action before they got there. At Librecourt they encountered five German parachutists, all of whom were shot. On the way back form this engagement they saw 'a man and a girl, civilians, necking on the roadside. They seemed to be enjoying themselves no end. The Field Security Police brought them in just after we passed, so I was told later: both were men and both shot.'

Stories of men dressed up as women, often nuns, were scoffed at later as being figments of somebody's imagination. However, whereas the presence of a man and his girl in a lonely wood might seem natural enough (even if the wood was close to an important military target) and attract no stronger comment than an amused, perhaps envious, smile from a passing soldier, the presence of two civilian men would be highly suspicious. The Germans were no novices when it came to spying. German 'tourists' had carefully reconnoitred Norway, Denmark and Poland before their invasion and left agents in position. Both sides used prostitutes in enemy countries to spy for them; there may have been more truth in some of the spy stories than their desk-bound critics thought.

Having arrived at the front line – or what passed for it in Belgium – Infantry Officer's regiment found they were not to stay there but instead to take part in the general rearguard action. At various points they were told that this was where they would make a stand, 'meet the Hun and hit him hard'. Hardly had they dug in than they were told that 'in order to conform with the Allies' plan of defence we must withdraw to new positions'. There were, of course, variants on that phrase which became all too familiar to the British public until after the battle of Alamein in 1942. Sometimes they were 'prepared positions', sometimes 'straightening of the Allied line', sometimes 'tactical withdrawals'. It was not long, however, before everyone recognized them as euphemisms for defeats and the loss of important ground.

Infantry Officer had a great affection for France, tempered though it was with realism:

The next morning a squadron of French Cuirassiers arrived to support us. They were as good as only good French troops can be. They had fought back from Sedan, losing over sixty per cent en route, and yet they were still of good heart and excellent discipline. They were only with us for a few hours, as they got orders suddenly to move, and we were sorry to see them go. We had seen so much of the rottenness of France, the selfishness and gutlessness of it all, that it came as a real joy to meet the real France again, the France that we had loved. . . .

Having come abroad with the expectation that in a few days they would be engaged in a desperate struggle with the Germans, they found the reality was very different. At short intervals they were bombed and at other times they were engaged in skirmishes with German reconnaissance units which had somewhere managed to penetrate the Allied lines.

That afternoon we were bombed rather heavily by six Dorniers which dived low on to us. It's not so bad when they come low; it gives you a chance to retaliate. We had quite a lot of the other sort, off and on, with Heinz flying at about 7000 feet in huge formations, and all the bombs coming down on you at once. You can see them fall out of the bellies of the brutes, hundreds of them and they all seemed to be coming straight at you, at first terribly slowly, then faster and faster till at last there's a blackish flash and a scream.

Skirmishes with enemy units began suddenly and ended quickly:

We had been expecting the Boche for days and a Hun reconnaissance Henschel gave away the fact that he was about. Nothing happened for a couple of hours then . . . suddenly there was a burst of fire from my left-hand section. I raced down to see what was happening and was just in time to see a Hun motorcycle combination go head-over-heels into the canal, with the crew of three, all dead. Another was turning in the road when a shot from our anti-tank rifle knocked the engine out and into the lap of the man sitting in the sidecar. The other two leapt off and ran into the wood, dragging their pal with them. A third vehicle stopped on the corner and got a machine-gun into action against us in double quick time. A long burst of bullets hit the wall by my head and I got down quick. Then came the shot of the century. It was our anti-tank man again. With one shot he hit the gunner and knocked his head clean off his shoulders.

On the road lay the smashed motorcycle and the now deserted machine-gun. I shouted for a volunteer and Barnes and Fox, two old soldiers with pretty grisly crime sheets and the hearts of lions, ran up. We hopped into a small boat and rowed across the canal. Fox then ran for the machine-gun and I got some maps out of the motorcycle and a couple of boxes of ammunition . . . we rowed back like hell with the booty and, just as we landed on our side, the Bren and the anti-tank rifle opened up again, and an answering stream of Boche stuff came back at us. We ducked and ran for cover. At the top of the road a tank appeared and blazed away at us: the bullets, at the rate of a thousand a minute, plopped, skidded, and screamed at our feet. Stewart, behind the anti-tank rifle, was shooting like a man possessed. Corporal Squire, the section commander, quite fearless, was standing in the open, shouting orders and controlling the fire of his section. The tank was far from happy and reversed back into cover. All was quiet for a minute or so: then hell broke loose again.

Out from behind the corner came a large anti-tank gun being pushed along by the nose of the tank. The Hun gunner was sitting behind the shield, thus covered from small-arms fire. 'My bastard,' shouted Stewart. 'You watch the —— jump!'

He and the Hun fired simultaneously. The Hun shot smashed through our little emplacement, about an inch from Stewart, and between Squire and myself. Stewart's bullet went through the shield of the gun, hit the Hun gunner and threw him, spread-eagled, on to the top of the tank. Bits of wall and masonry covered Stewart and blinded him from view. We pulled the muck off him, and he got a couple of shots into the tank as it was trying to retreat round the corner again. What shooting! He must have hit the driver through his vizor, I think, because the tank staggered backwards and stuck, bottom-down and belly up, in the ditch behind.

Then it was our turn to play hell. We put twenty shots through the belly and into that tank and it looked like a colander by the time we had finished. Then we had a wallop at the gun, splitting the barrel in half and smashing up the breach. . . .

Half an hour later we received orders to withdraw 'in order to comply with the Allies' plan of defence'. I could have cried my eyes out!

We got into Fromelles in the late afternoon and had just settled in when sixty bombers came at us at about 7000 feet. Then the most incredible thing happened. The air was suddenly filled with little puffs of black smoke -- anti-aircraft fire and extremely accurate. What beautiful shooting too. Every burst seemed to be just in front of the leading planes, blocking their passage. The leader faltered, jinked and, rolling slowly on its back, started spinning down with black smoke pouring out of it. From the side appeared three little blobs which at once became men. A parachute opened behind one of the figures but nothing happened to arrest the fall of the other two.

The two men hit the deck at about one hundred and twenty miles an hour and we didn't know whether to scrape them off or just paint over them. The third fellow came down slowly, eventually to land bang in our midst. He was a Fifth Columnist but he was a brave type, and kept his mouth shut, giving nothing away. He had on him a pass saying he was a French lunatic and so was of no military value to anyone – but the thorough Hun had forgotten to sign the thing!

In between actions such as this the young subaltern found himself using his platoon in order to try to re-establish some sort of order in villages from which the inhabitants had fled. Of one he wrote:

> I tried to find some civic authority but the mayor had been the first to leave, ten days earlier, and he had been quickly followed by the one policeman and all the male members of the community. In fact the only beings who seemed to be left were one pretty little woman who owned the pub, which I made my headquarters, one old chemist who was bed-ridden and had been left behind by his family without food or water, and a number of very hungry dogs. So we British soldiers were left to deal with the pathetic and ever-increasing lines of waifs. Ours was the only bridge for miles around so we had more than our share of it. An added complication arose after I had pulled a handful of sweets out of my pocket to give to a small child. I was nearly killed by the rush of adults trying to get one. This made me realize that the poor devils were famished, so we set up a food counter and issued a tin of something and a packet of biscuits to each person.

Soldiering, as this young officer, who could not have been more than twenty, now began to appreciate, was not merely a matter of killing the enemy, but of helping the helpless and at times taking over civilian administration. Nowadays the Army calls this 'assisting the civil power'. All too often, as in France in 1940, there is no civil power to assist.

A few days later Infantry Officer received the surprising

information that evacuation from Dunkirk had already begun and that six officers and six NCOs from his brigade were to join them without waiting for the rest of the unit. The news was not welcome, for 'we were about to rush for our lives in high-speed trucks, leaving behind the men we had fought with and, in the past few weeks, had come to love'. The reason given by brigade HQ for their sudden departure was that they would be needed in the future for important appointments in an army which would shortly be landing in the South of France. This explanation, although somewhat bizarre, did at least indicate that the BEF had not given up the struggle and accepted defeat, but was planning to continue the battle elsewhere.

In his journey to Dunkirk and onwards to Britain Infantry Officer saw more bodies and violent death than he had seen in the entire previous campaign, for so far war had hardly touched him. Others were less fortunate: 'We patched up one fellow, a Tank Corporal, who had been an Army goalkeeper. His left foot was shot away, and he had sixteen machine-gun bullets in his chest and belly. He took three hours to die, and never once complained, though he was conscious the whole time.'

By this time Staff Officer, whose diary was referred to earlier during the taking of the Maastricht bridge, was obtaining a fuller, more realistic, view of the campaign:

Oxborrow and I were thinking this morning how strange it was that we two English soldiers could be 250 miles from the BEF, and be among the very few English to have any idea of the implications of these extreme moments in the world's history. I feel certain that the Cabinet can have no idea of what was happening yesterday or their actions would have been different. From the newspapers it is evident that the people at home have so far had their complacency very little disturbed.

At 10 p.m. on 18 May he was writing:

The Panzer divisions are insatiable. They should be short of food, their tracks should be giving trouble and by the law of averages a good proportion of them should be suffering from mechanical defects by this time. Their crews ought, by the ordinary laws governing physical endurance, to be completely exhausted.

None of these influences seem to have developed. The Panzer

111

divisions, with the bit between their teeth, are going as strong as ever.

However, he had grave misgivings about the morale of the French: 'I am amazed that more heroic measures have not been taken. A few 75s shoved into every road in the path of the Panzers and to the flanks firing point-blank would blow them to Kingdom Come.'

Staff Officer noted that 'The Allies send out orders calling for immediate action, but they send them in code, and this means that by the time the message is coded by the sender and decoded by the recipient some hours have elapsed, and the fleeting opportunity target will no longer present itself for attack.' He might have added that if there had been a mistake in encoding, transmission or reception, the process would take twice as long. Such mistakes occurred frequently until more efficient mechanical methods of coding and decoding were introduced.

On 21 May he noted in his diary that 'Amiens is full of enemy troops. The Germans have crossed the Somme at Abbeville. The Allies are now separated; the Germans stand between them from Belgium to the Channel at Boulogne. Calais is reported to be burning. No news of any counter-attacks destined to close the pocket . . . it seems to indicate that France, like Poland, will be conquered in three weeks.' A particularly disturbing piece of information was that Merville airfield was reported deserted with sixteen Hurricanes, half of them airworthy, standing on the tarmac. This mysterious news about an airfield believed to be some thirty miles behind the Allied lines was confirmed by an Allied pilot who landed there. A full explanation was not forthcoming, but the supposition was that it had been shot up by a roving Panzer division and then by-passed.

On the 22nd he recorded that:

General Georges was asked point-blank why the promised counter-attack had not been delivered. His liaison officer spoke for him and answered that the General could not give orders so far in advance of the inclinations of his divisions. This was an eye-opener and it is only now that it is brought home to me that the formation of soldiers' committees [the military equivalent of trades unions], regularized in the French Army in 1936 by Monsieur Léon Blum's regime, have so far undermined discipline. GHQ is definitely handicapped by the spirit of internationalism [he meant communism] which exists to such a great extent among the rank and file. Another point that was brought home today by a French officer is the fact that at least one-third of the French Army is recruited in the densely populated North. It is this northern area which is now in German occupation, with the result that one man in three has already lost his home and his place of employment. The argument seems to be that, human nature being what it is, there is no longer any inducement to those men to resist since all they have is already lost.

The argument seems more of an excuse than an explanation. In such circumstances one might feel the northerners would fight like demons to recover their lost lands.

However, Staff Officer's own views often contained much wisdom. He was puzzled by the absence of movement in the wake of the Panzers, 'silent towns, empty roads, naked countryside'. Where was the German infantry, he asked, where was the main body of their army? He noted that in the British Army the main weakness was 'multiplicity of command, too much unnecessary secrecy, too much red tape as the British and French deliberate in whose area is a German target. By the time the problem is resolved the target has disappeared.' There is a saying in the British Army, 'Order + counter-order = disorder.' It certainly applied in France in 1940.

At 1230 hours the CGS [Chief of the General Staff] got a message through asking for the cancellation of the Allied bombing attack on the [German] pocket. At approximately 1313 hours a message came through from CGS instructing us to lay on the Allied bombing. The whole area between the Somme and St Omer – that is to say the area Boulogne, St Omer, Béthune, Arras, Cambrai, St Quentin, Amiens, Abbeville – is to be a No-Man's-Land. It is crowded with enemy tank formations, BEF ambulances, French DLMs [Light Motorized Divisions] and columns of all arms marching and counter-marching. It is a mêlée of the first magnitude.

There are 14 Me 110s over here at the moment.

Yet optimism had not vanished entirely. The French were reported to have seven divisions ready to attack in a north-westerly direction while the northern armies struck southwards. If all went well the entire situation would be reversed, and it would be the Germans who would be in a desperate plight. But on 24 May at 8 p.m. Staff

Officer wrote:

> This evening General Georges' directive of this morning ordering an attack through Péronne and Albert to the North is called off. The BEF is left to its fate. This is an astonishing decision.
>
> It begins to look like a hard peace for France and England or a separate peace for France and England left to fight on alone.
>
> Meanwhile the nightingales sing full throatedly around the Chateau and, like the countryside in the loveliness of May, illustrate the great measure of delight that can still be drawn on in spite of the madness of the men who are responsible for this disaster.

However, there were still new plans. The 51st Highland Division was being rushed up to the Somme, and the French were about to try to recover the bridgehead on the River Nenne which they had lost the day before. The big counter-attack might still follow. On the other hand, the Panzers were reported to have reached the coast at Dunkirk. Food and ammunition were said to be very short in the BEF.

On 26 May he recounted what he described as a 'sidelight': 'A BEF staff officer was talking to a French officer from the Troisième Bureau. The English officer asked, "When is the French offensive going to take place?" The Frenchman answered, "Not yet. The armies are *épuisé* [exhausted]." "But surely too the Germans are *épuisé*," the Englishman answered. "But they are drunk with success and we are sober with defeat," the Frenchman replied, "and the drunkard has the strength of seven men."'

On the 27th Staff Officer, far from being a reliable source of information, appeared to have been relying entirely on hearsay. He understood that the French suspected the BEF were going to move out (some had already done so, though he did not know it) and in that case were not prepared to risk a full-scale attack themselves.

Later that day he wrote: 'The sad thing is the war's unpopularity – an effect probably due to twenty years of League of Nations windy exaltations. It is one of the main causes of our reverses. We have no shouting and singing of national anthems. The troop-carriers have killed marching songs and it is only German throats that are sore with singing the strains of Horst-Wessel [a Nazi anthem].'

On 28 May he recorded: '0830 hours. No news of importance. Phantom, No. 3 Mission, which has done such fine work hitherto in Belgium, has closed down. Our main source of information in the north is gone – I suppose to England. Last night we heard that some 2800 odds and sods had been shipped from Dunkirk.' Phantom had not in fact closed down and departed for England but was busy elsewhere with the BEF. This unorthodox intelligence-gathering unit of good linguists and intrepid motorcyclists continued to function throughout the war in many theatres, and had a number of members who were later to distinguish themselves in other spheres. They included the actor David Niven, and future ambassadors, sportsmen and academics.

However, there was no shortage of alarming news. All the French armies were reported to be so battered that they had virtually ceased to exist. Morale appeared to have been extinguished, as Staff Officer recorded:

An officer who got marooned in Le Touquet, waking up there one morning to find the Germans in possession, gave me an interesting account today. He has a French wife and has lived in France for a number of years, and so had no difficulty when dressing up as a fisherman in passing himself off as a Frenchman. For four days of the German occupation he stayed in the town. It appears that the Le Touquet-Abbeville area is very lightly held. The Germans are only policing the area: no tanks came into Abbeville at all. Just a handful of motorcyclists; a few of these stood about at the crossroads and here and there there was an occasional machine-gun and so forth. He told me that in hiding there are at least five French soldiers for every German in the area. He says the Germans are behaving in the most gentlemanly way: they have given passes to all the tradesmen and the latter hurry hither and thither to execute the invaders' orders. This officer collected a handful of British Line of Communication soldiers, who were also marooned, and got them away in a boat. He told me that French soldiers were wandering about in great numbers in uniform but, of course, unarmed. They had thrown away their rifles. One of these was heard to say that if only their officers had not run away and they had someone to lead them they would soon mop up the Boche. There were far too many French soldiers to be handled by the Germans as prisoners and for some days they allowed them to roam about at will. Eventually they were mopped up and taken away unresisting in motor lorries to a cage somewhere inland.

He continued: 'There is something very phoney about this warfare. It is so unreal. The lack of conviction, the irresolution, the sense of resignation – and, above all, the sense of indifference, is wholly disillusioning. This war will not last long – in France.' Hardly had he written these words when he had to add even more dramatic ones. The news that King Leopold of the Belgians had capitulated had just reached them. There would be much subsequent recrimination over the Belgian king's surrender, until many years afterwards it was proved that he had done his best not to let down his allies.

A French officer, Captain Denis Barlone, who subsequently served in the Free French forces, also kept a diary in these eventful days. Before the German invasion he felt that the international situation was highly dangerous for France, with the German success in Norway, the Italian menace in the Mediterranean and Japanese threats in the Far East, and he noted 'a considerable lowering of morale on the home front'. However, he comforted himself with the thought that in the previous war the French Army had suffered disaster after disaster but eventually began an offensive on 18 July 1918 which culminated in the Germans' signing the Armistice on 11 November that year.

On the evening of 9 May he had dinner in the mess with a dozen friends – lobster à l'américaine, truffled fowl and so on – after which he played bridge until 1 a.m. At three he was awakened by the incessant noise of planes passing over the house, but was tired and soon fell asleep again. At 5 a.m. he received the order to stand by. 'Contrary to all the forecasts of the British and French Staffs, who apparently knew nothing, the Germans have invaded Holland and Belgium.'

Soon he was moving forward with his regiment, passing through Valenciennes on the way. The town had been heavily bombed and 'an enormous flame of gas spurted from the broken roadway'. A damaged German bomber fell in the town and its bombs exploded, but 'life in Valenciennes has not been interrupted for one minute, no sign of fright, even of nerves'. When they entered Belgium he noted that 'everywhere the welcome is most cordial, the French soldiers inspire absolute confidence'. But he also observed that many cars full of refugees from the Liège region were racing towards France, bringing pessimistic accounts. He wondered if they were trying to justify their flight. 'Treachery and the fifth column are the sole topics of conversation. We listen, but we remain rather sceptical and not a little amused.' They were billeted with a Belgian, M. Pollet, 'who gives us cause to reflect when he tells us of the political manoeuvrings by which the Walloons [French-speaking Belgians] have been ousted from the King's Staff and replaced by distinctly germanophile Flemings'.

At first Barlone could not believe what he was hearing. 'Fantastic reports go around about the fall of the forts of Liège; the Germans are supposed to have crossed the Albert Canal and the great south-eastern line of defence. These reports can only have been spread by spies who are everywhere and have been dropped by parachute.' On 14 May he recorded: 'No newspapers, but the radio announces that Holland is invaded and that Rotterdam is in flames. The Dutch government has taken refuge in England after three days' fighting. Fortunately our *poilus* have no more idea where Rotterdam is than Pekin so the news does not worry them. They say that so long as the Boches have to deal with the Belgians and the Dutch anything may happen, but when they meet our army, the party will soon be over.'

On 15 May, although morale still remained high, Barlone voiced a note of concern about the increasing refugee problem. Everywhere he found traffic blocks and a complete absence of 'army traffic control'. He was completely mystified because he knew from experience that in 1917 French Army traffic control had worked perfectly. Although he saw plenty of German bombers, some of which caused casualties in his unit, he did not see any French fighters. Optimistically he decided they must be 'some miles ahead at the front'. On the same day he was told to organize a retreat to as far back as Maing.

By now everyone was beginning to blame the Belgians for the débâcle. 'Contrary to their pledged word the Belgians had prepared no positions,' wrote Barlone bitterly. 'Not a single position was prepared, not a trench dug, not a yard of barbed wire run. They were supposed to hold the Albert Canal for seven days, so that we could organize our positions on the Dyle. They didn't hold six hours, nor even blow up the bridges.'

Undoubtedly the Belgians had been taken by surprise, and it was for this reason that, like the Dutch, they had put up less resistance than had been hoped. The Nazi invasion had been planned for years, and there seemed to be two main reasons for the Belgian collapse. First, the countryside had been meticulously surveyed by German 'tourists' or others who had found temporary jobs in the local administration. The Germans had a long tradition of introducing their nationals or sympathizers into railways and other service industries. Secondly, they had also been working to increase the animosity between the Flemish element in the population and the French-speakers – antagonisms which went very deep and had existed for hundreds of years.

In 1940 Belgium was a small, highly vulnerable country, with an independent existence of barely a hundred years. In the First World War it was attacked without warning by the Germans and occupied for four years. After that experience it tried desperately to preserve its neutrality, doing everything within its power to avoid giving its large, powerful, belligerent neighbour, Germany, an excuse for violating that neutrality. Unfortunately, while the Germans paid no heed to Belgium's neutral posture, knowing it would mean nothing when their own armies started rolling forward, Belgium's attempt to stand on one side made the Allied task infinitely greater. The treacherous surprise attack on Eben Emael and the loss of the frontier forts could have damaged the morale of a stronger country than Belgium. After an initial effort at resistance the Belgians realized their cause was lost. But not all Belgians gave up, and later in the war some of the strongest resistance against German occupation was to be found in that country. Some Belgians escaped and joined the Royal Navy, RAF or regiments of the British Army.

Having dismissed the Belgians, Barlone meanwhile noted that the French troops who had taken the full weight of the German attack had fought heroically: 'They let themselves be crushed by tanks rather than give way.' On 16 May he reported that his machine-gunners fired three thousand rounds at the German aircraft which were bombing and machine-gunning them, but 'without any visible results'. He heard stories of magnificent French resistance elsewhere, but also of heavy losses.

'The men want to know where I am leading them but I conceal the fact that we are returning to France,' he wrote with mounting pessimism. 'They feel that things are not going too well, but do not suspect defeat.' They were not left in doubt for long. When they reached the French frontier they were astonished to find the blockhouses empty. 'Why did the High Command adopt these tactics?' Barlone asked rhetorically, and answered himself: 'This beats me.' He was in an extremely vulnerable position. The convoy he was leading extended over seven miles of road and included over eight hundred horses and fifteen hundred men. Every time he saw German aircraft in the sky he wondered if his convoy would now become their target: the prospect was daunting.

But there were happier moments. When they reached St Amand they were told they could take what they wanted from the cellars of the principal hotel. Barlone took fifty bottles, mainly burgundy, bordeaux and champagne. Everyone's spirits were raised by seeing a Canadian Curtiss attack three Messerschmitts, bring down two and put the third to flight.

On 21 May they were much cheered again by the news that a French Army corps elsewhere had repelled heavy German attacks. But they were very worried by the prevalence of fifth columnists: 'Every night, blue, green and red lights appear everywhere.' Bombing followed, but ceased when the regiment moved out. On 22 May Barlone wrote: 'Our orders are to shoot all spies and strangers who are unable to justify their presence in the zone: also those who give orders to retire or start panicking. No fuss or bother, merely keep an account of the total number dealt with.' As the countryside must now have been full of terrified refugees who could scarcely justify their presence – for they probably did not know the name of the place they were in – and there were stragglers who had lost their original Army units, Barlone and other recipients of this somewhat sweeping order would seem to have been given a busy programme. But as they themselves had been ordered to move on at 10 p.m. next day there would be little time for such drastic measures.

On arrival at a place called Le Riez, Barlone was told to disperse his men in the orchards and to order them to dig slit trenches. The order was not welcome, for it implied that the unit was not expected to play anything but a passive role. 'There are no newspapers, and there is no radio. The whole region is without electricity,' he recorded. Fortunately food was plentiful. 'Gamelin,' he heard, 'has been superseded. . . . What a disappointment is this man. Weygand has taken his place. He surely will pull us through.'

But then, to his horror, he learnt that the Germans had reached Boulogne and Calais. 'So we are encircled.' He wondered whether they would succeed in breaking out or be taken prisoner. It seemed incredible to him that all their fortifications, their hundreds of thousands of men and immense quantities of material would now fall into the hands of the Germans. He now realised why no attempt had been made to hold the frontier forts: the position had already been turned.

He and his men set off towards Dunkirk, where they had been ordered to assemble, moving between fifteen and twenty-five miles a night. But on 26 May hope flared up again. A French army from the south was marching north to Bapaume. The remains of the French armies in Belgium, although down to less than half strength, were heading south and the Germans had been trapped in this pincer movement after heavy fighting. 'The German advanced units would now all fall intact into French hands. 'That shows the Weygand touch,' he recorded gleefully. 'The German manoeuvre will end disastrously. We dance for joy.' But the next day he was writing: 'Alas, all the information was false. The High Command appears to have given up all hope of saving us. We must reach Dunkirk at all costs.'

On the way to the port they were told to billet in a wood on the other side of the Lys, but then suddenly had to retrace their steps because it was already partly occupied by Germans. Adding injury to insult they were machine-gunned and dive-bombed by twenty-seven German aircraft, which appeared to be playing with them. All they had for retaliation was a small number of obsolete instructional machine-guns which would be ineffective even if they were not worn out. Barlone waited for further orders and occasionally heard of infantry regiments being told to counter-attack. The aim of these orders was to delay the Germans while other units reached Dunkirk, but the cost to the infantry of these desperate last battles was heavy. Most of their officers had already been killed and the regiments were being controlled by NCOs.

At Neuve Eglise he was heartened to see British preparations for a counter-attack with infantry and tanks. Although the British infantry looked very tired, and German aircraft attacked them relentlessly, the counter-attack party moved ahead with success. Unfortunately, when the British had cleared the road to Dunkirk they barricaded the sides of the route with tractors. As this move blocked the French route, an inevitable incident occurred, and the French artillery threatened to fire on the British. Barlone, as the senior officer present, told two artillery officers to take a hundred men and drag away the tractors. Meanwhile he went off to find a British officer and within two minutes of meeting a major all was smoothed over, different routes for French and English troops were agreed, and the columns flowed swiftly on in the direction of Dunkirk.

But as they came to within twelve miles of the town the congestion and disorder were indescribable, and it was not improved by periodic German shelling and bombing. Previously abandoned horses rushed from the adjoining fields and tried to join Barlone's convoy; there were hundreds of horses and thousands of vehicles. Only about 7 per cent of the division's original manpower had made it to Dunkirk to be evacuated. What made the situation worse was the fact that the division had never been able to go into battle as it should have done. By brilliant manoeuvring, Barlone recorded bitterly, the Germans had cut holes through the Allied defence and made them twist and turn until they had become an exhausted, dispirited shambles.

12 The Sweep to the Channel Ports

How had this sorry state of affairs for the Allies come to pass? General Guderian had some of the answers. On 19 May he had been crossing the old First World War battlefield of the Somme. As the Germans had been advancing north of the Aisne, that river and the Serre and the Somme had served to guard their left flank, although it was also covered by reconnaissance troops and anti-tank units. He knew that there might be minor trouble along this flank, as the French 4th Armoured Division, under a certain General de Gaulle, was known to be in the area and had already made one or two attempts to harass them, but no serious danger was anticipated from him. Nevertheless there had been an uncomfortable moment when some of de Gaulle's tanks came to within a mile of the German advanced HQ. As that forward position had no more than a few 20-mm anti-aircraft guns for its protection, it was hoped that de Gaulle did not know how well his tanks were doing.

There were reports of another French army under General Frère, but this caused little apprehension. The Germans had made a careful study of the characteristics of the French generals they were likely to encounter and had learnt that General Frère did not like to commit his forces until he had a clear idea of where his enemy was and what he was doing. Guderian decided that Frère should be denied that satisfaction by the simple process of keeping the German armies moving forward. Nevertheless, as they penetrated into areas where the Allied armies were likely to be more concentrated, he thickened up the defence of his left flank by deploying 2nd and 10th Panzer

Divisions along the route. When needed they could be brought into the main attack again.

First Panzer, having been relieved from escort duties along the flank, could now be brought into the impending attack on Amiens. However, an incident now occurred which infuriated Guderian when he heard of it. When he visited Péronne and spoke to 10th Panzer, he learnt that they had arrived to find the town empty of German troops. First Panzer, instead of waiting for 10th Panzer to relieve them, had moved out and positioned themselves for the forthcoming attack on Amiens. The commanding officer of 1st Panzer, Lieutenant Colonel Balck, was determined that the division should be in the forefront of the attack on Amiens and was not prepared to wait for his relief. When rebuked for his conduct by the commanding officer of 10th Panzer, who pointed out that if the French had counter-attacked Péronne would have been lost, Balck airily replied: 'Never mind. If we lose it you can always take it again. I had to capture it in the first place, didn't I?' This little interchange indicated that the German Panzer leaders were such intense rivals that they were prepared to jeopardize the entire tactical plan if they thought that doing so might bring them a little extra prestige. But Guderian was not in a very strong position to complain of insubordination among his successful Panzer leaders. He himself had constantly flouted his superior's intentions, even to the extent of disobeying orders, and in doing so had achieved great success.

So great was the confusion in this area that the Germans were themselves now driving through throngs of refugees. By this time these unfortunate people had no idea of where they were going; their only wish was to remove themselves as far as possible from the battle zone, wherever that might be. Guderian was rather amused to note that some British vehicles had mingled with the German columns, hoping that their thick covering of dust would prevent them from being detected, and that in this way they might perhaps reach their own lines and join their comrades. Had he known that just over four years later German troops would be employing the same tactics when the Allied armies were sweeping across France and north-west Europe towards Germany, he might have thought it less humorous.

Guderian moved on quickly to Albert, where he was pleased to find that 2nd Panzer had captured an English artillery battery; drawn up on the parade square and equipped with training ammunition only, it had been unaware of any threat until it was suddenly surrounded.

All this was very pleasing but a discordant note was struck in Amiens, where his headquarters was attacked by the Luftwaffe. The infuriated German anti-aircraft batteries opened fire, knowing exactly what they were doing. One aircraft was shot down, but its crew of two were able to parachute to the ground. On arrival they found the general was waiting for them. 'When the more disagreeable part of our conversation was over,' said Guderian, 'I fortified the two young men with a glass of champagne.' No doubt they needed it.

At this point Guderian noted that some of his forward troop commanders were beginning to report a shortage of fuel, or even that their stocks were exhausted. He simply did not believe them, interpreting their statements as another way of saying they wanted a rest. No doubt they were exhausted and realized that their vehicles badly needed maintenance, but that was not an excuse that would be accepted. Weariness seldom affects victorious troops, though to the defeated it can be the last crushing blow. As long as the tanks were able to move and fire their guns there was no point in halting for maintenance: improvisation must be the order of the day. Fuel, as Guderian knew, was plentiful, both from captured stocks and from base supplies. The only possible shortages would come from imperfect distribution. As long as the Army was moving forward, it would capture more stocks.

This was, of course, the sort of calculation which would lead the German armies into serious trouble later. Unlimited stocks of fuel would not be found in the Western Desert, still less in the snowy wastes of Russia. Thus the triumphant advance in France, where Allied stocks were abundant, would cause the Germans, and Hitler in particular, to assume that a conquering army could live off the countryside. Napoleon could have told them differently. In view of Guderian's knowledge of military history, it seems strange that he did not ponder its lessons even in the moment of victory.

On the 21st, Guderian was told he could continue his advance northwards with a view to capturing the Channel ports and thus cutting off the Allied supply line. He had made a plan to capture Dunkirk, Calais and Boulogne by the co-ordinated advance of his three Panzer regiments; but he had reckoned without his Higher Command. Still cautious, his superiors had decided that 10th Panzer should be withdrawn and held in reserve. It seems a reasonable precaution, for the Germans had every reason to believe they were now about to run into a desperate last-ditch battle with every man, tank and gun the Allies could lay their hands on. Tenth Panzer had been earmarked for the capture of Dunkirk, and there seems little doubt that if it had been allowed to go forward at that point it would undoubtedly have done so and there would have been no mass evacuation. But it did not.

The decision to withdraw 10th Panzer was probably one of the most momentous of the war, for it undoubtedly saved Dunkirk and thus allowed the bulk of the British Army to get away. With this nucleus a new Army was then built, trained and equipped in Britain, and an Allied landing was made in 1944. Hitler should have pressed home his advantage and invaded Britain immediately after the fall of France. He was deterred from doing so partly because he knew he had neither air nor naval supremacy, but also by his belief that Britain had twenty-four trained and equipped divisions waiting for him in south-east England; 338,000 men, the number evacuated from Dunkirk, represent approximately twenty-two divisions; and twenty-two divisions, however battered and however badly equipped, represent a formidable threat to any invasion force which has to cross twenty-one miles of potentially turbulent water, all the while being harassed by a formidable navy and air force. In hindsight it is clear that Guderian could hardly have failed to reach and capture Dunkirk, and the world owes a debt to the unknown source of the order to withdraw 10th Panzer.

In place of his cherished 10th Panzer Guderian received the infantry regiment Gross-Deutschland, which had acquitted itself well at Sedan but could obviously not be an adequate replacement. At the same time he learnt of the counter-attack by British tanks at Arras. Guderian reflected that the main German opposition in that area was provided by the SS Totenkopf Division. This, though bearing a daunting title (Death's Head), had not previously been in action, and had reacted badly, even showing signs of panic. But the information did not worry him. He had expected the British to make a counter-attack soon and the fact that it had had some success against an inexperienced infantry unit did not seem to him surprising or particularly disturbing. In fact he was encouraged by the realization that the British tank attack had achieved little and then quickly given up its temporary gains.

But the effect on von Kleist and his staff was very different. In their view this could only be the forerunner, perhaps the first testing probe, of the desperate counter-attack which could spell complete disaster

for the Panzers. Strung out over a vast area, badly in need of maintenance, and probably with both crews and fuel stocks at the point
of exhaustion, they would now encounter a desperate Allied army,
fighting with the dangerous resolution of a cornered animal. These
fears were not entirely without foundation, for in certain sectors of
the line the Allied forces had clung tenaciously to their positions and
inflicted heavy casualties on the Germans. The thought of this being
repeated on a large scale sent a shiver of apprehension down von
Kleist's spine. Many great victories have been snatched from the jaws
of defeat because the attacker had over-extended himself, and von
Kleist hoped that this would not be another to add to their number.

On 22 May the Panzers rolled forward again. According to
Guderian neither 1st nor 2nd Panzer were at full strength any more
because they had been obliged to leave detachments guarding their
vital bridgeheads over the Somme. But they were a formidable force
none the less. They had some brisk encounters with mixed French,
British and Belgian forces on the way to Boulogne, but were not
held up seriously. Their casualties were mounting, as was inevitable,
and the process of getting up replacements took longer than it did
for the Allies, who had plenty of men nearby. Some of these had
provided the counter-attacks of which Denis Barlone had written.
The Luftwaffe was giving Guderian's Panzers very little help at this
point; instead, they were receiving increasing and unwelcome attention from British and French aircraft. Guderian doubtless guessed the
reason for the sudden withdrawal of the Luftwaffe. No air map could
possibly predict where the Panzers were, and after learning that
they had bombed Guderian's headquarters in Amiens the Luftwaffe
would be unwilling to take chances with targets in the forward areas
where the situation might change from one hour to the next.

Second Panzer reached Boulogne at the end of the day on 22 May
and surrounded the landward side. At approximately the same time
1st Panzer reached Calais. This left Dunkirk, a little further up the
coast, as the only port with an approach route still under the control
of the Allies – a route packed with exhausted troops, abandoned vehicles, transport and casualties. But with all its drawbacks, the Dunkirk
road was a vital lifeline to the Allies; and so for the moment Guderian
decided he must concentrate his attacks there.

Late that night, Guderian received a message from von Kleist
telling him that, as the threatened Allied attack had not material-
ized, he could now bring 10th Panzer back into the main action.

Guderian's reaction was not to waste energy deploring the timidity of his superiors which had upset his plans of the day before, but to make up for lost time. If he could move his Panzers along the coast in this area, capturing the ports as they went, the whole Allied army would be trapped. It did not occur to him that in doing so he would also be preventing an evacuation, for that possibility had occurred to nobody except those close enough to Gort to know how bad the situation was; but Guderian realized that with Calais and Boulogne virtually in the bag Dunkirk was now the only port through which supplies could come to keep the Allies in being as a fighting force. If they lost Dunkirk they would become a beleaguered army. They might, of course, with their vast numbers, still break out by land and perhaps head in the direction of Le Havre, Cherbourg or Brest. They might even eject 2nd Panzer from its position around (or, perhaps, in) Boulogne. These were possibilities, but even if they became realities the German stranglehold would be immensely strengthened by the possession of Dunkirk.

As Calais was already invested by 1st Panzer and could not easily be reached by the Allies, Guderian decided that the best tactic would be the slightly risky one of pushing up 10th Panzer along the route to Calais to allow 1st Panzer to move on to Dunkirk. In its present position at Calais 1st Panzer was very favourably situated for a swift move to its neighbour. On 23 May, Guderian issued the necessary orders. 'Move at once to line Audruick-Ardres-Calais and then swing eastwards to advance east through Bourbourgville-Gravelines to Bergues and Dunkirk.'

Total victory was now coming within the German grasp. With the three vital Channel ports captured the BEF would still be a dangerous fighting force, with some twenty to thirty divisions, but its unsupported position would be desperate and, if it did not surrender readily, it could doubtless be battered into submission by the German guns and air force later. Guderian was, in fact, visualizing a situation which the BEF avoided but which, ironically, would be met by the German armies in France four years later. In August 1944 the German 5th Panzer and 7th Army were caught in what became known as the Falaise pocket by the convergence of American, British and French forces. After five days of desperate fighting, the retreating Germans left behind fifty thousand prisoners and ten thousand killed. But whereas in 1944 the Germans had virtually no chance of escape, the Allies in 1940 still had Dunkirk, the port which on 23 May 1940 Guderian was planning to capture, he felt with every chance of success. He had 10th Panzer back under his control and the Higher Command was, at last, leaving him to his own devices. In his moment of victory all earlier matters of insubordination would obviously be overlooked. The Führer would be delighted. It could only be a matter of two or three days.

13 Halt Before Dunkirk

O<small>N</small> 22 MAY, with the Channel ports under threat of capture, Churchill flew to Paris, as this seemed to be the only way he could obtain a full and up-to-date account of events. He did not realize that the French government in Paris was even more out of touch with the course of events than was the government in London. All he discovered was that within twelve days the Allied armies had been reduced from a mood of joyous confidence to the immediate expectation of complete defeat. When he asked Weygand if he could get the French Army to fight back, even at this late stage, Weygand had replied, 'I will try.' The answer did not convey much confidence.

That evening Ismay, Churchill's Chief of Staff, told him that he was afraid the Germans would now offer such generous terms that the French would be bound to consider them. But before accepting they would ask Britain to help them with another forty divisions and fifteen more fighter squadrons. It would clearly be an impossible request, and when Britain refused, as she must do, the French would shrug their shoulders and say, 'In that case we have no alternative but to accept the German terms.' Churchill did not entirely agree with this pessimistic view: he thought the French would not stoop to making such a bargain. Had he known what the Vichy government would do later, he might not have been so sanguine.

The following day news flowed to London continuously, all of it bad. The BEF was reported to be short of food, a statement which probably meant it had been cut off from its main supply depots. It was no longer considered possible that the harassed BEF could turn south and link up with the French, for German forces of unknown strength were already across the route they would have to take. The news that Boulogne, Dunkirk and Calais were all under threat from the rampaging Panzers caused further gloom. It was reported (wrongly) that the Germans were already in Boulogne. But when Churchill spoke to Weygand on the telephone the mood suddenly changed, for Weygand now reported that the French had recaptured Amiens and Péronne. This startling announcement was greeted with joy, but in subsequent conversation doubts were voiced as to whether it could actually be true.

The worse the situation, the more extravagant the rumours. It is never possible to trace the source of most of the wilder fantasies in wartime. It was, of course, perfectly feasible for the French to have recaptured Péronne and Amiens once the Panzers had moved on and before the German infantry had caught up to consolidate the position. But it was a false rumour. It may have had a fifth column source; there is value in spreading rumours among enemy forces, but they are usually of defeats rather than victories.

After the initial shocks, Churchill and the Cabinet were now grimly realistic. Suspecting that invasion might be imminent, they asked Parliament for absolute power for any emergency – which was agreed. Houses, factories, buildings of any kind could be requisitioned or demolished if need be. Labour could be conscripted. In his diaries Colville wondered if, when granted, such powers would ever be completely relinquished.

Grim though the situation was, Colville was able to leave his duties at No. 10 Downing Street and take a short weekend break in Oxford. At this stage England was virtually untouched by the war and Oxford was an oasis of calm and beauty. Later in the war it would become busier, crowded with members of the services in uniform, and not unfamiliar with the sound of enemy aircraft although it escaped unscathed. Many of the young undergraduates and many dons, too, would be taken into the services in the near future; some of those walking around while the BEF was being hounded out of France would be killed later in the return invasion of 1944; others would find their careers improved by the experiences the war would give them.

> Before dinner the sun came out and we were able to walk placidly in Christ Church Meadows. We dined once again at The Trout, but in glorious conditions this time: a blue sky, a setting sun and enough clouds to make the sun still more effective. We ate on a seat by the river, and then walked along the tow path watching children at play and listening to plovers calling. There had never been a more beautiful setting in which to be happy and I have never felt greater serenity or contentment.

Across the Channel there was no such serenity or contentment. But although the BEF was in dire straits, both it and the French Army still occupied substantial portions of France. Captain Basil Bartlett was concerned by the extraordinary number of German agents who seemed to be operating in advance of their armies. The most obvious sign of their presence was that wherever there were telephone lines, civilian or military, they were constantly being cut. When repaired, they were cut again. He suspected that many of the saboteurs were Belgians who were working for the Germans. Claiming to be refugees put them in a strong position for then they could not be expected to know where they were, still less that they were in a prohibited area.

'I've told people they'll be shot if they go out at night and arrested if they show lights after dark,' he wrote. 'But the Belgian peasant is *entêté* [stubborn]. He'll never pay attention to anything he's told.'

On the retreat through Lille, he and another officer found only one bar open. 'The proprietress seemed very hopeful about the outcome of the war. Her optimism was shared by an old man who was dancing by himself in the middle of the floor. "We'll beat them. We'll beat them. We'll beat them," he said. Then he sank down into a chair and went to sleep.'

This optimism was not much in evidence among those required to do the fighting, which had become piecemeal and disorganized. Outside Lille, 8th Brigade sent out a reconnaissance group to find out how strong the Germans were and to see if a counter-attack was feasible. The recce party was made up of two companies each from the 1st Suffolks, the 4th Royal Berkshires and the 2nd East Yorkshire, assisted by some machine-gunners from the 2nd Middlesex operating on their flanks. Their mission was successful in that they found that the Germans were in greater strength on their right and in the centre than on their left. After a brisk engagement the recce party returned. There were twelve officer casualties, of which three were missing and nine wounded. Four soldiers had been killed, four were wounded and ninety-seven were missing. Five Bren gun carriers had been lost. As this attack was not followed up by larger forces, and seemed to form no part of a general tactical plan, it was difficult to understand why it had been ordered.

Usherforce put up a spirited defence of the bridges at Gravelines. Apart from the 6th Battalion of the Green Howards, this force consisted mainly of Royal Engineers and Royal Artillery fighting as infantry. The Green Howards fought with success alongside 3rd Searchlight Regiment (who could hardly have imagined they would ever find themselves in such a position) and held off attacks from the German 1st Panzer. Gunners from 1st and 3rd Super-Heavy Battery, and 52nd Heavy, also fought with distinction as infantry.

British troops were now holding, or trying to hold, the Canal Line between St Omer and Aire. The first blows were countered by the 5th (Inniskilling) Dragoon Guards but, as the Germans brought up even stronger forces, the 5th DG were forced back. Having stabilized their position, they were joined by units from the 4th/7th Dragoon Guards, the 13th/18th Hussars, some machine-gunners from the 9th Northumberland Fusiliers, and a mixed unit known as 'Don Details' which consisted of a mixture of Signals, Ordnance, RASC and Engineers. Together this hybrid unit held the position, but were not strong enough to carry the attack to the enemy.

As the Germans made probing attacks, they were countered by Allied units which were already depleted by earlier actions. French troops relieved Usherforce and to the south-west of Raches blocked every attempt by strong German forces to drive a wedge between the two British fronts. It was perhaps as well that the general situation was so confused that units hardly knew who was on their left or their right and still less who was behind them. Had they realized that some German units had already reached the coast it would have done little for the morale of men who, tired with marching and being attacked, felt they were facing an apparently inexhaustible supply of fresh enemy troops. Those who survived the war would be interested to discover later what they were supposed to be defending and how greatly the dice were weighted against them.

However, those in a position to know the general trend, if not the

Top left: Von Rundstedt, whose fears about the vulnerability of the German columns caused him to check the Panzers – and unwittingly made the evacuation of Dunkirk possible.

Top right: Heinz Guderian, the mastermind of Panzer warfare, who led the German drive over the Meuse and through France.

Above: General Georges, Commander of the Allied Northern Army Group, in conversation with General Gort, Commander of the B.E.F.

Right: German parachutists spearheading the invasion of the Low Countries.

All photos from the author's collection.

Top: Bridge over the Albert Canal, destroyed by the British to prevent the Germans from using it.

Centre: Germans ferrying their troops across the Meuse on pontoons. Inflatable craft in the foreground.

Bottom: Germans making use of local transport during the invasion of Belgium.

All photos from the author's collection.

Top left: Civilians in the middle. Forlorn mother with her family in Enghien.

Bottom: British troops in the rubble of Louvain waiting to confront the Panzers.

Top left photo courtesy of the Imperial War Museum; bottom photo from the author's collection.

Opposite, top: German troops advancing through cornfields in Champagne.

Opposite, centre: A knocked-out French tank.

Below: The cost of war: would-be refugees caught by German low-level air attack.

Bottom: German infantry advancing through a burning town.

Opposite centre and below courtesy of the Imperial War Museum; opposite top and bottom from the author's collection.

Top: Waiting in line on the beach at Dunkirk.

Bottom: Dunkirk: troops waiting for evacuation take refuge in sand dunes against bombing and machine-gunning.

Top: The beach; deserted apart from bodies and wrecked transport.

Bottom left: Wounded French soldier being evacuated. Over one-third of those rescued were French, but many returned voluntarily to France while it was German-occupied.

Bottom right: Street scene in Dunkirk after the fighting.

THE FINAL STAGES.

Top left: Wrecked vehicles outside Cherbourg.

Top right: Members of the 4th Border Regiment holding up the German advance in the Somme sector. Though isolated, they still managed to harrass the Germans for five days.

Bottom: The *Lancastria,* a 20,000 ton Cunard liner is sunk by German dive-bombers off St Nazaire on 17 June 1940. 3000 of the 5000 aboard were drowned.

Top photos courtesy of the Imperial War Museum; bottom photo from the author's collection.

details of events, were surprised to find that the entire German front was not sent driving forward on the 24th. It seemed all too clear to Gort and his staff that if the German forces, who by now had caught up with all but the leading Panzers, had made a concerted drive, the BEF and the miscellany of French troops in the area would not have been able to hole it.

Von Rundstedt, fortunately for the Allies, took a more cautious view. Even after the enormous successes the Germans had already had, he felt that extreme prudence was necessary. He considered that the Panzers and other mobile units were too widely dispersed and that, in consequence, Allied counter-attacks could drive wedges between them and recapture huge sectors of important territory. He regarded the Arras counter-attack far more seriously than Guderian did and thought that it could be followed by others. The biggest danger, in his view, would occur if Allied forces, mainly French, with tanks which had not so far been used, drove up from the south and cut the German forces in half just as neatly as German forces had split the Allied forces by driving from Sedan to Abbeville. If that happened, the Germans would be trying to hold fresh French troops and tanks with exhausted German soldiers and Panzers desperately in need of maintenance.

It was an entirely sensible attitude to take; but von Rundstedt did not realize that the great force waiting to counter-attack from the south once the German Army was spread loosely over France was a myth. There were a few troops in the south who would try to continue the fight back, but they bore no resemblance to a formidable counter-attacking force. Perhaps von Rundstedt believed, in the absence of other information, that the French force of unknown strength had already recaptured Péronne and Amiens. The French believed it, and so, of course, did the British Cabinet. It could easily have been true if Gamelin had not been the original French Commander-in-Chief, for almost anyone else would have been certain to have had a strategic reserve of tanks.

Although von Rundstedt's caution allowed the BEF to escape, and therefore contributed largely to the subsequent defeat of Germany, it was not as bizarre as it is sometimes made out to be. His suspicion that Guderian's forward units might have reached the end of their effective fighting power appeared to be confirmed when he heard that they had reached Calais and Boulogne but had failed to take them. The Allies therefore still controlled both harbours and could, presumably, use these as well as Dunkirk for the base of their counter-attack. Exercising common sense, at 6 p.m. on 23 May von Rundstedt sent out a directive to the German 4th Army to halt.

At 11.30 on the following day Hitler visited von Rundstedt at his headquarters. He agreed entirely with his general's assessment of the situation and endorsed his plans for halting the Panzers along the line Lens-Béthune-Aire-St Omer-Gravelines. Hitler believed that the Panzers should now be rested and kept in reserve for any heavy fighting they might be required to undertake in the Allied counter-attacks. He felt that the destruction of the encircled BEF could now be completed by the Luftwaffe, but in order for this to take place it was essential that forward units of the Panzers should not be roaming casually on the chosen 'killing ground'.

Relieved that Hitler agreed with his strategic thinking, von Rundstedt now proceeded to safeguard his own position still further. He was well aware that frustrated Panzer leaders who saw final victory in their grasp would make critical comments on the order to halt. He was, however, equally aware that, whatever their thoughts, they would not dare voice them if they thought the orders came from the Führer. He therefore issued another directive (after Hitler had left his headquarters) which began, 'By the Führer's orders . . .' and then emphasized that the Aa Canal Line would not be passed. Vehicle maintenance was to begin forthwith. Years afterwards the Panzer leaders were still expressing their dismay that 'the Führer' should have intervened at that moment and robbed them of final victory. They did not, however, express these views until after Hitler was dead.

Although Hitler must have known from aerial reconnaissance that the BEF was already beginning to use Dunkirk as an evacuation port, he did not envisage it as being able to handle more than a fraction of the forces that the German Army had now trapped. But even if the numbers at this stage had been much greater, Hitler would not have been concerned. He had every confidence that Goering's Luftwaffe would demolish the port itself and then proceed to bomb the Royal Navy out of the water. The Navy could never be in a more vulnerable position than when it was trying to collect hundreds of men from open beaches.

The halt on the 24th was put to good use by the BEF. All the *ad hoc* forces, such as Frankforce, Petreforce and Macforce, were disbanded, as the defensive task they had managed so well could now be taken over by more orthodox units; they themselves could be held in reserve. A joint Anglo-French counter-attack was planned for 26 May. The British contribution was to be 9th and 50th Divisions and 1st Army Tank Brigade, although the last was now much below brigade strength. Artillery was redistributed to the support positions it would occupy normally. Regiments which had suffered heavy casualties were brought up to strength by amalgamation or drafts from other regiments.

Unfortunately this breathing space, which gave the Allies an opportunity to reorganize the defence, could not alter the fact that the BEF and the 1st French Army were now trapped in a salient, probably the most vulnerable of all military positions. The salient was seventy miles long and varied in width from twenty-five miles to thirteen. It was full of troops marching to their allotted positions, or trying to rejoin their parent units; it also contained hopeless, helpless refugees who tramped steadily towards the coast where they imagined there would be food and safety. Periodically it was bombed by the Luftwaffe who machine-gunned indiscriminately.

At this moment, making a bad situation worse, there was a serious rift in Anglo-French relations. Owing to a misunderstanding, the French Prime Minister sent a telegram to Churchill informing him that instead of conforming to the original plan for a combined pincer movement attack the BEF had withdrawn forty kilometres towards the coast and therefore had made the joint attack impossible. Reynaud also made the improbable claim that French forces from the south were making ground in their move to the north.

The BEF had not in fact withdrawn forty kilometres, but two divisions had retired half that distance from the Arras salient, which was no longer of tactical importance. The French forces from the south had made no progress at all.

Churchill replied as best he could, pointing out that there had been no change in the tactical plan. By the time Churchill's reply reached Reynaud, the latter had been informed by Weygand that the French plan to drive up from the south had now been abandoned as impossible. But it was disastrous that at a moment of such extreme peril Anglo-French distrust and suspicion should be in evidence. The French thought that Gort was failing to obey orders from his French superior, Weygand; the British thought that Weygand must be totally out of touch with the real facts of the situation.

135

Although Gort's military record and decorations caused him to be respected by the French, this did not extend to trusting that he and the perfidious British might not take any opportunity to withdraw from the battle and leave the French to their fate. But, it should be emphasized, this was not a view held by the French who were fighting side by side with the British; it existed only in the upper realms of the staff, which from the beginning had been very reticent about their own dispositions and slow to report the early disasters.

On the 25th Dill, who had just replaced Ironside after the latter's removal on grounds of his political connections,* flew over from England to obtain from Gort his view of the general situation. Gort had by no means decided that the battle was lost, but he conveyed to Dill that the position was acutely dangerous. On the northern side of the salient Gort was trying to hold eighty-seven miles with seven divisions; this would represent one man to every 150 yards if they had been strung out in a line. For the attack to the south, which would be in combination with two, perhaps three, French divisions, only two British divisions could be spared.

However, at this point the British Army had another stroke of luck, or perhaps it would be fairer to say was amply rewarded for initiative and daring. A fighting patrol from 3rd Division had spotted a German staff car close to their front and had attacked it, killing the driver. The passenger ran back towards his own lines and escaped; he was a lieutenant general, and in his haste left his papers in the car. They were of the greatest importance, mainly because they disclosed the details of the German plans and the numbers involved. Armed with this information, the Commander of the British 2nd Corps, Lieutenant General A. F. Brooke, later

---

*Ironside's sudden removal from his post of Chief of the General Staff, his subsequent appointment as Commander-in-Chief, Home Forces, and retirement in the same year as a field marshal, conceals a mystery. He had a distinguished military record in the First World War and at the end of it had been Commander-in-Chief of the Allied Troops at Archangel in Russia; he spoke Russian, Polish, German and several other languages fluently. However, in May 1940 the Field Security Police reported to the War Office that a staff car had been observed making frequent and lengthy visits to a house in Holland Park. The car was identified; its occupant was General Ironside. Malcolm Muggeridge, then in the FSP, was told to investigate. The occupants of the house were said to have 'dubious political associations'. Ironside was reputed to have had Fascist associations in the past. Muggeridge was inclined to think that Ironside's visits were 'personal rather than political', but was surprised that a man in Ironside's position at this time of crisis should be able to spend so much time away from his office. The evening papers carried a headline 'Ironside sacked' the day after Muggeridge made his report.

Field-Marshal Lord Alanbrooke, was able to make the best use of his thin line of troops. This was especially important at that moment as there was a dangerous gap between the British and Belgian forces which had been opened up as the Belgians fell back. The critical area was between Menin and Ypres; if the Germans made a successful thrust there they would slice through the middle of the Allied salient, separating the bulk of the British army from Dunkirk. When Gort learnt of this immediate danger he decided to close this gap at all costs. He therefore abandoned the abortive attempt to make a south-westerly attack in company with the French, and instead rushed up 5th and 50th Divisions to the Menin-Ypres sector.

As the Panzers had been halted on 24 May, it now seems strange that 9th Corps and 6th Corps of the German Army were still pressing forward. There was, in fact, some confusion in the German Higher Command over whether the attack should be renewed, but this mainly affected the armoured divisions around the southern areas of the salient, notably on the Canal Line. It would not affect the Panzers attacking Boulogne or Calais. In the northern sector the pressure was coming from units which had already forced their way through Belgium. When they arrived, 5th and 50th put up a tremendous defence against the German attempts to penetrate this sector. Knowing how vital this area was, Brooke stiffened up the defence with as much artillery and other support as he dared move from other areas.

In view of the fact that after the campaign was over there was a general assumption in Britain that the Panzers had cruised through France without meeting much resistance, the casualty figures of the German 39th Corps are interesting. By 24 May, the one motorized and two armoured divisions had *each* suffered average casualties of 50 officers and 1500 other ranks. One third of their tanks had been put out of action, and losses of guns had been high. Although these figures only relate to three divisions, they were considered to be average for the other units. The British public may have thought the German Army had had an easy victory in sweeping aside the badly commanded French and inadequately armed and trained British, but the Panzer leaders would not have shared that view.

By the 26th, Gort had made an appreciation of the situation which confirmed his worst fears. Even if the Belgians fought on and did not make a separate peace (which they would soon do), they could not affect the eventual outcome. He had no hope of reinforcements, nor of further supplies of ammunition or food. He had little hope that the French would now make an attack to the south, though it was theoretically possible for them to do so. He did not, of course, know that Weygand had abandoned his plan for a thrust from the south combined with the attack from the north. He knew that his men were outnumbered, very tired and at the end of their resources. He knew also that the French Army was in no better state. His only comforting thought was the manner in which many British units had accomplished feats that no one could have anticipated in their wildest imaginings. One of the many was that of a Pioneer battalion, the 6th King's Own, which had held the southern bridge at Merville against determined enemy attacks. Pioneers are not rated as the cream of the Army and, because of their lower physical standards, are usually allotted mundane tasks such as road-making or trench-digging. These men produced something more. They held off repeated German attacks, using a field gun they had acquired to knock out three tanks and two armoured cars, and captured twenty prisoners.

But although this action was typical of the way in which many units were facing their near-impossible tasks, it did not alter the fact that the German firepower was now so great that a further Allied withdrawal would be necessary if the defensive perimeter was to be kept intact. The general situation was precarious but not disastrous. The French 1st Army was defending with skill and resolution, and the defence of the Canal Line, though severely strained, appeared to be holding.

To the north-west, where the Belgian Army seemed to be crumbling fast, the picture was less happy. When 5th Division rushed up from the south to close the gap in front of Courtrai, they arrived to a welcome of shells; the German Army was advancing to the same area from the opposite direction and was softening up any potential opposition in advance. When the 12th Lancers, covering the right flank of 5th Division, came up to Ypres they found it undefended and without a Belgian soldier in sight. There were none closer than Zonnebeke, five miles to the north-east. News of the vulnerability of the Allied line in this sector soon reached Gort, who made up his mind that the perimeter must be shortened by a retreat to the River Lys.

A week earlier he had decided that, if the worst came to the worst, the BEF and as many French as possible might eventually have to leave the country via Dunkirk, Calais or Boulogne, and return to France at a later date. Now Calais and Boulogne were blocked, leaving only Dunkirk. But Gort was not the only person thinking that the BEF might have to leave via Dunkirk. The Luftwaffe had come to much the same opinion, and in consequence was bombing the docks and installations as vigorously as possible. The RAF was providing as much fighter cover as possible but, as it was now mainly operating from airfields on the other side of the Channel, its task was exceptionally difficult. Boulogne and Calais meanwhile had been receiving close attention from Guderian's Panzers.

14 The Battles for Calais and Boulogne

O N 19 MAY both Calais and Boulogne appeared to be safely in Allied hands and unlikely to experience more than bombing; however, if the general situation continued to deteriorate either or both might have to be used for evacuating non-essential troops from elsewhere. The arrival of Guderian's Panzers in the neighbourhood caused a rapid reappraisal of these ideas. Realising that the two ports had suddenly become highly vulnerable, the War Office sent out anti-aircraft guns, the 3rd Royal Tank Regiment, and the Queen Victoria Rifles, who arrived with no transport and few weapons. On 23 May these were joined by 2nd Battalion King's Royal Rifle Corps (60th Rifles), also then known as the Greenjackets, and 1st Battalion The Rifle Brigade.

The commander of this small but stout-hearted force was Brigadier Claude Nicholson. He was well aware that most of his troops had never seen any form of action, that they had insufficient weapons, and that the most critical shortage was in tanks and field artillery. They would soon be confronted by the experienced 10th Panzer Division, which had considerable battle experience, artillery of every variety, and powerful aerial support. The odds would still have been overwhelmingly in favour of the Germans even if Nicholson had been sent the artillery and ammunition he requested. The only commodity which he had in abundance was absurd orders; the War Office, aware that it had no control over the main battle, was determined to show that in this area, at least, it could make an attempt to demonstrate its authority. Nicholson was therefore informed that he should help the hard-pressed garrison in Boulogne but in the same breath that he should be ready to assail the troops around St Omer. He was told that his forces must be evacuated immediately and then that they should stay and fight to the end. Meanwhile he could see the destroyers in Calais harbour which had been ordered to stand by and wait for the evacuation.

The muddles seem almost incredible, even allowing for the confusion created by the general situation. There was a critical shortage of arms and ammunition, which had been left behind because of an alleged lack of space in the transports; and most of the anti-tank guns which would have been invaluable in the defence of Calais were still on the dockside at Dover. Even more astonishing was the fact that when the troops had been put ashore at Calais their ships were sent home before they had completed unloading what stores they had been able to bring with them. Incredulously they watched these vessels depart carrying their essential needs.

In recent years Calais and the surrounding countryside have become familiar to large numbers of people who have visited the area as tourists. Although much of the town, including the old part, was destroyed during the war, most of it has been rebuilt. The town lies in flat country and is overlooked by a ridge of high ground to the south-west from which it can be shelled easily and accurately, but it has the advantage of once having been fortified by Vauban. Its defences include water-filled moats and sturdy, though ancient, ramparts. The perimeter extends over eight miles; this, of course, was much too long for Nicholson's small force to defend properly. Mobility inside the town was greatly restricted by the refugees who had flocked there and could now go no further.

The 3rd Royal Tank Regiment (RTR) was sent to reconnoitre the situation at St Omer; they found it unoccupied but in flames. However, before it could be occupied 1st Panzer Division arrived on the scene, blocking the approach road. After 3rd RTR had lost twelve of its tanks, it realized that further progress was impossible and withdrew to Calais. A spirited defence was put up by 1st Searchlight Regiment at Les Attaques, but this too was overwhelmed by the heavy firepower which was brought to bear on it. So far Calais had only encountered the superior numbers and weapons of 1st Panzer; in a short time it would also be contending with the massive strength of 10th Panzer. With a good idea of what to expect, Nicholson set out the defences with the Rifle Brigade and the 60th defending the ramparts and Queen Victoria's Rifles (QVR) manning the outposts.

With everything now set for a crunching battle as the Panzers approached the ramparts and the ditches, Nicholson could not hope for a miracle but planned to make the Panzers pay dearly for their gains. At that moment he received the near-incredible order to escort rations for 350,000 men to Dunkirk, which lay to the east, beyond Gravelines. He was informed that the order must be regarded as 'over-riding all other considerations'. As the convoy formed up, he withdrew infantry from the positions to which he had just sent them. At the same moment, 10th Panzer reached the slopes to the south and began shelling Calais from that vantage point.

Third RTR now sent a squadron forward to test the road to Dunkirk. Inevitably they ran into the rear of 1st Panzer, an experience which lost them all but three of their tanks; however the three which survived managed to break through the German lines and reach Gravelines. This was, of course, completely unknown to Nicholson, who could only assume that their failure to reappear meant that they were still clearing the path ahead. He therefore sent another squadron from 3rd RTR, accompanied by one company from the Rifle Brigade, to help the advanced party and then secure the road for the convoy to pass through. Their mission was soon found to be unrealistically optimistic. As they moved up the road, they found their progress blocked by a strong force of anti-tank guns and field artillery from 1st Panzer. After pitting itself against this immovable obstacle for some hours and suffering casualties for no territorial gains, the squadron was ordered back to Calais. There were now twenty-one light and medium tanks left to oppose the combined strength of two German Panzer divisions – 550 tanks. The defending force was concentrated on the ramparts, on which forward units of the Panzers had now begun a series of sharp, vicious attacks which had so far all been repulsed.

The harbour too had come under fire from the Panzer artillery. This led to yet another muddle which in retrospect seems inexplicable, although in the conditions of the time was probably only to be expected. On the quayside was a hospital train full of wounded waiting for a boat to evacuate them. As there were ships in the harbour which were still engaged in unloading equipment (which included weapons and vehicles) for the hard-pressed infantry on the other side of the town, it was decided that the wounded must have priority. In consequence the stevedores were told to stop unloading and to put the wounded men into spaces which had already been cleared. The transports then sailed off back to England taking with them various non-combatants and the stevedores who had been doing the unloading.

The War Office had now made up its mind that Calais was virtually lost and all but the few troops still trying to delay the inevitable should be evacuated. It was as well that these did not know that the weapons and ammunition they so sorely needed were now sailing away again, or their morale might well have been dented. However, by now they were engaged in such a ding-dong, close-quarter battle with their attackers that they had little time to contemplate what might be happening elsewhere.

On the afternoon of 24 May, 10th Panzer made a determined effort to break through the British defences. After bitter fighting they made some progress in the west and south, eventually getting a foothold in the outskirts of the town. But they paid a high price. Their attacking units had now lost between a third and a half of their equipment, and their ardour for this particular battle was diminishing. Guderian asked the divisional commander if he would like to pause and let the Luftwaffe complete the obliteration of the town. The divisional commander, Major General Schaal, hesitated but then, having decided that the Luftwaffe's bombs would be ineffective against the Vauban ramparts, decided he must continue with the frontal attack. For the defenders, the attack was more than frontal. The Luftwaffe was already bombing them, shells were landing all round and behind them, and fifth-column snipers, who had infiltrated with the refugees, were operating from houses in the town and proving a deadly nuisance.

Nicholson was now informed by the War Office that the final evacuation of the fighting troops would take place at 7 a.m. the following day. He therefore withdrew his defensive force into a smaller perimeter so that they were mostly in the old town. Here they should have been able to hold out without difficulty if the bridges over the canal were blown. But owing to another misunderstanding, the French had not fitted them with demolition charges and the British forces had nothing which could be used as a substitute.

Accustomed as he was to conflicting and impossible orders, Nicholson was nevertheless astonished to receive one which, though it had come from London, originated from the local French commander in the area. This expressly forbade Nicholson to continue with the evacuation. Lest there should be any doubt about the matter, the message was reinforced by a note from the War Office saying that it must be obeyed 'for the sake of Allied solidarity'. As a word of comfort Nicholson was told that as he continued his battle to the end he would receive further ammunition but no troop reinforcements. Contradicting this last statement, he was also told that he would soon be assisted by 48th Division, which was already marching to his assistance.

Had 48th Division known of this piece of misinformation they would have been interested though perhaps sceptical, for they were already fully occupied on the western line of the salient confronting the 2nd and 20th German Motorized Division, and had never at any time heard that there were plans for them to be withdrawn and used elsewhere. Nicholson, a regular soldier accustomed to obeying the latest order without questioning it, received this one philosophically. Apparently his only comment was that he thought he could hold on for quite a while. Sadly, Nicholson died in 1943 in a German prisoner-of-war camp, so he was never able to make any post-war comments on the bizarre situation he found himself in in May 1940.

Churchill was considerably less philosophical when he heard of the wording of the order to Nicholson. Although he realized that the French Commander of the 15th French Corps, General Fagalde, was within his rights in demanding that the British should abandon their plans to evacuate, for the Calais area came under French command, Churchill felt that Allied solidarity was not at that moment a primary consideration. Even if it were, he did not feel that a verbose order telling brave men to fight to the death – an order which they would certainly obey – should be couched in such terms. It has been suggested that General Fagalde issued the order because he was furious that Gort was proceeding with his plans to evacuate the rest of the BEF from Dunkirk, which Fagalde was powerless to prevent. In the event, Fagalde's order benefited the Dunkirk evacuation enormously by holding up 10th Panzer, which would otherwise have been free to leave Calais and proceed to harass Dunkirk.

Fortunately there was similar confusion among the senior officers of the German Army. On 24 May Guderian and his Panzer leaders were astonished to receive the order which stated that the Aa Canal

Line was not to be passed, and continued: 'Dunkirk is to be left to the Luftwaffe. If the capture of Calais proves difficult this port too is to be left to the Luftwaffe.' As the Germans had now established four bridgeheads over the Aa Canal, and the Leibstandarte SS Division, which had just been placed under Guderian's command, was also heading rapidly for Calais, the order to halt left Guderian, to use his own word, 'speechless'. Various explanations were offered by his colleagues for what must have been the most frustrating of all the orders for him to slow down his advance. It was suggested that Goering wished to have Calais on the list of battle honours of the Luftwaffe. In the event, the Luftwaffe's influence on the battle for Calais was considerably less than Goering had hoped for; a combination of bad weather and RAF fighters removed that prize from his grasp.

The real reason (mentioned earlier) for the Hitler/von Rundstedt order – that the French might counter-attack and the Panzers would all break down if they did – would not have occurred to Guderian or his staff. At this stage in the war they had not yet become accustomed to Hitler's view of his own omniscience, which extended to believing that he knew more than the man on the spot about what was really happening. Guderian took the fairly charitable view that, because both Hitler and von Rundstedt had fought in Belgium in the previous war, they assumed that the terrain around Calais probably resembled that of the tank graveyard at Passchendaele. In fact Hitler *was* apprehensive of what would happen if the Belgians opened the sluices and flooded the surrounding area. But his fears were unfounded: the sluices had already been opened, but they could not stop Guderian if he wished to continue on the route he had chosen.

Meanwhile Reynaud sent Churchill a telegram urging him to despatch troops to Dunkirk, just as he had done for Calais. This, he explained, would enable Gort to continue fighting the Germans. Reynaud, completely out of touch with the situation, was still expecting an Allied counter-attack. Churchill had no intention of sending more troops to Dunkirk, but he did send what was meant to be an encouraging message to Gort, mentioning that Calais was under attack but was still holding out; when Gort received this telegram Calais had already fallen, as he doubtless knew.

The scene in Calais resembled that in many other towns in France. There were Belgian soldiers who had lost contact with their senior officers and obstinately refused to take orders from anyone else.

There were French soldiers who were taking an active part in the fighting, and there were other French soldiers who stayed under cover until the town surrendered and then became prisoners. And there were disconsolate bands of refugees who had no idea of what to do next.

There was considerable confusion when French gunners from coastal guns which had exhausted their ammunition arrived on the beach and began to embark on French naval tugs: the French Navy had ordered that the French gunners should now be taken to Cherbourg. However, before the gunners left they were addressed by Capitaine Carlos de Lambertye, a French naval officer who did not believe that French soldiers should leave the British to fight to the end in defence of a French town. Admittedly the French were heavy gunners, but they all knew how to fire rifles and machine-guns and could be very useful. It was a historic moment. There were still French holding key positions on the ramparts, although casualties among them had been severe; some of them were Moroccans who were determined to fight to the end whatever the cost.

At first, de Lambertye's appeal seemed to have little effect. Then a wounded officer volunteered to stay; he could still walk. Soon he was joined by approximately a hundred others, who watched the tugs sail away without them and then marched into one of the surviving bastions. They became known as 'The Volunteers of Calais'. Altogether there were now some eight hundred French soldiers and sailors still manning posts around the town; their resolution was all the more creditable because they knew that many of their former comrades had given up the struggle and were hiding in cellars to await what they judged to be an inevitable surrender. The most valuable result of de Lambertye's call to fight for the honour of France was that the British in Calais no longer felt entirely on their own, deserted by those whose soil they were trying to defend.

As with all desperate last stands, many of the most heroic and stubborn actions went unrecorded simply because there was no one left to chronicle them when positions were overwhelmed. One of the key posts in the defence was Fort Nieulay, a crumbling old Vauban relic manned by a mixed force which included survivors of the QVR, Searchlights,* and French soldiers and marines. Although none of the varied arms they possessed was very formidable, they

---

*Troops manning searchlights for detecting enemy aircrafts.

had the advantage of thick walls to shield them from the pounding of the German artillery. However, when the Germans launched a tremendous bombardment in conjunction with an infantry attack, and the defenders' machine-guns were put out of action, it was clear that the fort was doomed. Nevertheless not until it was completely surrounded and ammunition was virtually at an end did the French captain, who was in overall charge, agree to surrender.

Although Nicholson had made several urgent requests to the War Office for field artillery there was no response. However, the Admiralty, well aware that this was now a battle to which they could make a useful contribution, sent four British and one Polish destroyer to join a French one in shelling suitable land targets. The destroyers inflicted considerable damage, but not without cost to themselves from the Luftwaffe. One British destroyer was sunk and the Polish vessel and another British one badly damaged. They stayed in the waters outside Calais until 20 May, hoping to evacuate the remainder of the garrison if and when the town fell.

To those not on the scene the situation at Calais seemed inexplicable. Churchill could not understand why Gort did not send forces to relieve the blockage; he calculated that Gort had nine divisions at his disposal. Churchill's attention was particularly focused on the 3rd Tank Regiment which he seemed to believe must still be at full strength. The reality was very different. Five of their cruiser tanks had been destroyed because of an order which seems to have been the result of yet another muddle. The tracks of others were giving trouble and, in the circumstances, could not be repaired. Back in London there was surprise that Nicholson appeared to have made no attempt to break out. In fact he had given the idea full consideration but decided that the forces at his disposal were too weak for him to do so.

As the hours passed, the 'fifth column' problem became particularly troublesome. Some, though German, had acquired French or Belgian uniforms and were using machine-guns. Not least of their profitable activities was spreading false rumours. The late Airey Neave, who was wounded in the fighting for Calais, learned in 1971 that there was a well-organized 'fifth column' group of Germans based at Gravelines, and that since 1945 they had been holding annual reunions during which they visited the graves of their members who had been caught and executed in northern France.

Some idea of the intensity of the fighting may be gained from the fact that no official casualty figures were ever subsequently obtained from either side. Neither 1st nor 10th Panzer could ever produce a figure for their own losses, still less could the French Army and Navy. The Rifle Brigade and the 60th Rifles each had 60 per cent casualties; the QVR, 3rd RTR and other units suffered heavily also. By the third day of the battle so many buildings in Calais were burning that a thick pall of smoke hung over the town. Rubble from shattered buildings lay in the streets and every shell sent a cloud of dust into the air. By this time the garrison had reached such a point of weariness, from the noise, heat and lack of sleep, that they seemed to be fighting automatically.

The Germans, well aware of the state that the British were now in, realized it held many dangers for themselves. They too had had many casualties and were tired; if at that moment the British managed to land reinforcements the battle might take a turn which would not be at all to the German liking. In consequence Nicholson was twice sent demands to surrender 'to save further bloodshed'. He ignored them, determined to fight to the end whatever the cost, and moved around himself to the various defensive points, encouraging those holding them.

Finally he established himself in a crumbling fortification known as the Citadel. This was a key point in the defences and the Germans were giving it their full attention. When a steady bombardment appeared to be having little effect, Schaal increased it by adding dive-bombers. Finally he ordered that it must be completely destroyed, an order easier to give than to carry out; not for the last time in this war would commanders with all the latest artillery at their disposal learn the frustrating truth that fortifications from previous centuries could absorb almost unlimited punishment from modern weapons.

At this moment the British Cabinet had suddenly become aware of the dire straits to which Calais had been reduced, and how great a contribution its stubborn defence was making to the evacuation now proceeding from Dunkirk. In consequence Anthony Eden sent one of those telegrams which are meant to encourage defenders of lost causes but which usually merely amuse or irritate them: 'The Defence of Calais to the utmost is of highest importance to our country as symbolising our continued co-operation with France. The eyes of the empire are upon the defences of Calais and HM Government are confident you and your gallant regiments will perform an exploit worthy of the British name.'

If anyone had had time at that moment to give the telegram more than a passing glance, he might have wondered exactly what HM Government meant by 'to the utmost', and whether anyone expected the defence to do more than it was doing already. Before the war was won 'the eyes of the empire' would have to focus on many more targets than Calais: Hong Kong, Tobruk, Singapore and Malta would be prominent among them.

Meanwhile Schaal sent another deputation to Nicholson, calling on him to surrender on the basis that further resistance was clearly useless. Nicholson's answer politely but firmly refused, saying it was 'the British Army's duty to fight as well as it was the Germans''. Guderian was impressed but annoyed. He knew better than anyone that every hour spent at Calais was delaying 10th Panzer and therefore preventing it from playing havoc with the increasing evacuation from Dunkirk. Although not personally directing the battle, he knew that some of Schaal's commanders were saying that because of their troops' extreme tiredness a forty-eight-hour rest was virtually essential. Schaal, of course, was not listening: uppermost in his mind was the thought that if Calais was not taken within the next day the British could easily land fresh troops and keep up the fight in the rubble of the town. With backing from Guderian, he was able to obtain more heavy artillery and the promise of continued air strikes from the Luftwaffe.

As the bombardment intensified on the night of the 26th, Calais became virtually untenable from heat, smoke and shortage of water. But the fighting continued. The French under de Lambertye held their positions. Sadly, on the morning of 26 May the gallant French officer, no longer young and in indifferent health, collapsed and died of a heart attack. Nicholson's main problem now was the lack of men to hold the inner perimeter: many of those doing so had already been wounded, some several times. The Gare Maritime went, then Bastion 1, and finally the Citadel; the last was totally surrounded by German tanks and infantry and did not give up until they were in the central courtyard. Here Nicholson himself was taken prisoner.

Although organized resistance was now at an end, small detachments were still trying to keep up the fight. When an order came from the senior officer, Lieutenant Colonel (later Lieutenant General Sir Euan) Miller, for survivors to try to break out individually, many attempts were made by land; all, however, were blocked by surrounding German infantry or tanks. Those who tried

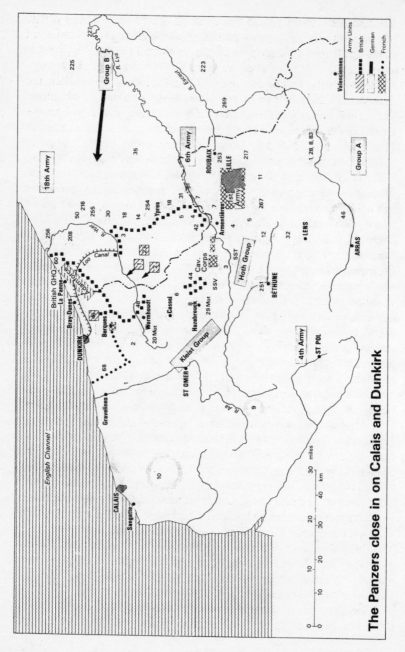

The Panzers close in on Calais and Dunkirk

the port were luckier, and some two hundred were taken off by the brave and skilful crews of two yachts. One second lieutenant in the QVR found a dinghy and rowed himself across the Channel alone.

Subsequently Guderian made the astonishing claim that the defence of Calais had in no way interfered with any of his plans, and that if Hitler had not endorsed the original order to halt the tanks he, Guderian, could have prevented the Dunkirk evacuation. That view is not upheld by German historians.

Perhaps the most astonishing contribution was made by Queen Victoria's Rifles, a London Territorial regiment attached to the Rifle Brigade – which was, of course, a regular regiment of great military distinction. QVR had a total strength of 566 (which was well under battalion strength); half of these were young and totally inexperienced in war. Their commanding officer was a college bursar at London University, for in peacetime the entire regiment consisted of civilians who turned up at their drill hall once a week and normally had a fortnight's training camp in the summer. The Territorial Army was not highly respected by either the rest of the Army or the general public: they were nicknamed 'the Saturday afternoon soldiers'. Nevertheless many of its members were full of energy and enthusiasm and did their best to learn soldiering with equipment which the regular Army considered sufficiently obsolete to be passed on to the TA.

QVR were a motorcycle reconnaissance battalion whose task was to reconnoitre in front of the main army in the way the cavalry would have done before horses were abandoned and the army was 'mechanized'. In QVR the mechanization process had not gone very far, for during the early part of the war they had had to train with hired civilian motorcycles and vans. When it seemed that they would be sent to Norway in the spring of 1940 they were given some motorcycles and scout cars, but these were all taken away again when their embarkation was cancelled. Eleven days after the invasion of France they were still in England. When they were ordered to France on 22 May they had no transport, a few Bren guns and even fewer Boys anti-tank rifles (said to be more intimidating to the user than the enemy). Approximately two hundred of the battalion had revolvers, but had never practised with them.

When they were sent to Dover for embarkation, the movement order was not given until 9.45 p.m. on the evening of the 22nd. It informed them that they must be on the train by 5.15 a.m. next day for an 'unknown' destination; this turned out to be Dover. Before leaving that port they had the mortification of seeing the scout cars which had once, briefly, been theirs parked on the dockside. On arrival in France they had to manhandle all their own equipment, and as they did so they were able to observe French and British wounded being put into its place on the ship. Civilians gave them the encouraging information that fifty German tanks were rapidly approaching the town. After these helpful boosts to morale they were allotted the stretch of the perimeter they were expected to defend. Needless to say, it was vastly in excess of what would have been normal even for a battalion equipped with the correct amount of transport, ammunition and weapons. There was no possibility of digging trenches, for all their picks and shovels had been left behind in their vehicles. They had one day to settle into their positions and distribute their ammunition, stores and equipment, most of which they had had to carry themselves. It was clearly a ridiculous situation. Nobody could except them to put up more than a token resistance before the weight of the German Army flung them to one side.

In the event it was not quite like that. On 24 May they were attacked by 10th Panzer, and made such excellent use of their limited equipment that the pride of the German Army was delayed for twenty-four hours. Then they were forced to fall back but, fighting in small groups, they battled on to the end, astonishing the regulars and themselves alike. As they fell back they acquired ammunition and weapons from their dead comrades. They were among the last to surrender.

The heroic defence of Calais has, unfortunately, been overshadowed by the huge evacuation from Dunkirk, which it did much to make possible. The general public seems unaware of the remarkable efforts of the Rifle Brigade, the 60th, the Searchlights, the QVR and many French soldiers who showed what France could really have achieved if the leadership at the top had been adequate. The battle of Calais was soon followed by what became known as the 'epic of Dunkirk' and then by the Battle of Britain. The attention of the public was diverted elsewhere – to Alamein, Sicily, Italy, Kohima, Imphal, Leningrad, Stalingrad, Arnhem and many other battlefields. Calais was all over in May 1940 and the survivors were marched off to prison camps in Germany; five years later, when the prison camps were opened, the public had forgotten there had ever been a battle of Calais. Yet without that battle the others might never have taken place. They would no doubt have been replaced by other battles, which in all probability would have been German victories.

Boulogne, which fell first, was another problem which Guderian had underestimated. Before 20 May it had not occurred to the Allied Command that that useful little port would ever need defences; fortunately, like many other European towns, it had ancient earthworks which would prove extremely useful. However, the rapidly deteriorating situation in France in mid-May jogged the War Office into despatching some guns for its defence. As these totalled eight 3.7-inch anti-aircraft guns, eight machine-guns and one battery of the 2nd Searchlight Regiment (the 1st Battalion was engaged at Calais), it was not likely to make much impression on the armour and firepower of 2nd Panzer Division. The French had managed to muster four guns and two immobile tanks. The guns consisted of two 75-mm, which were in far from mint condition, and two 25-mm anti-tank guns. For manpower there was a mixture of French of all arms, most of whom had become detached from their original units. There were a number of recruits, both French and British, who had not yet begun any military training, and there was the usual collection of refugees, except that in Boulogne they were French rather than Belgian.

The War Office was now taking the situation seriously and on 21 May ordered elements of 20th Guards Brigade, which at the time was training at Camberley, to move to Dover immediately for embarkation. The battalions chosen for this interesting assignment were the 2nd Irish and 2nd Welsh Guards and the Brigade Anti-Tank Company; they arrived in Boulogne on 22 May, accompanied by 275 Battery of the 69th Anti-Tank Regiment. The commander of the mixed force was Brigadier W. A. F. L. Fox-Pitt. On arrival he reported to Wimereux (where rear GHQ was now established) to be briefed by the Adjutant-General, Lieutenant General Sir Douglas Brownrigg. Brownrigg imparted the encouraging information that, although the Germans had been sighted a mere sixteen miles from Boulogne, the French 21st Infantry Division was now moving up to block any further German advance. Furthermore Fox-Pitt would soon have the benefit of a British regiment of tanks and a British infantry battalion to supplement his force. These last two units were named as the 3rd RTR and the 1st QVR; Brownrigg seemed blissfully unaware of the fact that these would be more than fully occupied in Calais.

Boulogne lies at the point where the River Liane runs into the sea. There is a small area of level ground around the harbour, and then the land slopes up fairly steeply to the old town which has stout earthworks. Boulogne's defences date from the Roman period and have been steadily added to through medieval and more modern times. It was the port from which William the Conqueror set out with eight hundred boats to invade England in 1066. Napoleon attempted to emulate William's feat in the early 1800s, but decided against it after his battle fleet was destroyed by Nelson at Trafalgar. The most formidable of the ramparts date from the thirteenth century, before guns had been invented.

The old town, known as the 'Haute Ville' or the 'Citadel', encloses an equally ancient cathedral. Outside the town the country is undulating, which gives an advantage to an attacker if the forces available to the defender are thin on the ground, as Fox-Pitt's were. As with Calais, possession of the higher ground to the south-east would give enemy artillery an enormous advantage.

Fox-Pitt deployed the Irish Guards along the south-eastern part of the semi-circular perimeter defence line and allotted the Welsh Guards the north-east. As the perimeter was approximately six miles long, this meant that if they had been in line each man would have been covering some seven hundred yards. Fox-Pitt also had fifty men from the Royal West Kent Regiment and one hundred Royal Engineers.

At this time the notorious order to halt the Panzers had not been made, and 2nd Panzer Division was under orders to press on to Boulogne and try to capture the town before a proper defence could be mobilized. Guderian had not sought the approval of Group Headquarters before issuing his orders, but was once again relying on the formula that if successful he was more likely to be rewarded than reprimanded.

In consequence, 2nd Panzer rolled forward and, although checked by stubborn French resistance at Samer for a while, reached the Irish Guards on the afternoon of 22 May. At 5 p.m. they launched a full-scale attack, but lost one tank and sustained numerous casualties for no gain whatsoever. They then turned their attention to the Welsh Guards at 8 p.m., but with no more success. For the moment there was a stalemate. Reports were received that the German attack would shortly be strengthened by other Panzers (presumably 1st and 10th Panzer) from the north-east, but Fox-Pitt was assured that they need not alarm him, as he would shortly be reinforced by 3rd RTR and 1st QVR. There was, of course, the comforting thought that the French 21st Division would also be available to throw a protective screen around Boulogne, if that was necessary. Unfortunately 21st Division had already been disposed of by Guderian's tanks while it was still on the trains taking it to its destination. In fact, apart from the anti-aircraft gunners already mentioned, 20th Guards Brigade and the few attached troops were the only Allied ground forces available to defend Boulogne.

However, it is important to remember that both the Royal Navy and the RAF made a very considerable contribution to the battle at both Calais and Boulogne. They operated under immense difficulties. The Navy took enormous risks in standing off the coast in order to shell the advancing Panzers: no target is more tempting and easily seen than a slowly moving ship. Likewise the RAF was at a disadvantage in that its airfields were on the other side of the Channel, whereas the Luftwaffe now had an abundance of captured airfields and could operate from very close to its targets. Even so, Luftwaffe losses were considerably higher than those of the RAF.

On the morning of the 23rd the Germans resolved to clinch the Boulogne battle with a massive display of firepower. The pressure was so strong and so continuous that casualties to soldiers and weapons mounted up disconcertingly fast. It was clear that the existing perimeter was becoming untenable and in consequence the two battalions were withdrawn to a shorter line, closer to the town. As it seemed that Boulogne must soon fall a start was made to the destruction of port installations, and the evacuation was continued of all troops who for various reasons could not be employed in the fighting. During the afternoon of the 23rd, the Luftwaffe made a determined attack on the shipping in and around the harbour. Eight German aircraft were shot down but three RAF planes were also lost. This attack gave a slight breathing space to 2nd Panzer, which had requested it after suffering heavily from the naval bombardment. Most of the naval forces were now within easy range not merely of the Luftwaffe but also of German artillery, mortar and even machine-gun-fire.

At 6 p.m. on the evening of the 23rd, the War Office sent a message to GHQ BEF that 20th Guards Brigade was to be evacuated from Boulogne immediately. It was an order easier to give than to carry out. The Germans had now succeeded in ringing Boulogne with guns, and inevitably the entire harbour was being swept with shell-fire. Two British destroyers, *Whitshed* and *Vimiera*, steamed into the middle of the maelstrom, firing back at the German batteries as they did so.

The Irish and the Welsh Guards, accompanied by some Royal Marines, went aboard, each destroyer taking a total of some thousand men. As they steamed out of the harbour, their places were taken by *Wild Swan*, *Venomous* and *Venetia*. By this time, with the Guards Brigade withdrawn, the Germans had come so close that while the embarkation of the next batch of troops was proceeding the German tanks and machine-guns were being engaged at point-blank range. *Venetia* had been so heavily damaged as she entered the harbour that she had to back out again immediately. Her place was taken by *Windsor*. Some time after midnight *Vimiera* made a second trip, and took a further 1400 men on board.

There were still three hundred Welsh Guards in the town but the destroyer *Wessex*, which had been instructed to take them off, was instead sent to Calais. Some of them tried to break out, as ordered, but were captured; others, supplemented by a mixture of troops, including some French infantry, retreated to the mole, where they held out for thirty-six hours. In that position they were under constant attack from arms of all variety, but only surrendered when their food and ammunition was exhausted. The French who were holding out in the Citadel surrendered at the same time.

In his memoirs Guderian wrote:

> On 23 May the 1st Panzer Division set off towards Gravelines against strong resistance, while the 2nd Panzer Division was involved in heavy fighting in and around Boulogne. The attack on the town itself assumed a curious form, since for some time neither our tanks nor our guns managed to penetrate the old town walls. By the use of a ladder from the kitchens of a nearby house, and with the powerful assistance of an 88-mm flak gun, a breach was at last made in the wall near the Cathedral and an entry forced into the town itself. There was fighting in the harbour area, during the course of which a tank managed to sink one British motor torpedo boat and damage several others.

Almost as soon as 2nd Division had captured Boulogne, Guderian was ordered to repair the defences against a possible Allied attack and invasion. He was not pleased.

Even less pleased than Guderian over the course of the Boulogne battle was the French general, Lanquetot, who had been the commander of the ill-fated 21st Division. He had arrived in Boulogne ahead of his troops with the intention of planning their disposition. Hardly had he arrived when he learnt that they would not be coming, having been intercepted by 2nd Panzer. Most of his command therefore consisted of British troops – until the majority of these were evacuated on the 24th. Unfortunately for Anglo-French harmony, the bulk of the small British force had been evacuated without prior notice to the French general.

15 Evacuation at Dunkirk

Once Boulogne was in German hands, and Calais about to follow suit, the chances of the BEF making successful counter-attacks and forcing back the Germans seemed out of the question, whatever Reynaud may have thought. From all fronts the news was bad. The Belgians were said to be at the point of total capitulation, and pressure on the eastern side of the Allies' salient seemed to be so great that unless more troops were sent to Brooke there could be a German breakthrough with disastrous consequences. The western side of the salient was no better, with all the Allied troops heavily outnumbered. Weygand's belief that a strong French counter-attack could still be mounted was clearly fantasy.

Although the Panzers had been ordered not to move further forward, this had not stopped them consolidating and expanding their bridgeheads over the La Bassée Canal. However, for the moment they were contained in that area.

Gort now received a telegram from Anthony Eden, who seemed to have made a realistic appreciation of the current situation. It ran:

I have had information all of which goes to show that French offensive from Somme cannot be made in sufficient strength to hold any prospects of junction with your armies in the north. Should this prove to be the case you will be faced with a situation in which the safety of BEF will be predominant consideration. In such conditions only course open to you may be to fight your way back to west where all beaches and ports east of Gravelines will be used for embarkation. Navy would provide fleet of ships and small boats and RAF would give full support. As withdrawal may have to begin very early preliminary plans should be urgently prepared. You should also consider urgently security of Ostend and Dunkirk to which latter port Canadian brigade group is being sent night 26th/27th. Prime Minister is seeing M. Reynaud tomorrow afternoon when whole situation will be clarified.

It was optimistic to assume that any situation would now be clarified, but at least Gort now knew the way the Cabinet was thinking. But hardly had he received this telegram when he was informed by another that the Canadian group would not be arriving after all.

From now on the French general Blanchard felt increasingly frustrated and thwarted. In the preceding days all he had received from his Higher Command was a series of lofty exhortations about fighting to the last man, counter-attacking and taking part in improbable Anglo-French manoeuvres. The only hard facts he had received had arrived via Gort, and as they were invariably depressing his own morale was beginning to weaken.

The evacuation plan, agreed by Reynaud, was for the British, French and Belgian armies to fall back together on an agreed timing towards Dunkirk. Such directives, difficult enough to follow under relatively stable conditions, are almost impossible to carry out when matters are already verging on chaos. In France at this juncture it was extremely difficult for each army to know exactly where the others lay; one false move and they would find themselves entangled with the Germans. Gort had great difficulty in keeping contact with Blanchard and was unable to inform him of the agreed plan until the morning of 28 May.

After all the stirring messages from Reynaud and Weygand, Blanchard was stunned when he learnt that the BEF and most of the French Army was now to be evacuated. The broad bridgehead around Dunkirk, into which all the best of the Allied fighting troops were now being withdrawn, was not, after all, to be used for a counter-attack supplied from the sea, but merely as a shield for an evacuation. So appalling was the news that he could scarcely believe it, and told Gort that he would be unable to withdraw the French divisions to their allotted stations in the time available; his men were tired, he said, and needed twenty-four hours' rest. He received a short, uncompromising answer. The Belgian Army had now ceased to exist as a fighting force, and if Blanchard did not bring back his armies immediately Gort would be forced to leave him to fend for himself.

Relations between the British and the French were becoming tense elsewhere too at this stage. The evacuation procedure from Dunkirk was being handled by a British joint naval/military team. Not surprisingly, perhaps, when weary French officers finally reached the town they resented being told by their Allies exactly where to go and when. Some of them did not consider the battle of France already lost and did not realize that they would be lucky if they escaped with their lives; with more optimism than realism they persuaded themselves that after being evacuated from Dunkirk they would land again at St Nazaire, or even Cherbourg, and stage that massive, long-delayed but unstoppable counter-attack which would eventually push the Germans right back off French soil. Reynaud and Churchill had agreed that French and British would be taken off in equal numbers, but their views of what would happen next differed considerably.

Evacuation from Dunkirk had been in progress for nearly a week before the decision was made to evacuate the *whole* of the BEF. The first troops to go were construction workers and others, such as administrative troops, whose skills were no longer of use in France but who, because they were highly skilled, would be very useful in the next stage of the war, whenever that happened to be. These had been unflatteringly lumped together in a directive as being 'useless mouths'. The term dated back to medieval times when castles coming under siege hastily pushed out all those who would not be part of an active fighting force. They included the old, the sick, women and children. Often, in the peculiar chivalry which sometimes obtained in the Middle Ages, they would be allowed through the besiegers' lines, or even co-opted into their forces as labourers; sometimes, however, the besiegers would decide not to let them through but to let them lie in no-man's land, dying of starvation and exposure; it was hoped that such ruthlessness would intimidate those besieged in the castle and make them more prone to surrender. 'Useless mouths' was a particularly unfair description to apply to some of the administrative or behind-the-lines troops in France in 1940, for many of them took up arms and gave an excellent account of themselves when used as replacements for casualties in infantry battalions.

Like the other coastal towns, Dunkirk had been fortified by Vauban, and still had remnants of his defences. It was particularly suitable for an evacuation, for it lies roughly at the centre of a piece of coastline which for seventeen miles consists of sand, dunes and scrub. There are summer holiday resorts here, notably at La Panne, Bray-Dunes and Malo les Bains, names which most of those making for the beaches had never previously heard of but which would now become lifelong memories. It was open, uncluttered land at that time, but its open character left those who waited there clearly exposed to the attentions of the Luftwaffe. The British sector of the coastline was east of the Bergues Canal, which runs the six miles from Dunkirk to the old town of Bergues; the French sector was to the west of it. The area would have made a good defensive bridgehead if there had still been the resources to use it properly, for behind the beaches the land is drained and abounds with banks and ditches. Tanks which probed into it could have a very unhappy time if a reception had been prepared for them. This fact was well known to the Germans who therefore decided that the Luftwaffe and infantry, supplemented by artillery fire, could make the Dunkirk area untenable. But for the moment, very few troops were there. Most of them were making a weary way back along congested roads, or fighting an enemy who seemed to have inexhaustible supplies of ammunition, and troops and guns to use it.

Once the decision to evacuate the BEF was taken, in what was code-named Operation Dynamo, the Royal Navy and Royal Air Force knew exactly what their task was and set about it unflinchingly. In spite of the romantic legend that the Dunkirk evacuation was accomplished by little ships, dinghies, lighters, motor-boats and so on, piloted by amateur sailors from England, the facts are that the Navy achieved the bulk of the evacuation. This is not to say that the small-boat armada did not make an enormously valuable contribution – it did, and displayed great courage and resourcefulness in doing so – but the general success of the evacuation was owed to the Royal Navy.

The contribution of the RAF is also often overlooked; many people believe that it was now rehabilitating in England. In fact it maintained continuous fighter patrols by sixteen squadrons throughout all the hours of daylight. Inevitably the patrols were always outnumbered, usually by two to one; and, as mentioned earlier, their task was made more difficult by the fact that they were operating at a considerable distance from their bases. Perhaps the most important part of their task was preventing the Luftwaffe from sinking ships loaded to the gunwales with evacuated troops. The RAF was not invariably successful, but the success rate was encouragingly high. Early in the conflict fourteen Hurricanes and Spitfires failed to return after an air battle with double their number; however, when the German casualty records for the same day became available after the war it was noted that their losses totalled thirty-eight.

Unfortunately the RAF did not have the resources to prevent the Luftwaffe bombing the docks, harbour and a good part of the town of Dunkirk. The damage inflicted on the docks and harbour was supposed to make them unsafe, and this is what caused the evacuation to be carried out from the beaches which subsequently became so well known from photographs. Apart from the difficulties of evacuating large bodies of men from open beaches, it is a much slower process than moving them from docks. The destruction of the harbour gave the Luftwaffe ample opportunities for machine-gunning the long lines of men who stood patiently waiting for their turn to climb into one of the boats when it became available.

The evacuation was planned, organized and supervised by Vice-Admiral Sir Bertram Ramsay, the Flag Officer commanding Dover. Ramsay, a man of infinite resource and great personal charm, brought in craft from far and wide for the vital operation, which was not completed without considerable losses of ships and sailors. The Navy had a way of seeming totally imperturbable in the face of diving bombers, chattering machine-guns and deadly torpedoes, and the Army derived considerable benefit from the calm example they set.

By the final stages of the evacuation the Germans had brought up a variety of guns capable of shelling the harbour, the beaches and the approaches, and therefore many men who had sunk wearily on to the deck of a ship were flung unceremoniously off it again as the vessel took a direct hit. One of those with vivid memories of such an experience was Second Lieutenant G. F. N. Reddaway, a member of Phantom (GHQ Liaison Regiment) who, after beginning the war on the Belgian frontier, had now found a place on an overloaded merchantman called the *Aboukir*. Eight miles out from the coast, the *Aboukir* was torpedoed by a German E boat. Fortunately for Reddaway, he was both on deck and an exceptionally strong swimmer, so he stayed afloat long enough to be rescued, to fight through the remainder of the war and later to become British Ambassador to Poland.

Captain Sir Basil Bartlett, last encountered in Lille, did not leave Dunkirk until the 31st. He remained philosophical and noted that others were too: 'I met Arthur Marshall looking well and industrious. I cannot imagine any man less suited to fighting in a war than Arthur. But he seems to have adapted himself perfectly.' Indeed he did. After the war he adapted himself to becoming a prolific writer, well known for his humorous books and newspaper articles, and a very popular television personality. 'It's a truism', continued Bartlett, 'that unexpected people make good soldiers. I'm told for example that Ernest Thesiger was an exemplary private in the last war. He was the only man who habitually did petit point in a front-line trench.' Thesiger was a well-known actor who was also the author of books on needlework and embroidery.

Bartlett was amazed at the optimism shown by French staff officers, even when the Dunkirk evacuation was well under way. At best they thought that the Germans would be defeated in one great battle somewhere near Cambrai; at the worst they admitted: '*Il ne faut pas désespérer.*'

In spite of his close contact with the staff of both the French and British armies, he himself was not very well informed. When he was ordered to proceed to Dunkirk he enquired of a Frenchman in Furnes, about fifteen miles from Dunkirk, whether he could recommend a good hotel in the town where they could wash and sleep.

He looked at me in amazement. I soon discovered why.

As I entered the town there was a roar of engines overhead. I looked up and saw about thirty pale-green aeroplanes with a black cross on their under-wings flying very low above me. There were no air-raid shelters to be seen, so I dived down a side-street and hid myself under a stone seat. At that moment the bombs began to fall. Each aeroplane dropped a 500 lb screaming bomb. Then they all scattered hundreds of little delayed-action and incendiary bombs which rained down like heavy hail. By a miracle I escaped being hit. I crawled out feeling rather shaken.

The next day he was told to make his way to the beach with as many of his command as he could still find:

All night men came trickling down to the dunes. I found myself in command of my bit of the beach. It was a little difficult to keep control – especially as the men were strange to me. But they were all extraordinarily patient and sensible. They allowed themselves to be directed into groups of about twenty-five and tucked themselves quite happily away in the sand. I don't think the Germans spotted us, although they put up flares which illuminated the whole landscape with a hard white light. The men pretended to be shadows.

Bartlett helped load up the boats as they came in.

It was queer to be loading up strange soldiers into strange boats and handing them over to strange sailors. Even the sergeants who worked with me were strange. We shared water-bottles, and biscuits and chocolate. But we never saw each other's faces.

The French got very worried by all this secret activity. There were a lot of them around. And they kept on coming down in the middle of our embarkations and asking to see our papers. I don't know whether they thought we were a German army landing. I was glad of my Field Security Police pass. It had a magical effect, as indeed all passes – false or genuine – always do on all French officials.

Night was the best time, for it was relatively quiet. Bombing and machine-gunning began at daybreak and continued steadily all day. At midday on the 28th, Bartlett and his party moved up to Bray-Dunes, and as the hours passed the situation grew ever worse: 'Wave after wave of bombers came over. And it became necessary to keep everyone off the beach except the actual party being embarked. Loading took a long time as the destroyers had only two boats each and these had to row to the beaches and back, half a mile each way, with a dozen men on each. In consequence it took 6–8 hours to fill the destroyers to capacity.'

There was a hospital on the dunes and it was full of casualties. All who could move were evacuated. 'The doctors and Sisters of Mercy were carrying on patiently just as if nothing was happening round them,' he wrote. Finally Bartlett himself went aboard, where he sat down and fell fast asleep.

But not for long. At 3 a.m. the destroyer was torpedoed. Having awoken in pitch darkness he stumbled on to the deck where he was told 'Keep down. They're machine-gunning us.' The bullets were coming from two German motor torpedo boats which were themselves being attacked by a British destroyer: eventually both MTBs were sunk. Bartlett found that, apart from damage to his teeth, he had escaped unscathed. He was one of the lucky ones. Among many others, the captain had been killed; there were mangled bodies all over the deck, which was a tangle of twisted steel. Their destroyer had been struck by two torpedoes while trying to pick up survivors from another ship which had just been sunk. As her engines were out of action, she would now have to wait until someone took her in tow – if the Luftwaffe did not reach her first. As he waited on deck, wounded men were brought up from below; thirty-five officers had been killed when a torpedo went through the ward room; nobody knew how many other bodies were still below.

Fortunately for Bartlett, a ship which had been trying in vain to get into Dunkirk harbour during the night now came to the survivors' rescue. They were transferred to it, and then the destroyer with its cargo of bodies was sunk. Those of the crew who were still alive rowed to a nearby cruiser, from which they continued the rescue work. The voyage to Dover took ten hours. The most heartening feature of the Dunkirk evacuation, as Bartlett remembered it, was the courage, patience and self-discipline of the evacuated soldiers, and the totally unfearing dedication of the sailors.

It should not be overlooked – though it often is – that French troops played a considerable part in making the Dunkirk evacuation a success. They covered the western side for the major part of the time, and also the last two days on the eastern side when most of the British troops from that area were being taken off. There were plenty of brave and indomitable Frenchmen, like Captain Denis Barlone:

After six miles of tramping we arrive at Bray-Dunes. There the confusion is unbelievable; with difficulty one dodges between thousands of lorries and vehicles abandoned by English and French units already embarked. By chance we come across . . . the Ambulance Corps doctors. They tell me that the division is being re-formed on the Belgian frontier, in the dunes near La Panne. We get there by walking down the railway track. From the top of the dunes we overlook the plain where the water slowly mounts and we see the heart-rending sight of tens of thousands of abandoned vehicles and wandering horses. An impression of awful and irretrievable disaster.

Barlone's morale had taken some blows and withstood them all but this final assault on it was almost too much. Buoyed up by hopes that his division was still continuing the fight, he stumbled over a rough railway track in order to reach it. But on arrival he saw all too clearly that this, like all the other brave rumours which had cheered him up previously, was farcical in its unreality.

For those who may think that the French did not put up much of a fight, Barlone's account includes some interesting figures. The general who commanded this excellent North African division had been wounded and taken prisoner; the regiments had been in some form of action every day and had sustained heavy casualties – out of the nine colonels in the division, seven had been killed or wounded. Of the original 18,000 men only 1250 remained.

He was now given orders to embark from Dunkirk itself. Although most of the docks had been destroyed, it was still possible to take soldiers off the mole protecting the harbour. Reaching Dunkirk was not easy and conditions on arrival were depressing: 'Not a single building intact, many have collapsed or have been burnt out.' As the 551 men under his command waited for their turn they were continuously shelled by 77-, 88- and 105-mm shells: these ploughed into the rubble and inflicted further casualties.

The westerly wind beats down the immense column of grim, black smoke from the flaming oil tanks. Truly this is the suffocating breath of the last judgement. Long sheaves of bright flames shoot up from the huge burning buildings. Broken bricks and mortar, windows, paving stones dislodged by shells, strew the ground. Immense open spaces stretch further than the eye can see with only a fragment of wall standing up here and there, and the carcasses of monster cranes in the docks desperately hold up their great black arms towards a ghastly sky, rent unceasingly by the explosions of the whining shells.

And, as if the shelling was not enough, squadron after squadron of German planes circled above, dropping sticks of bombs in quick succession. Goering's Luftwaffe, which had been given the task of annihilating the BEF before it could embark, was making up for lost time. But by now most of the birds had flown.

Eventually, having pushed their way through the rubble, frequently diving to the ground for some slight measure of protection, Barlone and his men arrived on the quayside at the point arranged. There they were informed that there had been a mistake and the boats allotted for their party had been used for other troops. At best they might expect to be taken off by tramp steamers in the middle of the night or perhaps the next morning.

As four of his men had been killed, and a number of others seriously wounded, on their way to the quayside, Barlone was reluctant to take them back to their original assembly point in the middle of the town; instead he led them to the dunes where they lay out in the open, completely unprotected. Here they fell asleep, in spite of the ear-splitting noise of the shells.

At 1 a.m. they were told that four cargo vessels were at the entrance to the harbour, and a sailor was sent off in a motor-boat to find these ships and pilot them in. An hour later he returned to say he could not find them. The commander of the naval embarkation party – who looked completely exhausted, not surprisingly – told the Frenchmen that they must now wait for dawn when they would be able to see the ships. Barlone, grimly aware that daylight would also make his troops completely visible to the Luftwaffe, insisted that the sailor should have another try. He went out, but returned half an hour later having still seen nothing. This seemed to the naval commander to settle the matter; both he and his men were desperately tired and wished only to sleep. Barlone then pointed out that his own men were even more tired, for they had marched two hundred miles before they even reached Dunkirk. Barlone persisted, and the naval man, realizing he was not going to get any sleep unless he made a further move, now sent out the sailor in the launch for a third time. Twenty minutes later he returned, having found the ships.

Perseverance having paid off, at 3 a.m. Barlone and his party embarked on two small cargo ships. They were not comforted by the discovery that the boats contained bombs which were destined for the defence of Dunkirk. The boats were shelled as they left the port area, but eventually they arrived off the British coast.

At Dover Barlone was astonished by the quiet order and discipline, so totally in contrast with the conditions on the other side. He and his men were given food, and they slept. Eventually they were put on a train and travelled for twelve hours, stopping frequently on the way. He was surprised to find that at every station there were crowds of young women and old gentlemen who gave them cakes, tea, post-cards, sandwiches and cigarettes. He wished to send a telegram to his sister: an elderly man took it and refused the money offered in payment. Barlone wrote: 'These people cannot do enough by way of being kind. They receive us as brothers rather than allies.'

Every dazed and exhausted survivor had a similar story to tell. On the first day of the evacuation, which was 26/27 May, 7669 men were rescued. This was a promising start but it also revealed the difficulties of the task ahead. The first of the ships detailed for the evacuation, *Mona's Isle*, reached the Dunkirk docks as they were being bombed and took on board 1420 troops: 23 of these were killed and 60 wounded by Luftwaffe machine-gunning and shore-based enemy artillery. Five other transports met with such heavy German shelling that they could not even reach Dunkirk and returned empty to Dover.

On the second day 17,804 men were evacuated and on the third day, 29 May, the total shot up to 47,310. This figure exceeded by ten thousand the number which had been forecast as being the maximum which could be evacuated. On 30 May this figure too was passed, for 53,823 were taken off; while 31 May saw the record number evacuated in one day: 68,014. This was an astonishing achievement, for there was a heavy swell; on the other days the sea was remarkably calm. Had the weather deteriorated in the nine days of the evacuation, as can happen all too easily in that area, there might have been a different and sadder story to tell.

On 1 June the numbers evacuated fell away slightly to 64,729, and on the three following days the fall was much more dramatic, though consistent. On 2 June 26,256 got away, on 3 June 26,746, and on 4 June 26,175. The grand total was therefore 338,526, of which 125,000 were French. Sad to say, many of the French troops, who were evacuated in conditions of great danger to their British rescuers, opted to return to France later as ordinary civilians while it was still occupied by the Germans. However, a considerable number joined the Free French Forces, determined to return to their homeland as a liberating army. Four years later they did, fighting with great gallantry in the process.

These are the bare statistics. But before the evacuation was complete there would be much more to tell. And even when the Dunkirk operation had ceased, the battle of France was not yet over. The final surrender of France to the Germans would not take place until 22 June, nearly three weeks after Dunkirk.

In times of crisis it is entirely natural to blame somebody else. France and Britain felt that the Belgians had let them down by adhering to a policy of strict neutrality when common sense should have told them it was pure folly to hope for clemency from Hitler.

In the period immediately before King Leopold's capitulation, the Belgians had pleaded with the Allies to mount a counter-attack on the Germans who were coming through Belgium. Their appeals met with firm refusals. This was not because it was felt that the Belgians deserved the fate which had now overcome them, but because a counter-attack in that sector could be of no benefit to anyone. Even if successful, it would be of no strategic importance and whatever happened could only serve to weaken 2nd Corps, who were holding a more important sector. Nevertheless, when Leopold unilaterally surrendered his country to the Germans on 27 May there was widespread Allied indignation that he had left the Allies in the lurch. The accusation was both untrue and unfair. There was nothing the Belgians could now do except get themselves killed in ever-increasing numbers, and the King had, in spite of opinions to the contrary, told the Allies of his intention. The Allies, on the other hand, had not informed Leopold of their intention to evacuate the bulk of the Allied army through Dunkirk and, in fact, did not do so until after Leopold told them he had surrendered. In fact, King Leopold's reputation comes out of this period considerably less blemished than that of the Allies.

Up until 29 May, Alan Brooke had been commanding 2nd Corps with considerable skill in extremely difficult circumstances. But on that date he was ordered to return to England, handing over his command to Montgomery. Brooke was extremely upset. Like any professional soldier, he had always aspired to a major command in the field and he now suspected that he was being withdrawn for administrative duties which would never permit him to command troops in battle again. Subsequently he became Churchill's right-hand man and, as much as anyone, the architect of final Allied victory. Probably the best general of the war, at one point he thought he was about to become commander of the D Day invasion force in 1944; but because he was too valuable in his administrative post he was denied that opportunity.

The fall of France was a testing time for generals, as catastrophic defeats usually are. Brooke came out of it well, and the future Field Marshal Alexander also created a good impression, though mainly for imperturbability rather than intellectual insight. Montgomery's personal characteristics were well known in the Army by that time: his egotistic vanity and often intentional discourtesies had made him less than popular. However, in France he surprised everyone by his calm and sensible behavior in crisis. No doubt the experience left its mark on him, for later in the war he tended to be over-cautious and never to fight a battle when there was any possibility of his being outnumbered or outgunned.

Another officer whose name would become known nationwide during and after the war was the then Lieutenant Colonel Brian Horrocks. He had been an instructor at the Staff College at Camberley when the Germans invaded the Netherlands, but was hastily removed from that post and sent to command the second battalion of the Middlesex Regiment in France. A veteran of the First World War, when he met his new command he was shocked to find that they were using the retreat as an excuse to stop shaving and let their personal standards decline. Horrocks put a stop to that, knowing from experience that a regiment which keeps up appearances even in the worst circumstances will probably do everything else well also. After seventeen days in command, Horrocks was promoted brigadier in the general step-up into vacancies caused by Brooke's departure.

However, Horrocks had little time to enjoy his new status. His first task was to supervise the evacuation of troops from La Panne, which was now being shelled and bombed: most of the surrounding houses were on fire. Horrocks arranged with one of his officers that he himself should stand up to his chest in the sea and signal with a torch when there was space for another twenty men on one of the boats. Eventually the long exposure in the water gave him cramp and he returned to the beach to find which troops still there belonged to his brigade. Having learnt that they had all been sent on to Dunkirk, he set off after them, being, as he put it, 'a very wet, very tired and very temporary brigadier with no staff and no troops'. He refused to leave Dunkirk before any of his soldiers, and then found he had to wait a long time before he received another offer. Then, as soon as he was aboard a destroyer, it was hit by a bomb and began to sink. Horrocks managed to scramble aboard a tug which had come alongside, and eventually reached Ramsgate.

One result of all these adventures, most of which happened to senior officers who had long before lost the figures and fitness of their youth, was that hard physical training became an obligatory part of the army curriculum. Physical training for recruits and certain other ranks had always been compulsory, but after the battle of France, when almost everyone had to march long distances carrying weapons and kit, it was pursued with almost fanatical resolution. Montgomery weeded out many of his senior officers by proving they were below his exacting standard of fitness even though they would probably never be required to use such physical ability in battle. Ten-mile runs carrying full kit became obligatory, even though officers collapsed and sometimes died in the process.

Probably the most frustrated general of all at this time was Guderian. Having been ordered to halt his Panzers outside Dunkirk, he spent the next two days inwardly seething as he heard how the BEF was slipping from his grasp. He was pleased when he learnt that Calais had fallen, giving him twenty thousand prisoners, but noted that only some three thousand were British; the rest of them were French, Dutch and Belgians who were only too willing to surrender. In spite of the order to halt, he indicated that he would not be displeased if his Panzers began to edge forward again; unfortunately for his plans, his Higher Command was well aware of what he probably had in mind and renewed the halt order. From his headquarters, Guderian could see Dunkirk and beyond it the armada of boats by which Britain was evacuating the remains of the BEF. Gloomily he watched the sorties of the Luftwaffe, thinking how much more damage his own ground troops could do.

Late in the afternoon of 26 May he received the information that he could attack once more. But it was too late. The BEF and the Royal Navy were both organized for the evacuation and the Luftwaffe had failed to prove that it could defeat the RAF, even though the latter was operating at a considerable disadvantage. On 28 May Guderian's forward troops reached Wormhoudt and Bourbourgville. On the 29th 1st Panzer took Gravelines. And then the final accolade of victory, the capture of Dunkirk – albeit a Dunkirk after most of the BEF had gone – was denied him. Instead Guderian received orders that he was to hand over command in this area to 14th Army Corps and take his own 19th Corps 150 miles to the south end of the front; there they were to destroy whatever French resistance they might still find. He was not pleased at being told they must put another 150 miles on to the 400 they had already covered, and was still bitterly disappointed by what seemed to have been an asinine order to halt the Panzers on the 24th, but he put a brave face on it and kept his thoughts to himself until after the war, when he set down his memories on paper.

While Guderian was kicking his heels in frustration, the withdrawal to Dunkirk was proceeding as smoothly as harassment by the

Luftwaffe and German infantry permitted. The French were holding the coastline which extended four miles west of Dunkirk, and in the process were putting up an excellent defence against the German attempts to break into the perimeter; while the BEF was holding an enclave with a seventeen-mile-long boundary.

Gort now had the unwelcome duty of encouraging the troops to fight hard while at the same time withdrawing senior officers and other key personnel, who he knew would be essential to the making of a new British Army. Generals Pownall and Adam were both despatched home and so too was Montgomery on the 31st, having held his Corps command for two days only. Gort himself, as befitted a VC from the previous war, moved around among the men on the beaches showing complete indifference to shells and bombs; sometimes he borrowed a rifle from the nearest man and took a shot at a low-flying aircraft. He had every intention of staying to the end, but he reckoned without Churchill.

The Prime Minister knew what was in Gort's mind, for it was what would have been in his own had their positions been reversed; he therefore arranged for the War Office to send Gort a telegram – which he himself had drafted to allow no possibility of misinterpretation. It instructed Gort to leave when the BEF had been reduced to the last three divisions – that is, to less than fifty thousand men. Knowing that Hitler and his propaganda minister, Goebbels, would have made maximum use of the capture of the commander of the BEF who was a renowned First World War hero as well, Churchill ensured that they would not have that satisfaction by adding these words: 'This is in accordance with correct military procedure and no personal discretion is left to you in the matter. On political grounds it would be a needless triumph to the enemy to capture you when only a small force remained under your orders.'

Reluctantly, feeling like a captain deserting a sinking ship with many passengers still on board, Gort handed over to Alexander on 31 May. By now the number to be evacuated, including French, was down to forty thousand. On 1 June he crossed the Channel to England in a fast motor-boat.

Gort never received another field command, although he later held the prestigious appointment of Governor of both Gibraltar and Malta. Although in the opinion of many he had made the right decisions and been largely responsible for saving the BEF when the collapse of Gamelin's policies had lost the battle for the Allies, he was nevertheless criticized for his conduct of the campaign. Some of these accusations came from disgruntled commanders, but Gort was unable to refute them, for during the war he was not allowed to publish his despatches lest they should upset the French. Undoubtedly they would have done so, but the decision seems harsh none the less. His main complaint was not against the French soldier as a fighting man when properly led, as sometimes he had been during the campaign, but against the lesser generals who, on being told that there were orders for them to retreat at specific times, invariably began those retreats six hours earlier than they should have done, constantly leaving the flanks of their British allies exposed. However, Gort was a realist and knew that as a commander-in-chief who had presided over one of the most catastrophic military defeats in history he could never hope for a similar post. Such an appointment would now seem an invitation to defeat.

16 Rearguard Action

ALTHOUGH THE German Army seemed at the time to have had an easy victory, those actually engaged in securing it would have been unlikely to agree. When the order was given for the BEF to withdraw to Dunkirk, this meant more hard fighting for many rather than less. Many British units were told to hold certain positions until further instructions and, while doing so, were killed, wounded or captured while resisting the invaders. But orders to withdraw were often delayed or lost. Radio communication was unreliable and uncertain, and the main method of transmitting information and orders was by despatch riders or staff officers travelling in vehicles. Of the two, the despatch riders of the Royal Signals, who were all proficient motorcyclists, were the most successful, but their task was made more difficult by the fact that the roads they should have traversed were blocked by refugees and other traffic. The units to which their despatches were addressed were rarely still in the position they were supposed to be in, and the Luftwaffe and fifth columns tended to make any form of travel difficult. A major factor in the difficulty of holding a continuous line against sharp, probing German attacks was that there were insufficient troops available for the purpose. But most units did their very good best.

At 8 a.m. on 28 May the 2nd Warwickshires found themselves under heavy attack from bombing, artillery and mortar fire in Wormhoudt. This 'softening up', as it is called, was followed by tanks and infantry, but the Warwicks had not been softened up and the German attack was repelled. Then it was renewed from

174

two sides, and soon the whole town was in flames and desperate fighting was taking place in between blazing buildings. By afternoon the Warwicks, who had started the day approximately seven hundred strong, were down to one hundred all ranks. These were ordered to withdraw. By that time the Germans were entering in their War Diary: 'The Corps Commander is not counting on any success from this attack, and is of the opinion that further useless sacrifices must be avoided after the severe casualties which the 3rd Armoured Regiment has suffered during the counter-attack.'

There were many other examples of dogged and courageous fighting in what must have seemed to all taking part a lost battle. Among these were the 5th Battalion of the Gloucestershire Regiment. When they received orders to fall back from the village of Ledringhem, they were already surrounded by German units who were attacking them fiercely in the hope of causing them to surrender. The Gloucesters would have none of it and vigorously repelled all German onslaughts all day. During that night the remains of the regiment broke through the German lines and joined the rest of 144th Brigade on the Yser.

In the same division (48th South Midland) was 145th Brigade which comprised the 2nd Battalion of the Gloucesters, the 4th Battalion of the Oxford and Buckinghamshire Light Infantry, and the 1st Battalion of the Buckinghamshire Light Infantry who were a TA regiment. These last were established in Hazebrouck, from which the Germans tried all day to dislodge them. Displaying considerable initiative, they picked off the German gunners who were trying to bring a battery to bear at close range and therefore limited their opponents to mortaring and rifle fire. Casualties mounted, among them their commanding officer, who was killed. Not until the end of the day, with ammunition exhausted and their temporary defence in ruins, were the gallant Buckinghamshires over-run by a combined German infantry and tank attack.

These tenacious fights were typical of the resistance, rather than exceptional; they made the Germans fight hard for their gains and gave them much food for thought in doing so: if these were the sort of performances put up by British troops fighting in a lost cause on foreign soil, what sort of resistance would they put up if the Germans put an invasion force over the Channel and tried to invade England? Even though the bulk of the BEF was being evacuated, there was no sign of defeatism in their comrades securing the retreat.

Particularly annoying to the Germans was the situation between

Caestre and Strazelee. Here the British line was held by troops of 44th (Home Counties) Division; these consisted of battalions drawn from the Buffs (East Kent Regiment), the Royal West Kents (who supplied five battalions) and the Royal Sussex (who supplied three). In this area the Germans were unpleasantly surprised to find that, having captured Rouge Croix, they had lost it again in a counter-attack. To make matters worse, Clyte Hill and La Motte had exactly the same experience, although at the end of the day the Germans managed to hold on to La Motte, which they had once again captured. In consequence the Germans temporarily abandoned the attempt to penetrate in this area, thus giving more precious time for the BEF to be evacuated.

Unfortunately all the British battalions involved were reduced to a third of their original numbers. There was no possibility that they could now be withdrawn and rested: the future held nothing but marching, fighting and, if they were lucky, a long wait on the beaches where they would be machine-gunned and bombed before making a hazardous sea journey home. Although they were not aware of it and would not necessarily have been too enthusiastic if they had been, their spirited resistance was causing the Luftwaffe to be diverted from the task of harassing Dunkirk and the surrounding beaches, and instead concentrated on troops still fighting. Even so, as the RAF knew only too well, that still left enough German aircraft to outnumber them by considerable numbers.

Forty-fourth Division, who had already shown their mettle in the preceding days, were on the 29th holding the important town of Cassel. Orders for them to retire from this point had already been issued the day before, but had not reached them. In consequence, when they began to move out that day the town was already surrounded. That fact had not prevented the Germans steadily shelling and mortaring the beleaguered garrison all day, although they felt it was now neutralized. Their mistake in making that judgement was soon revealed when 44th Division, headed by the 4th Oxford and Bucks, and with a rearguard formed of the remnants of the East Riding Yeomanry, moved out with considerable vigour.

The East Riding Yeomanry is a good example of how territorial and inexperienced troops took on the pick of the German Army and learnt their soldiering in the process. At the same time they gave some severe lessons to the Germans. The ERY, as they came to be called affectionately, knew that their task was to reconnoitre the surrounding countryside and test the German strength. They did so unflinchingly, though not without paying a heavy price. In the breakout they were completely exposed to furious attacks by the frustrated Germans. Rearguards have an especially difficult time, for whereas a vanguard may rely to some extent on surprise, those protecting the rear have no such benefit. Enemy troops who have had a hole punched through their lines close up quickly and have usually recovered in time to take their revenge on the rearguard. By the time 44th Division reached Dunkirk very few of them, and particularly the ERY, survived to tell the tale.

But few sacrifices have been made in a better cause. Cassel was a nodal point, as the military like to describe such important road or rail junctions. Five roads met there, and in order to cut off the retreat to Dunkirk the Germans had to control the town. Roads, as the Romans were among the first to discover, are essential to the movement of armies. In theory an army should be able to cross open country without difficulty, but when they try to do so formations tend to lose shape, supplies straggle behind, and unforeseen obstacles delay the advance. Roads, bridges, railways, valleys are essential to the movement of armies and a unit which blocks a vital point, even for a few hours, can destroy an entire plan of attack. Even with their vastly superior numbers, the Germans could not concentrate enough to destroy the dogged soldiers of the 44th Division in Cassel until the golden opportunity was irretrievably lost.

Similar tenacity was shown in other areas. The 1st Welsh Guards and the 8th Worcesters held the line on the western flank and the Sherwood Foresters had good cause to put France on their battle honours.

Another who would have a variety of experiences before he left France – not from Dunkirk during the nine days' sea evacuation, but from Nantes by air on 17 June – was Staff Officer. On 29 May he received the information that the 7th and 9th French Armies were no longer 'a fighting force' and that the 1st French Army had ceased to exist. However, the French still had fifty-one divisions in the field and another ten in the Maginot Line. The latter were to be withdrawn and used as a reserve. As the French would now be trying to hold a front 180 miles long with only 35 divisions, their chances of preventing a Panzer breakthrough were not rated very highly. Meanwhile, he was informed, 'The BEF is reported to be carrying out a successful evacuation under cover of smoke.' He commented: 'What does "successful" imply, I wonder.'

When his colonel and adjutant set off to make a personal reconnaissance of the Aisne area, where they had been assured by General Georges that the line was strongly held, they discovered that there was no trench system, no trace of digging at all, no anti-tank traps, nor any proper barricades, 'only a few groups of sentries cowering behind inadequate protection. Not a machine-gun nest anywhere, not a gun trained, not a zone of fire marked out.' They discussed the position with the French commander, 'an unshaven, dirty little man, very little like a soldier'. When asked why there were no trenches, he told them that the troops he commanded were Algerians and: 'Algerians never dig.' This, commented Staff Officer, was bad luck for the Algerians but even more unfortunate for those whom they were supposed to protect. When these points were put to the French staff they confirmed that Algerians never dug, but added that the French 6th Army was *épuisé*, having lost 50 per cent of its equipment. '*C'est la guerre,*' they said, and there the matter ended.

Reims was a deserted city, with taxicabs still on the ranks and food and wine in the restaurants, but no inhabitants: they had all fled from fear of the German bombers. However, rumours still abounded; they heard that, *somewhere else*, the French had made a magnificently successful counter-attack. General Georges was saying that 'A new spirit had become evident among the French troops. The spirit of Verdun was aroused.' This information was received cautiously.

Staff Officer was fortunate in that he did not appear to have come across the darker side of the German fighting machine. Although Guderian and many other German generals had high ethical standards about the conduct of war, there were, unfortunately, several commanders – fanatical Nazis and/or members of the Waffen SS – who did not share them. Most of the major atrocities of the war would be committed by the SS (Schutzstaffel), Hitler's personal troops, of which the Waffen SS was the essentially military part. During the war the SS built up their numbers to nine hundred thousand, of which two hundred thousand were foreigners. The latter were recruited from territories which the Germans over-ran in Europe: France, Holland, Norway, Belgium and so on. In the days of German victories it was not difficult to recruit impressionable but bone-headed young men of strong racist, anti-semitic, Fascist views. When the tide of war turned against Germany later, the German generals derived some satisfaction from plugging awkward gaps with these aliens in the hated SS uniform, who fought hard because they knew only too well what would happen if they were captured alive by their own countrymen.

As the German Army came within sight of victory in France in 1940 SS units which were frustrated by isolated pockets of Allied resistance showed their true colours. The notorious affair known as the Paradis or Wormhoudt Massacre took place on 27 May.

After their position had become hopeless, the remnants of the 2nd Battalion of Norfolks surrendered to a force from the SS Totenkopf Division in the hamlet of Paradis. About a hundred prisoners were rounded up and marched into a field, where they were machine-gunned. Those not obviously dead were finished off by the SS troops with bayonets, while their officers also fired rifles and revolvers into the mass of bodies. Amazingly, there were a handful of survivors, who after being secretly cared for by local people were taken to a military hospital and eventually became prisoners of war. One of the more severely wounded of the men was repatriated in 1943, when he told his story. No one believed him at the time – only later would the full extent of SS atrocities during the war be revealed, when the Allies discovered the truth about the mass deportations and the concentration camps, and the massacres of civilians at Oradour-sur-Glane and Lidice.

But the behaviour of Waffen SS units, though unwelcome, was not a matter of great concern to the German High Command at this time; they would think about it more carefully when the Nuremberg trials began after the war and the search for German war criminals was intensified. For the moment, even in the hour of triumph, German generals were digesting some facts which had not been palatable. Guderian and his tank theories had been proved right, and the victory in Poland had not been a mere flash in the pan – but the realization that the young, revolutionary theorists of tank warfare had now triumphed over the more conservative thinkers in the German Army was not pleasing to the reactionaries. It appeared to the old guard that the recent spectacular triumphs could well encourage Hitler to believe they could be repeated everywhere. In this view they were right, and the disastrous invasion of Russia, which took place a year later, was one of the results of over-confidence that tanks could win rapid victories anywhere at any time.

But even among the tank protagonists there were some

murmurings of discontent. The victory which was being won in France and Belgium was a victory of tactics, not necessarily of new weapons. German tanks had been successful and had appeared to be invincible because they had probed at weak points in the Allied defence; by invading France around Sedan and then cutting in behind the Allies who were pushing rapidly into Belgium they had been able to throw the Allied armies into confusion. In this, they had been greatly assisted by their professionalism and Gamelin's ineptitude.

None the less, there were disconcerting features about the victory. The German tanks were not, as had been hoped, superior to the French and British when they met in equal combat. The French Char Bs and the British Matildas were better quality than the German tanks and tended to get the better of head-on clashes; had the British and French tanks been well handled tactically, the outcome of the campaign might have been very different.

The thought that even after the Dunkirk evacuation the British and French might be able to mount an offensive in the south made the German High Command distinctly wary. Although the Allies believed that the Germans had already won the campaign, that view was not shared by the Germans, and for that reason Guderian and his 19th Corps, which had already proved their worth, were being rushed headlong to another sector. In the meantime there was some hard thinking about the type of gun the Panzer IIIs and IVs would need for future conflicts; one of the first to benefit from the larger-calibre guns and tougher armour would be Rommel when he was rampaging in the Western Desert in 1941 and 1942.

On 5 June the Panzers were on the move again and soon penetrated the alleged defence line at several points. Staff Officer gloomily contrasted the French Army of 1940 with that of 1918. The latter would have been well dug in, and the Germans, with tanks or not, would have been checked. On 7 June the Germans took Montdidier and Compiègne, then reached Beauvais, some twenty miles from Paris.

The 9th was a difficult day for Staff Officer. The French reported that the Germans had broken through on a ten-mile front on either side of Soissons. His new headquarters was to be at Orleans, but by then they would be well out of any fighter cover from Britain. It seemed as if the Germans were beginning a giant pincer movement in which one arm would drive to Orleans via Chalons-sur-Marne and the other come in from the west via Rouen. The Germans would then

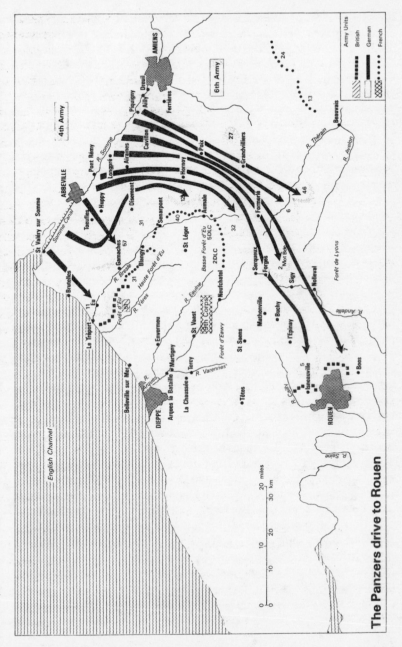

The Panzers drive to Rouen

be able to occupy France as far south as the Loire; there would be nothing to stop them.

By 10 June Staff Officer was becoming very tired. He had been on duty for forty-eight hours, and food appeared only once in every twelve hours. He was depressed to learn that the French had mined the bridges at Rouen and Orleans, which he described as 'venerable', but comforted himself with the thought that if the demolitions there were no more effective than they had been elsewhere most of the bridges would be left intact. Survivors of one of the British armoured divisions, who still had some tanks, used them to drive over the shallow trenches that the Germans had built between their strongpoints. Those Germans who were not crushed by the tanks were killed by the British crews firing revolvers from open turrets down into the trenches.

On the evening of 10 June the Italians declared war on France and England. Mussolini had jumped to the incorrect conclusion that the entire war was now as good as won and that the Italians must appear on the victory parades.

The next day Staff Officer went by car to visit another headquarters, near Briare. Here the news was no better. On the return journey he was caught up in a stream of refugees from Paris. This contingent owned a large number of cars and resembled a Derby Day trek to Epsom in appearance, though not mood. Each car had a mattress tied to its roof; the owners apparently believed that as well as serving as a bed at night it would serve as a shield from Luftwaffe machine-gun bullets in the day.

On 12 June he learnt that the Germans had three fresh army corps south of Reims, which they had already occupied. The following day it became apparent the Germans had crossed the Seine at Pont de l'Arch and Andelys, with forward Panzer units as far south as Evreux and Dreux. Among the miscellaneous information Staff Officer received that day was the fact that the French government was now at Tours, and that many soldiers of the estimated thirty-five French divisions, who were outnumbered two to one by the Germans, were now throwing down their arms and running to the south of the Marne. Sixty per cent of the French shells were 'dud'; he gave the latter figure as a confirmed statement, though how the confirmation was made was not disclosed.

The 14th June brought the sad news that Paris had been abandoned by the Allies and was being occupied by the German 14th Army.

The Germans who marched into Paris that day were surprised when their arrival was greeted by cheering crowds. The explanation, of course, was not that the French citizens were pleased to see German soldiers triumphant in the streets of their capital – they were delighted because their presence signified that the war was over and that normality would soon be restored.

The war was, of course, far from being over. Even the battle of France had not yet finished. Then, after a dictated peace, there would be the years of occupation, resistance and reprisals, Allied bombing, the invasion and the liberation battles. The period of suffering for France was not ending but beginning. There would be no return to normality for many years. The worst period would be when the Nazis began to draft the young men to Germany to work in the factories.

At midday on 14 June General Georges announced that the French Army was to retire to the line of the Loire and that the Maginot Line was to be abandoned completely. Even he was probably unaware that a part of the 'impregnable' Maginot Line had been penetrated by German infantry. Later that afternoon they received a further message from General Georges. It read: 'All organized resistance over.'

Organized resistance may have been over, but there were still seventy-five thousand members of the BEF in France. Staff Officer left Orleans for Angers, then departed from Angers even more hurriedly, for the Germans were then only fourteen miles away. After he had crossed the Loire he and his group were stopped at every village by elderly but very tough-looking French civilians. Doubtless many of them were veterans of the previous war, and they had no arms more powerful than shotguns and rifles, but they were clearly not people to be brushed on one side. He reflected that if the younger French soldiers had had an ounce of the determination shown by these grizzled old warriors the outcome of the campaign might have been very different. Staff Officer was flown out of Nantes airfield at 6 p.m. on 17 June and arrived at Heston at 8 p.m. The Germans arrived in Nantes soon after he left.

The collapse of much of the French Army – though not all – which so disheartened Staff Officer, was subsequently the subject of painful self-analysis by the French themselves. Daniel Vilfroy was one of the first to enter this field. His conclusion, though not indisputable, contained much truth. He noted that modern war differed in one important respect from its predecessors: it was total.

Previous wars had involved only a part of the population and had often left whole areas of a defeated country virtually untouched. Fortified by this view, many people in past eras have hoped to keep invaders out of parts, or even the whole, of their country by building strong defences, which have varied from the Great Wall of China to Hadrian's Wall in northern Britain. Sometimes a chain of border forts has been considered to be the equal of a continuous fortification. Nowadays our amazement at the labour and skill required to build these ancient barriers is only exceeded by our wonder that their sponsors and architects should not have learnt from experience that such fortifications never succeed in their main purpose: apathy or treachery in their garrisons, or tactical skills in the attackers, usually enable attackers to find a way through. The Maginot Line was not a new idea but an optimistic continuation of a long-discredited theory.

Equally, natural physical obstacles seldom deter a determined aggressor. It was the French, not the Germans, who regarded the Ardennes as 'impassable to tanks'. Before the war was over, other 'impassable' frontiers would have been crossed: the waterless waste of the North African desert would have been conquered by enterprising young men of the Long Range Desert Group and the SAS; the impenetrable jungles of Burma, Malaya and the Philippines would be crossed by the Japanese, and then the Allies; the great barrier of five thousand miles of water between America and Japan would be breached by aircraft carriers and long-distance aircraft. The only natural barrier which would thwart an invader was the vast area of Russia, which would swallow up Hitler's legions before freezing them to death in the ice of winter. But in 1940 France was clinging resolutely to the defensive image of the Ardennes and the Maginot.

Although Vilfroy, writing as early as 1942, could not take his argument as far as this, his conclusions are broadly correct. He found that the French Army of 1940 differed dramatically from that of 1914–18. Much of the artillery was horse-drawn still, but the horses were now used to drag the guns to strategic positions where they were dug in so deeply that they could not be moved before the Germans over-ran them; in the previous war horses had been used to give the guns mobility. But above all, he felt, the failure of the once so magnificent French Army was a failure of morale, a realization that, in spite of all that the soldiers had been told, this war would not be won easily and without heavy bloodshed. They believed that accepting early defeat would save lives. A fact about war which is not usually recognized is that in countering wars of aggression no loss of life in the fighting is likely to be as great as the loss sustained subsequently by the unfortunate victims. In previous wars the defeated were often massacred as they tried to escape from the battlefield on which they had clearly lost. In the present century aggressive wars have often been followed by a policy of genocide.

Perhaps the most distressing aspect of the French defeat in 1940, as far as Vilfroy was concerned, was that it was virtually self-inflicted. France had the advantage in numbers of soldiers and tanks, but was inferior in dynamic leadership, in her air force, and in her tactical doctrine. The most damaging factor was lack of leadership from the top. Vilfroy emphasized that when the Germans had broken through the Sedan sector they were extremely vulnerable to a flank attack. At that moment they needed a Marshal Joffre to organize an attack into the vulnerable German flank. This would have ruined Guderian's plan and no doubt given satisfaction to von Kleist; it would certainly have prevented that lightning thrust across the rear of the BEF which brought it headlong back from Belgium. But there was no Joffre in 1940 and no counter-attack.

In the long run the greatest victims of the Blitzkrieg theory were the Germans themselves, particularly Hitler, for the easy victory in France gave them the impression that there would be easy victories everywhere for minimal efforts, provided those efforts were properly co-ordinated. Blitzkrieg tactics gave them easy victories in Yugoslavia (where they had to maintain a strong holding force for the rest of the war), took them through Greece and into the expensive necessity of holding on to the Aegean islands, involved them in Crete where they had so many losses in their airborne attack that they never attempted another like it again, and gave them mixed fortunes in the Western Desert where, at the end of less than two years, a quarter of a million German and Italian troops surrendered to the Allies. Because of the ease of the German victory in France, Mussolini thought the Germans must be invincible; he threw in his lot with them irrevocably, and in consequence suffered defeat after defeat before his ignominious death at the hands of partisans.

But the most gullible victim of the Blitzkrieg delusion was Hitler, who considered he would have an easy victory in Russia, and therefore delayed his invasion of that country until he had settled, as he thought, the Balkans. So if the French had deceived themselves about the natural and man-made defences, their self-delusion was as nothing to that of the victorious Germans who overestimated their military powers so much that eventually they reduced their own country to a devastated ruin occupied by and eventually divided between their former enemies.

17 View from the War Room

BACK IN NO. 10 Downing Street, John Colville was writing about the state of the war as the politicians saw it on 31 May:

> Everybody is elated by the progress of the evacuation. One of the world's greatest defeats is being redeemed by an outstanding achievement of organisation and gallantry. . . .
>
> Meanwhile the secret service reports from Germany show that the difficulties there are increasing and that the Nazis are terrified of failing to win the war this summer. There is general apathy at home in Germany, the casualties have been heavy, the shortages of food and raw materials are making themselves felt, and the production of tanks and aircraft is falling off by forty per cent. If these reports are true, the war may well be over by Christmas, despite the German people and army's famous staying power.

The reports were not, of course, true, the war would not be 'over by Christmas', and German tank production doubled during that year. In fact the Germans were overjoyed by their victories and confirmed in their view that Hitler was truly a miracle-maker. Food from the Scandinavian countries was already pouring into Germany: it was reported that the first trains from Denmark, loaded with butter, cheese and many other foodstuffs which the Germans had been denied by the 'guns before butter' policy, set off for the Reich within one hour of the German soldiers' arrival in that country. Colville reported other wishful thoughts in the Cabinet at this time. 'Although Italy is making every preparation for immediate war I think there is still a chance it is all a stupendous bluff. If Musso were serious he would scarcely be so blatant about it.' One realist, Edward Bridges, later to become head of the Treasury, commented on the euphoria surrounding the Dunkirk evacuation: 'Evacuation is becoming our greatest national industry.'

Churchill flew to Paris on the 31st, accompanied by the future Labour Prime Minister Attlee, but gained little from his brief visit. On his return he was asked if the pictures in the National Gallery should be sent to Canada. 'No,' he growled, 'bury them in caves. None must go. We are going to beat them.'

Gort returned from France on 1 June and made a statement about the situation, past and present, which impressed everyone at No. 10. On the 2nd Churchill was showing considerable irritation over Reynaud's request for more fighters, bombers and troops to help him withstand the expected German attack across the Aisne. In view of the almost hopeless situation in France he did not feel he could waste any more resources there, but instead wished to retain all he could to build up the defence of Britain and create a new army. On the other hand, he did not want to refuse completely because that might be the final fatal blow to French morale and give an excuse for its complete collapse.

Churchill was also concerned about British morale at this point. He decided that Britain had now had enough of being on the defensive and should be striking back at German territory. This was, no doubt, the point at which he began formulating his idea to 'Set Europe Ablaze' by Commando raids and sabotage by SOE (Special Operations Executive). The SAS had not yet been created, but if it had been, he would have welcomed it heartily.

On 4 June, there was some dismay in the Cabinet because the evacuation of the last British troops from Narvik was being delayed. After the disasters in France, most people had forgotten that there were still troops in Norway. Apparently the Swedes had formulated a plan for a peace treaty between Norway and Germany which would allow the King of Norway to retain sovereignty over the northern half of the country. As that would include the port of Narvik, through which the Swedes, though 'neutral', were shipping vast quantities of iron ore to Germany, it was obvious that the Germans would not countenance such a plan for a moment. In the event, the last British troops left on 8 June, but not without perilous moments.

Churchill had much to worry him, but this only seemed to spur him on to be more pugnacious and determined. Although the RAF had now suffered such heavy losses over France that it could not possibly spare any more aircraft, something had to be done to boost French morale; it was decided therefore to send two Army divisions to land somewhere in the west of France, possibly around Cherbourg.

That same day, with the world falling about his ears, Churchill stood up in the House of Commons and made one of his greatest speeches.

Even though large tracts of Europe have fallen under the grip of the Gestapo, and all the odious apparatus of Nazi rule, we shall not flag or fail. We shall go on to the end. We shall fight in France. We shall fight on the seas and oceans. We shall fight with growing confidence and growing strength in the air. We shall defend our island, whatever the cost may be. We shall fight on the beaches. We shall fight on the landing grounds. We shall fight in the streets and fields. We shall fight in the hills. We shall never surrender. And even if, which I do not for a moment believe, this island, or a large part of it, were subjugated and starving, then our Empire beyond the oceans, armed and guarded by the British fleet, will carry on the struggle until in God's good time the New World with all its power and might sets forth to the rescue and the liberation of the old.

This was the sort of speech that the French needed one of their leaders to make, or preferably to have made already. Reynaud had already hinted at the possibility (he hoped) that America might step in and insist on the Germans now making a peace treaty which would preserve the integrity of France. Churchill took a more realistic view. He did not believe that America would abandon its neutrality until the situation became infinitely worse in Europe; in fact he was by no means sure that she would ever change her attitude from that of 'Fortress America'. Not until the day eighteen months later when he heard that Germany's ally Japan had attacked Pearl Harbor, and thus brought the USA into the general war, was he really confident that Germany might be defeated.

By 4 June the Dunkirk evacuation was over, and already the

following day Churchill was full of ideas for striking back at the Germans in the territory they now occupied. He thought the Australians would make ideal Commandos and that raids should be begun as soon as possible.

How far the Commando raids were the product of Churchill's own mind and how far they stemmed from the creative thinking of Lieutenant Colonel Dudley Clarke, at that time Military Assistant to the CIGS (now Sir John Dill), is not a question which can ever be satisfactorily answered. Clarke had had experience of guerrilla warfare in Palestine and was now given the authority to recruit a force to mount a raid on the French coast in that same month. When it took place, near Le Touquet, on 23–24 June, France had just capitulated to the Germans. Although that particular raid achieved very little, it showed the Germans that Britain was in no mood to follow her ally into surrender. Churchill thought that the earlier a raid could be mounted the better it would be tactically; for on 5 June he was still under the impression that the French had a large intact force south of the Aisne. He had correctly forecast that once the Dunkirk evacuation was over the Germans would switch their best forces to the south, leaving their lower-quality troops to look after the northern coastline.

At this stage, of course, Churchill had no idea that the resistance put up by the French army of the south would be negligible; he imagined the two armies being locked in combat while Britain made life unendurable for the Germans in the north. His imagination ranged freely and he also envisaged the raids growing in power until they could capture a town such as Calais or Boulogne, hold it until the Germans had mounted a strong relief force, then disappear as quickly as they had come, only to reappear unexpectedly somewhere else.

On 6 June the French government was pressing hard for Britain to send more fighters to France. They implied that if the request was not met they would probably have to capitulate. They also hoped to spur Churchill into action by saying that the RAF contribution to the battle of France had been useful, but slow to arrive and inadequate. Churchill was infuriated, but not sufficiently so to lose his head and commit military follies.

An example of the complete failure of the British Cabinet to understand how bad the situation was in France occurred on 10 June. Churchill had just decided to go to Paris and obtain an up-to-date account of the situation for himself. He was about to leave for Hendon airport that afternoon when he received a telegram informing him that the French government was going to leave the city. Irritated though he was at having his plans disrupted, he concluded that this was a good sign: it meant that the French must be intending to carry on the fight in the south rather than wait in the capital for the German victors to arrive and dictate terms. However, the news which followed, that the Germans had occupied Rouen, was not encouraging. Churchill was having his afternoon nap when the news came in that Italy had entered the war; on hearing it, he decided that Mussolini should be given a quick taste of the medicine of war by receiving a heavy bombing raid. He added: 'People who go to Italy to look at ruins won't have to go as far as Naples and Pompeii in future.'

The 12th was a critical day. In spite of the grim news from Paris, which the Germans had not yet reached (that would not happen until the 14th), Churchill had made another swift flight to France the previous day. It seemed that although Reynaud was willing to fight to the bitter end, Marshal Pétain wished to sue for peace. Pétain was clearly going to be the source of considerable trouble. He had had a distinguished record in the First World War, acquiring the title 'Hero of Verdun', had subsequently been Minister for War and from 1934 to 1939 had been French Ambassador to Spain. Recently he had joined Reynaud's government. Although the French had great faith in Pétain, who was already eighty-four years old, he was destined to become a person whom they would regard with shame. During the German occupation he collaborated vigorously with the Nazis, and even condemned de Gaulle to death in his absence for not doing the same. At the end of the war Pétain was tried as a traitor and collaborator, but his sentence of death was commuted to life imprisonment. He lived to the age of ninety-five.

There was a foretaste of Britain's relationship with the future Vichy French government on 12 June when the news came through to Britain that the 51st Highland Division had reached St Valéry but had no prospect of being evacuated. It had been ordered by the French to surrender, but its commander had refused. French troops at St Valéry were already hanging out white flags. In the south other French were reported as trying to prevent British bombers taking off to raid Italy; they were said to have placed lorries on the runways of the airfields the Wellingtons would be using.

Later that day Reynaud rang up Churchill and suggested he should visit France once more. Although Reynaud, in contrast to Pétain, still seemed full of fighting spirit, this sudden request to see Churchill looked ominous. He seemed unaware of the risk the British Prime Minister would be taking in crossing to France when the Luftwaffe was now in control of the skies. As Reynaud had promised to consult Churchill before he took any dramatic step, it looked as if that moment had come. Unfortunately, the fact that Reynaud was discussing the idea of Churchill's visit over an open telephone line suggested that the French Prime Minister was rapidly losing his grip. However, Churchill made the risky journey on the 13th, visiting Reynaud at Tours, and heard from him that the French wished to be released from their pledge not to make a separate peace.

However, as Roosevelt chose that moment to send a telegram to Reynaud, promising him American support, the outlook brightened temporarily. Unfortunately the Americans were in no position to support Reynaud, nor would be for at least a year. Roosevelt's continuing support was all the more welcome – and surprising – because the American Ambassador in London, Joseph Kennedy, was firmly of the opinion that Britain had no chance at all of winning the war and should surrender on the best terms obtainable. Joseph Kennedy, father of the future President John Kennedy, lived until 1969, so he had ample time later to ponder his earlier views.

The principal worry for Churchill at this time was what would happen to the French fleet if Reynaud surrendered. If it fell intact into the hands of the Germans, it would tip the balance of power at sea decisively into their favour. The action Britain was forced to take, in sinking the French ships when they refused to join Britain, caused lasting bitterness among certain elements of the French population.

On 16 June telegrams were sent to France to the effect that there was no possibility of being released from its pledge not to make a separate peace. They were followed by the astonishing proposal for a union between Britain and France. This, though a dramatic announcement for Britain, had little impact in France. On the 17th Reynaud resigned and his place was taken by Pétain; in his government was Laval, who would be condemned to death after the war as a collaborator. The Declaration of Union between Britain and France had proved to be a stillborn baby. Nothing would now prevent Pétain from accepting the German terms, however harsh. In the event they seemed reasonably conciliatory.

France would be divided into two regions, occupied in the north but unoccupied in the south, where the French would have their own government based at Vichy. The Germans did not insist that the French Navy and colonies should be handed over as part of the peace terms. No doubt they thought both would be acquired without difficulty later. It was one of Hitler's many mistakes.

18 Personal Initiatives

'CONFUSED' IS A WORD which is often used to describe military situations, and is usually extremely apt. It would certainly have applied in both France and Britain. The British government knew little enough about the real progress of the war, and the French government seemed to know even less. The Belgian surrender came as a surprise, although there had been ample warning. Staff Officer, the Field Security Police and the various infantry regiments knew little except what was happening in their immediate neighbourhood. Even Gort's headquarters was often out of touch. In France, some four hundred thousand British soldiers experienced war and formed their own views of it. The stories of individuals often reveal more of the truth than the official communiqués.

Accusations that every disaster was someone else's fault were inevitable. In fact there could be no single scapegoat for the fall of France. The French and British could blame the Belgians for not having adequate defences to keep out the German invader, but the Belgians could retort that events had proved that her allies had shown in the course of the war that they were incapable of saving her. Even if they had been allowed into Belgium before Hitler attacked, they would still have had to come scurrying back when the Germans broke through at Sedan. The French could be blamed, as they were, for letting the Germans break through at Sedan and cut right through central France to the coast. Both Belgium and France could blame Britain for not having larger forces in France, not having a larger air component and, finally, removing the bulk of the BEF via Dunkirk. These critical views obscured the fact that the Belgians, placed in a virtually impossible position, produced units which fought well. Similarly, although the British numbers were not as large as they might have been, the soldiers fought stubbornly to hold the Panzers. And, whatever claims were made to the contrary, the last troops to leave Dunkirk officially on 4 June were 383 French soldiers who were embarked on the British destroyer *Shikari*.

Having been evacuated from Dunkirk, Denis Barlone had immediately returned and landed at Cherbourg, which was still in Allied hands. Unfortunately, or perhaps fortunately, for him, his feet and ankles were badly swollen from the effects of fatigue in the previous days and his first destination was a naval hospital. Here he was able to catch up with the latest news, although he found it hard to distinguish truth from rumours.

Criticism of the Higher Command was rife. Everyone was certain that, if the evacuation had been organized better, large numbers of guns could have been taken out of Dunkirk and used to equip forces for the reconquest of France. Instead they had been delayed until all the cranes which could have lifted and loaded them had been made useless by bombing. There was general agreement that the French Air Force was totally inadequate against the Luftwaffe. There was tactical criticism, too: many of the men from anti-tank units said that they were too small and badly positioned to be able to check the Panzers. What seemed most extraordinary was the superiority in numbers of the German tanks. However, as Barlone may have learnt later, it was not superior numbers overall which made the Panzers so effective, but their concentration where most needed. This, of course, was in conformity with the military principle of 'concentration of force', which Gamelin and his staff seemed to have ignored.

Spies and fifth-columnists had been everywhere, apparently, and still were. Even at the naval hospital in which Barlone was being cared for, five people had been shot for showing lights and thus guiding German bombers to a nearby chemical factory; one of these spies had been a beautiful young girl. Two other people had barricaded themselves into a loft, from which they were no doubt able to transmit messages; they were shot through a skylight. The release of patients from mental hospitals had given the fifth-columnists a wonderful opportunity to pretend to be escaped lunatics and wander about in restricted areas. When asked for their papers they gibbered insanely. Another interesting story circulating in the hospital was that all over Belgium the advertisement panels for Pacho brand chicory were used to hide information useful to the enemy. Fanciful though some of these stories seemed, there appeared to be an element of truth in many of them.

Here too Barlone heard about a new apparatus the British were using to track the path of German aeroplanes. This, of course, was radar, but its powers were exaggerated, for it was said to be strong enough to track the German aircraft from the time they left their airfields. The Germans were said to have developed highly sophisticated parachute techniques which enabled them to drop not merely men but also guns and light tanks; this information seems to have been somewhat premature.

Inevitably, Barlone heard many complaints about the French Ministry of Munitions, which was dubbed 'sixth column'. Some of them centred on the fact that, a month before the invasion, all the officers in the French Army received an instruction telling them to send back into reserve any man who declared that he was a 'skilled worker'. Not surprisingly, there were thousands, all of whom were sent home a week after signing a statement to that effect. Barlone had had considerable doubts about the truthfulness of some of the declarations, but had no power to prevent the removal from his unit of trained soldiers who claimed civilian skills. On being released from military service, these 'skilled workers' were put into reserved occupations in factories which could not be brought into production in less than a year.

After five days in the hospital at Cherbourg, Barlone and all the other patients were moved to Auray. He was still unable to walk properly but he was anxious to return to the fighting line as soon as possible, so he lay down for a whole afternoon, 'so that my foot may be fit to stand the fatigue of the journey'.

On 13 June, after an uncomfortable journey in a goods train and a lift in a civilian car, he rejoined his division once more; they were at St Corneille, twelve miles from Le Mans. When he arrived he found that this was merely the remnant of the artillery staff; the rest of his headquarters was elsewhere, but no one knew where 'elsewhere' was. That evening they all listened to the radio and were appalled to hear that Reynaud had just made a despairing plea to Roosevelt to bring America into the war. It was not so much the appeal to Roosevelt that he found so unpalatable as the fact that it was broadcast. This, he felt, must have had a very bad effect on the morale of French troops. If their Prime Minister was in despair, what hope could the soldiers have?

During the next five days he was still retreating, though at the same time trying to link up with others wishing to continue the fight. But on 18 June he learned that Pétain and Weygand had asked for an armistice. Some of the officers who heard the news began to weep, but Barlone was merely made grimly determined to escape to England and fight on. On the 19th he was told by French people who had been listening to the London radio that a young general by the name of de Gaulle had made a broadcast saying that he was already enrolling a French army in England. De Gaulle had emphasized that the superiority of the English equipment would soon enable the French to 'smash the Boches' on other battlefields.

Barlone was greatly cheered. He felt that de Gaulle was 'very convincing, very inspiring'. He was greatly impressed by Churchill's statement that thenceforth British and French would have dual nationality, and felt that de Gaulle must have the full backing of the British government or he would not have been allowed to broadcast such an address.

Unfortunately the euphoria did not last long for the French radio (now under the control of Pétain and his colleagues) repudiated de Gaulle, who, they said, had been recalled to France. Barlone tried to look at their viewpoint philosophically, imagining that Pétain was bound to take this attitude while he was negotiating armistice terms with the Germans.

On 21 June Barlone heard that Cherbourg had now fallen to the Germans. He found the news almost incredible. Cherbourg, a military town with warships in the harbour and forts with guns on the shore, had apparently surrendered without even making an attempt to fight.

As Barlone joined the general trek to the south, he and his fellow officers wondered why there were no arrangements to evacuate a large portion of the French army from the Atlantic and Mediterranean ports, such as Nantes, Bordeaux, Toulon and Marseilles. Unlike Pétain and his friends, Barlone did not trust German promises: he felt that the fate of France would be the same as that of Poland, Czechoslovakia and Austria. He recalled that those countries had believed Hitler's promises, and their subsequent fate was not enviable.

197

He was now faced with a difficult decision. In Bayonne on 22 June he was told that the embarkation of all men between the ages of seventeen and forty-five had been forbidden that morning. As he was over forty-five he could still have left, but he felt that to do so would be deserting his comrades. Soon after learning about the restrictions on embarkation, he heard that an order had now been issued for all unattached officers of the French Army in Bayonne to be arrested and taken to a depot.

Fortunately, this, like most of the other rumours with which he was surrounded, turned out not to be true. Eventually he managed to embark on a boat leaving Marseilles, found his way to Lisbon and arrived in England on 1 October. By that time he had heard of the sinking of the French fleet in harbour at Mers-el-Kebir. Unlike many French people, he was delighted. He considered that the British attack was eminently sensible, for if the French fleet had not been incapacitated, the whole of it could have come under German and Italian control.

Barlone subsequently achieved his ambition and joined up with de Gaulle and the Free French Forces in Britain. His morale had remained high and his belief that France could fight back and avoid a humiliating peace had stayed with him until he left French soil. He had had the advantage of belonging to a first-class unit and being able to share his opinions with others of similar viewpoints.

Hans Habe, an Austrian refugee, was also a soldier of high morale but had a very different viewpoint from Barlone as he was serving in the French Army in the 21st Foreign Volunteer Regiment, a unit which appeared to have been raised in some haste. Having been trained as a scout, he was sent to inspect the front line observation posts in the Alsace region. He had been warned by his captain that he would probably find most of them very comfortable, but quite useless for observing the enemy. He was told that he would probably also find them full of cases of champagne, which he would be well advised to put a bullet through. He encountered a family which, he was told, was typically Alsatian. The father, who had grown up when the province was occupied by the Germans before 1914, had fought throughout that war in the German Army; but he was now an ardent French patriot and passionately desired a French victory. His son, who had grown up in France and was now in the French Army, hoped for a German victory.

In Habe's regiment most of the men had rifles with dates ranging from 1891, many of which were so rusty that it was impossible to load them; they lacked slings, so these were taken off the gas masks the soldiers were supposed to be carrying. The condition of the rifles was typical of the other equipment, such as lorries: all were obsolete and lacking spares. This was hardly the way to encourage a volunteer regiment, but presumably the 21st were the ones who received what was left when all the other regiments had made their selection. The 21st were put in a train and told they were *en route* for Belgium. Before leaving each man was issued with what was described as 'reserve stocks'. This comprised eleven pounds of biscuits, one tin of sardines and a tin of meat. The last was covered with thick brown paint; when this was scraped off, the tins were seen to bear dates of manufacture between 1916 and 1920.

At St Mihiel the 21st was inspected by a general, and it was recorded that, out of 2300 men, 800 had no weapon at all. As they continued their journey on foot, they were constantly warned to be very careful because 'the enemy is stronger'. They therefore took cover as often as possible, even though there was no threat in sight. In fact, although they continued marching, no one, including the adjutant, had any idea of where the Germans were and what their ultimate destination would be. When they stopped for the night they usually camped in cemeteries from the 1914–18 war.

In the regiment, Habe's company commander, a veteran of the previous war, was named Captain Billerot. Billerot was fifty (their colonel was fifty-eight) and enjoyed nothing so much as telling stories of the narrow escapes he had had in the earlier war. Over and over again he would recount how he had twice lost 75 per cent of his company. He repeated this once more as the company stood in pouring rain among the graves at Verdun, emphasizing that when they eventually met the Germans each man must say to himself, 'From now on my life is not worth a sou.' Subsequently, whenever the regiment came under fire and they looked around for Billerot, expecting an example of heroic conduct, he was nowhere to be seen. He usually turned up later, without an explanation.

Habe was more cheered by a Romanian named Mayer, who marched alongside him. Mayer had been turned down three times by regimental doctors before finding a fourth, who, 'blind or senile, no doubt', had passed him. In their target-shooting practice he missed not only the bull's eye but usually the whole target. He

199

fell over at intervals on the march but always picked himself up; and he trembled with fear but tried not to show it.

Belleville was the first wrecked town that Habe saw and it was more bizarre than frightening. One side of the street was intact while on the other most of the houses had been cut in half, leaving a heap of rubble on one side and a virtually untouched bedroom or kitchen on the other. As they marched in, the shelling began again and continued for the next six hours.

The accuracy of the German artillery stemmed largely from an aircraft named the Arado. It had originated as a German training aircraft, was very slow, with a top speed of 85 m.p.h., and carried one machine-gun but no bombs. However, it was so heavily armoured that it could not be shot down by ground fire or even by pursuing aircraft. The Arados roamed freely over the French lines, reporting the location of their defences and of gaps which could be penetrated by German soldiers. When Arados appeared, the French gunners stopped firing, knowing that if a plane spotted them they were certain to be the recipients of concentrated German artillery fire. Once Habe's unit was caught in an intensive barrage 'in a wood that was so small that God had obviously made it for a solitary pair of lovers and not for two companies of infantry'.

By now the company was isolated and lost as far as the battle was concerned, although they noticed that geographically they were near Châtillon. Everywhere they went they came across soldiers, either solitary or in small groups. When they asked these what regiment they belonged to, and where these were, most of them gave the names of their units promptly but had no idea where their former comrades now were. All of them claimed to be looking for their regiments, which they had last seen under shellfire. All had been well until someone called out, 'Sauve qui peut.' 'Sauve qui peut' had not been interpreted as 'Everyone for himself', but as 'Run for your lives.' They repeated it monotonously; even the wounded who could hardly speak contrived to mumble it. As there were fifth columnists in the area, Habe wondered whether that disruptive phrase could have originated from them.

Eventually the 21st arrived at the sector of the front which they were going to hold for three weeks: it lay between Le Chesne and Les Petites Armoises. This was approximately twenty miles south of Sedan, where the Panzers had made their first breakthrough and destroyed General Corap's army. The Panzers had pressed on, thrusting forward to the west and north, where they created further havoc; the German infantry, following behind, was now trying to widen the gap made by the Panzers and by this means get in behind the Maginot Line. Habe recorded proudly that whereas in the north, west and south the Germans were able to advance a hundred kilometres a day, the 35th Division, to which his own regiment belonged, held their front until the final French collapse.

The fighting qualities shown by Habe's regiment and the morale of Barlone and his comrades on a different part of the front give some slight idea of what the French might have accomplished if there had been adequate leadership from the Higher Command. The resilience of the 21st was all the more surprising in view of the absurd restrictions put on them.

'From the first day,' said Habe, 'our bitterest enemy was hunger.' In order not to betray the position from the smoke of the cooking fires, the battalion kitchens had been sited seven miles behind the lines. However, although the kitchens themselves were not under artillery fire, the route between them and the 21st undoubtedly was. This meant that food, both frugal and stone cold, arrived at intervals of twelve hours, twenty-four hours or, on one occasion, forty-eight hours.

While thus deprived, the 21st were surrounded by food on the hoof, which they were strictly forbidden to touch. These were the cows which had been left behind by their former owners. There were hundreds of them. As there was no one to milk them, the wretched animals often ran bellowing along the fields, their udders almost touching the ground. As the 21st starved, they watched these cattle decline and die; occasionally one was shot in no-man's land, but it would have been certain death to try to haul it in. The only excursions into no-man's land were at night for mine-laying.

There was never a shortage of volunteers when there were dangerous jobs to be done. One mine-laying party contained a Hungarian, a Romanian Jew, a Spanish refugee, a Portuguese miner and a large number of Galicians from the Polish ghettos. Habe shook hands with them and before they left said to each, surprisingly, '*Merde*'.* Five of the thirty-five volunteers were killed when the Germans attacked them.

In this area were the dugouts which had been used in the

---

*It also means 'Good luck!'

previous war, many containing relics from both the French and German armies of that time. The 21st improved some of them, thinking as they did so that this would make them useful for the soldiers of the next war, when it came. There were few comforts, but among them was the fact that many of the German shells failed to explode. This was attributed to the fact that these were of Czech origin, made in the Skoda works which the Germans had taken over in 1939, thereby breaking the Munich Agreement. Happily, the French shells always exploded.

In spite of the complete air superiority of the Germans, Habe's fellow soldiers were more than a match for their enemy counterparts. Every dawn and every dusk the German infantry attacked, and on every occasion they were thrown back.

As the days passed, Habe and his companions began to feel increasingly cheerful. Then, one morning, they received orders from their headquarters to destroy all their papers and codebooks. This was puzzling, in view of the success they had been having, but when Habe looked through his telescope he could see opposite on the hillside dozens of German tanks; they themselves had none. The German tanks were not moving; they squatted 'like prehistoric beasts'. From the noise it was clear that others were coming up from behind to join them. The 21st sent out a patrol and captured two prisoners. One was too badly wounded to be able to talk; the other refused to answer leading questions or simply said 'Heil Hitler.' Habe asked permission to take over the interrogation. Instead of speaking quietly and amiably to the German, he ordered him to come up until their faces were six inches apart. Then Habe bellowed at the man. He did not threaten him, merely repeated the questions the interpreter had already asked. This time the German did not once say 'Heil Hitler', and he answered all the questions more fully than they had expected.

Out in front the Germans were now so confident that they were scarcely bothering to take cover. Habe saw one group of officers who spread out maps and then inspected the French lines through binoculars. Habe realized that this was the Divisional General Staff and hastily telephoned his artillery. Nothing happened. He repeated his request several times, although thinking as he did so that there must be good men among the German group who would now all be killed. He need not have worried – the French guns never fired.

Soon afterwards he learnt that they had exhausted their ammunition stocks two days earlier and nothing had come up to replace them. Habe did not realize that their division was an outpost of resistance in a sea of defeat and ruin. It was as well for their morale that they had no means of knowing about the disasters which had overtaken the French and British armies elsewhere in France.

The next day Habe was disturbed to notice that men from the battalions on either side were now falling back, although he and his comrades in their forward outpost had received no instructions. Attempts to make contact with headquarters by telephone received no response: the lines were obviously cut. To stay where they were meant certain death, but he had received no orders to retire. Habe sent a runner back to HQ to obtain instructions and information. They waited another night, during which they heard German voices passing their dugout. It seemed certain that Habe's runner must have been killed, but at last he returned. The woods where the colonel and the rest of the company had been stationed were completely empty, he told them. Habe wondered whether the runner could have lost his way and looked in the wrong wood. Hoping he was not leaving his post in the face of the enemy, Habe decided to go back with his party and see for himself. The runner's story had been true. There was not a soul in the company position. They *had* been forgotten. As dawn broke on the morning of 11 June they were surrounded by complete silence, which somehow seemed totally menacing. Habe reflected that they were completely alone; there were three of them and they were confronting sixty thousand German soldiers. . . .

They walked thirty miles before they found their regiment, mainly by guesswork. They marched past burning villages full of corpses. One of their members refused to believe everyone was dead and tried to turn over some corpses to talk to them; Habe ordered him to stop after he caught him shaking a corpse and shouting questions at it. At long last they came to a village where an old woman was sitting in front of her burning house. She could hardly speak, but when she did, she said: 'Are you hungry?'

'No,' they said. 'Are *you*?'

'Yes,' she replied. 'I'll get you something.'

She rose to her feet and, before they could stop her, walked quite erect into her burning house. 'The flames devoured her. We stood there grasping at the void.'

Near the Bois de Cornay they caught up with stragglers from the rearguard of the 21st and learnt what had happened. While they had stood firm, regiments on each side and behind had given way. One of the stragglers had just decided he could go no further and lay face down on the ground; he was a composer who, before the war, had put on his own revues. Habe persuaded him to get up and go on and at last they linked up with the 21st. They discovered that they had simply been forgotten when the regiment moved out, but now they had rejoined it they were soon once more on the march.

There was no proper news. They knew nothing of Calais or Boulogne or Arras or Dunkirk, of Paris or Pétain, but there were plenty of rumours. Russia was said to have declared war on Germany, forcing Hitler to remove most of his troops from France. The Poles and Romanians were marching with the Russians. British troops had landed in France. The RAF had set fire to the German munitions factories in the Ruhr.

Wild and bizarre rumours of this nature always seem to spread rapidly through retreating armies. Nobody seems to know where or how they originate; they have little effect on morale, for they seem over-fanciful even to the average soldier. On the other fronts, as mentioned earlier, there was the constant belief that a successful counter-attack had just been made *somewhere else*.

The 21st were not surprised to find that they were no longer being strafed by the Luftwaffe. They believed that the German aircraft were being heavily engaged elsewhere, possibly in defending Germany.

At the village of Manre the 21st joined the 18th Chasseurs de Pied, known as 'Les Joyeux'. Their nickname was ironic, for they were all hardened criminals which the French, logically, decided should not serve their sentences in safety while others fought the war. Their officers were not criminals, but had been sent to this regiment as a severe form of punishment. Les Joyeux were always sent to the worst places; if they survived, they *might* be pardoned. But here they were very friendly and were living very well. When they saw the remnants of the 21st they promptly gave them their own evening meal and said they would find something else for themselves later.

Here the 21st stopped. They were now told by their colonel that this was where they would stay and fight. It would not last long: most of Germany was in flames. However, the next morning they were ordered to march another twenty miles – away from the Germans. When they arrived at their destination, Vienne la Ville, that too was in flames. Here, for the first time in a month, they encountered civilians, hundreds of them, all refugees.

Habe went to his captain for instructions on the dispositions for the stand the 21st would make here. His captain seemed completely exhausted and did not open his eyes. 'We were going to make a stand here,' he said, 'but I have just had orders that we must march out on the stroke of midnight and retreat ten kilometres.' He explained that he was aware that his personal authority had now disappeared, and if he ordered them to march they would probably refuse; instead, he would tell them to make their own way.

At that moment Habe realized that France had lost the war. As he walked away he encountered his sergeant major, a man whom many suspected of being a German spy planted in their own ranks. The sergeant major told him, cheerfully, that the Germans had occupied Paris the day before. Habe was tempted to shoot him. Soon afterwards the sergeant major was said to have been arrested and shot as a spy, but an alternative story was that he had escaped and crossed over to the Germans.

It was not quite the end. The 21st once more began to retreat. Eventually they came to a village near Commercy where they were met by the mayor and some elderly citizens, most of them wearing medals from the previous war. To Habe's astonishment they were expecting the 21st and had dug trenches for them to defend. There was nothing amateurish about these trenches; they were well sited and expertly dug. The village was in an important strategic position, near to a river crossing and a railway junction. All the men and women in it were determined to support the 21st, and fight to the end. The 21st were heroes to them; and if need be they would all die together.

A day later, the 21st received another order. They were to retreat once more, leaving the village to its fate. As they marched out, the villagers who had greeted them with such warmth now spat at them and shouted obscenities. The mayor stood watching them, speechless. Habe recalled that he had never felt so ashamed in his life.

A few miles further on Habe was taken prisoner in the general surrender. As he was an Austrian, he thought the Germans would be likely to shoot him. He promptly changed his name, discarded his uniform and, dressed as a French peasant, headed for the Swiss border. It was 21 June. He escaped.

19 The Forgotten Evacuations

THERE WERE, of course, many units which were not evacuated from Dunkirk. Among them was 51st Highland Division, a territorial unit of high repute which had been deployed along the Saar. Their presence in that area, away from the remainder of the BEF, was due to the policy of giving British units experience of conditions in the French sector of the potential battlefield. The 51st's sector lay between Launstroff and Colmen; on the north they were flanked by the French 2nd Division and on the south by the French 42nd. They were commanded by Major General V. M. Fortune. In addition to the basic component of three all-Scottish brigades, they had a considerable number of English units among the attached troops, some French troops which had been put under General Fortune's command, and a squadron of the RAF.

Fighting began on 10 May with small-scale attacks which were beaten off, mainly by the 4th Black Watch. On 13 May the Germans made an attack along the whole front; it continued into the next day. All these attacks were repulsed. On 15 May the Germans made a dent in the northern sector, but this did not pose a serious threat.

During the next few days, as the situation was quiet, the French took the opportunity to relieve one of their divisions. At this point the Higher Command did not seem to appreciate that, as the Panzers had now driven deeply into France, they had cut off 51st Highland Division from the remainder of the BEF and, at the same time, separated the BEF from its supply bases at Nantes and Cherbourg. Within a few days of the start of the fighting 51st

Highland Division found itself, through no fault of its own, in the unenviable position of being separated from the rest of the BEF by roads which were already clogged with refugees, without clear instructions about future plans for its use, and pressed by heavy German forces coming from the east.

However, the division heard the encouraging news that the British 1st Armoured Division had landed at Le Havre. In fact only a small part of the Armoured Division had landed at that port, which was now being heavily bombed, and the remainder had had to come via Cherbourg. Furthermore, the 1st was just the skeleton of an armoured division, for one of the armoured units, the 3rd RTR, had been sent to Calais and with it had gone the divisional infantry, the 2nd King's Royal Rifle Corps and the 1st Battalion of the Rifle Brigade. First Armoured Division also had no artillery, no spares, no reserve tanks, no bridging materials and incomplete radio equipment.

Its commander, General R. Evans, was told on arrival to seize the Somme crossings and secure them before moving off to join the remainder of the BEF. However, as he had just been informed that the Germans were already over the Somme and had a number of units pressing towards the Seine, he decided that some urgent reconnaissance was immediately necessary to test the validity of these reports. GHQ had informed him that he would only encounter 'the mangled remains of six Panzer divisions'. It was encouraging to be told that his single, under-strength, untried armoured division would merely have to contend with the remains of six Panzers, but there was a fair chance that the six Panzers would muster many more tanks than the 114 light tanks and 143 cruisers in his own division. In the end the six Panzers turned out to be ten and not, unfortunately, mangled.

GHQ appeared to have been misinformed about the results of the counter-attack at Arras and were making plans based on almost complete ignorance of the true course of events. The possibility of ejecting the Germans from their crossing points on the Somme was diminished by the fact that these were now protected by strong German infantry units.

However, having received a firm order from GHQ, a divisional commander is in no position to tell his superiors they are talking nonsense and giving him orders he cannot obey, so Evans made preparations to carry out the instructions to the best of his ability. While considering the problem this procedure would involve he received a message from General Georges, the overall French commander in the area, that 1st Armoured Division should be prepared to follow the advance (*sic*) of the French 7th Army and mop up any small German armoured detachments it found on its way. For good measure he was also told by the 7th Army commander that 1st Armoured Division should cover the 7th's left flank. Of the three orders the last was the least problem, for 1st Armoured did not come under the command of French 7th Army.

Second Brigade of 1st Armoured Division was first into action. It comprised the Queen's Bays, the 9th Lancers and the 10th Hussars; the two latter were fighting the Germans within twenty-four hours of arriving at Cherbourg and subsequently making a sixty-five-mile journey. They lost two tanks from mines on the approach road to Longpré and found that all the bridges in their sector were protected by German troops and mines. By this time three companies from the 4th Border Regiment had been put under Evans's command, and one of these joined with a troop of the Bays to force a crossing of the Somme at Dreuil. Two platoons from the Borders managed to cross by a ford, but the tanks were unable to follow and the Borders were withdrawn.

More confusing orders now followed. General Georges produced the information that 51st Highland Division was now being transferred from the Saar and would shortly link up with 1st Armoured. He issued an order that 1st Armoured Division should destroy all German bridgeheads on the Somme and hold the Somme-Aisne line before linking up with 51st Division. Georges was clearly confident that the pincer movement mentioned earlier, of two divisions from the BEF striking south in a breakout from the salient outside Dunkirk, was already beginning. With this tactical manoeuvre firmly in his sights, he had obtained War Office approval for Evans to put his 1st Armoured Division under the command of the French 7th Army. When 51st Division arrived, the two British units would head north – having, of course, recaptured all the Somme bridges first.

Their next objective was the recapture of the Abbeville bridgehead. Evans tried to explain that his light tanks were designed for fast reconnaissance, not for smashing through well-protected infantry defences, but his superiors brushed the fact to one side. The attacks began on the morning of 27 May, but soon ran into German anti-tank defences which were set out far ahead of the bridgeheads they were protecting. Co-operation between the British and French forces was a total failure, and in consequence the French infantry did not come up to hold the ground the British armour had won at great cost but dug in some distance to the rear. Nearly a hundred British tanks were put out of action for no gain of any importance. The next day it was the French turn. Although they reached the river, they failed to loosen the German grip on the crossings at Abbeville and St Valéry.

On 29 May General de Gaulle's 4th Armoured Division arrived and plunged into the battle. It had already acquitted itself well along the flanks of the advancing Panzers and was keen to show it could do even better. But de Gaulle had no infantry to consolidate ground won, and very little artillery. He renewed the attack the next day, and the next, but none of them altered the German hold on the Somme crossings. By this time, of course, the plan for the other half of the pincer to close in from the north had long been abandoned; the divisions which would have taken part were now being evacuated.

However, 51st Highland Division, which, under French orders, had worked its way around the German flank, was now in Bresle. It had been a difficult journey, but they had accomplished it. They were now under the command of the French 9th Corps, although they were also likely to receive other orders from the War Office at home; it was hoped that these would not be contradictory. General Weygand was now the Supreme Commander Allied Forces in France, and General Georges was still commander of the North East Front. Fifty-first and 1st Armoured had an uncomfortable feeling that they were at the bottom of the heap.

There was an additional British division in the area, the Beauman Division, yet another of the formations which had been hastily assembled to deal with present and future emergencies. It took its name from the commander, Major General A. B. Beauman, who had earlier been the brigadier responsible for the defence of airfields, depots and other military installations in the northern area. Although it consisted mainly of specialist and older troops, who were not trained as infantrymen, it had done well in the fighting so far.

On 4 June a final attack was made to recapture the Abbeville

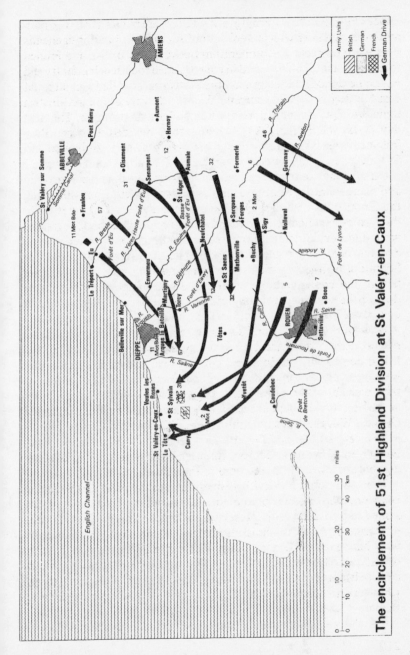

The encirclement of 51st Highland Division at St Valéry-en-Caux

bridgehead. On this day the evacuation from Dunkirk was completed and Bartlett and his comrades were recovering from the traumatic experience of the previous days. Barlone was now in hospital in Cherbourg, at which he had arrived after being evacuated to England and returning to France. Habe was blissfully unaware that the war was already lost and was taking pride in the way the 21st Regiment was standing up to taxing conditions. British troops were still in Norway, where they were pleased with having captured Narvik, but in a few days time they would all have left. This was the day Churchill made his speech in the Commons about fighting to the end and never surrendering. Of all these events the British troops fighting at Abbeville were totally unaware: they might have been happening on another planet.

Of more immediate interest to the troops deployed to capture the Abbeville bridgehead was the disposition of the German troops there, who had now had nearly a fortnight to consolidate their position. Unfortunately for the Allies, there was no means of knowing where the German strongpoints were until they came on to them; there had been very little opportunity for aerial reconnaissance, the Allied troops were not familiar with the area, and when the attack began a valley mist hung over the area. Co-ordination between Allied artillery, tanks and infantry was not good, with the result that tanks advanced without a covering barrage, and infantry often had to advance ahead of, instead of behind, tanks. German mines and anti-tank guns took a heavy toll, causing the loss of 50 per cent of the light tanks of 1st Armoured Division; 152nd Brigade, which had begun the day approximately three hundred strong, had twenty officer and 243 soldier casualties.

But there were also military successes. The 1st Black Watch pushed forward and then covered the advance of their comrades, the 1st Gordons. Both were eager to press on but, as this would have meant isolating themselves among strong German positions which had resisted attempts to destroy them, the Black Watch and Gordons were told to return to the position they had occupied at the start of the attack. Overall the assault had been a failure, but, as the next three days showed, it would have made no difference if it had been a success. Behind the Somme the Germans were massing the strength of Army Group B.

Their attack began on 5 June. The first to take the shock were the Argyll and Sutherland Highlanders, who were thinly disposed over the villages to the west of the Somme. Outnumbered and outgunned, they held out with diminishing ammunition and increasing casualties, but finally were overwhelmed; according to their War Diary the Germans paid a high price for their gains here.

This dour resistance was not limited to British troops. The French 31st Division took a heavy toll of the Germans before themselves being forced back. The 'Auld Alliance' between French and Scots worked well, though not now against England. This battle for the Somme bridgehead has never attracted the attention of writers and others who might have given it the credit it deserved. The Germans had every advantage: numbers, aircraft, heavy artillery and mortars. They were also rested before they began, whereas the Allies had marched long distances and then experienced the frustration and exhaustion of hurling themselves against well-prepared positions. The 51st Highland Division had gained an awesome reputation in the trenches of the 1914–18 war and now they showed why. Having marched this far and waited so long for a full-blooded fight with the Germans, they were going to have one. Orders to detachments of 51st Division to return when they were bypassed or surrounded meant little: many men decided to stay and fight to the end. The 5th was a day of blazing heat, and not least of the soldiers' problems was thirst. There was little available in the way of air support, for the AASF was now reduced to scarcely more than a dozen aircraft. On the other side, the Germans, determined that this would be the final battle which would crush all Allied resistance, had mustered 137 divisions, complete with air and artillery components; the Allies had nothing to match it.

The main German thrust eventually came well to the south of Abbeville, in the area between Longpré and Picquing. There was virtually nothing to stop it. By coming through in this area the Germans were able to slip past the southern flanks of the Allied troops deployed along the River Bresle and the River Béthune, both of which run south-east, parallel to the Somme. This was one of those devastating German breakthroughs with which the Allies were already all too familiar. If the Germans moved on swiftly to Rouen and then to Le Havre, 51st Highland Division would find themselves trapped in the Havre peninsula.

Urgent action was clearly required. By some means 51st and the French divisions must be assisted to cut a way through the encircling force before the latter's grip became too tight. In England Gort was informed that he was to command a new BEF, of which the first corps, under Alan Brooke, would be embarking within a week, preceded by a brigade group from 52nd Division which would be leaving immediately. For this counter-move to be successful, 51st and 31st Division should retire from their positions on the River Bresle, where they were already outflanked, and oppose the Germans in the Rouen area before the latter could set off towards Le Havre.

But the plan came to nothing. Weygand, who at the age of seventy-three had no intention of learning his trade from younger men, expressly forbade any retreat from the River Bresle. That position, he said, must be held at all costs. The War Office, no stranger to inflexibility, and realizing that nothing except brutal facts would influence Weygand, promptly abandoned this particular plan for a second BEF. General Fortune, accepting the fact that 51st Division was now going to stay on the Bresle until Weygand changed his mind or the Germans changed it for him, reorganized his battered division, whose losses had now been partly made up by the addition of a brigade from the Beauman Division. The German thrust towards Rouen, though posing a considerable threat, also offered opportunities to the Allies for a fresh attack, and it was therefore decided that one should be mounted from the slender resources of 1st Armoured Division. The tank strength of the division amounted to a total of seventy-eight, of which approximately half were cruisers and the others light tanks, so its chances of being a serious impediment to the Germans seemed to be limited.

However, at that moment Weygand arrived on the scene and had other plans. First Armoured Division was to proceed forthwith to the River Andelle, which lay across the German route to Rouen, and by deploying itself between Serqueux and Nolleval was to block the German columns squarely in a head-on clash. Astonished by Weygand's decision, General Evans pointed out that his division, which now lacked all infantry, anti-tank weapons and artillery, could not have been less suitable for such an action. Even when at full strength, it could not take on such a defensive role with the material at its disposal. But Weygand was adamant. Evans therefore had to send hasty instructions to recall his division, some units of which were already beginning to mount a flank attack on the German Panzers. Having reassembled the division, he set off for the Andelle line where he hoped to link up with French units or any

British troops who might be in the area. Adding to the confusion was the fact that 51st was under the supreme command of the French 9th Corps, Beauman was under General Georges, and 1st Armoured Division was now under the direct command of Weygand. In view of these arrangements, it was not surprising that nobody in the area – except perhaps the Germans – had a clear idea of what they were doing, what support they might expect, and what their next move should be, for better or worse.

In the circumstances it was inevitable that the German thrust would get through, but its success was not achieved easily or immediately. Ill-armed as they were, the defenders put up a fight which both surprised and delayed the Germans. Nevertheless the Panzers entered Rouen on 9 June, which was then empty of Allied troops.

Fifty-first Division were now in a desperate position, as were the other members of the French 9th Corps. They were still up on the Bresle, on the north-west coast, with ten German divisions between them and the other Allied forces in the south. Their best hope was to move along the coast towards Le Havre, hoping that the Germans would not arrive there before they did themselves. Withdrawal from the Bresle position would not be easy, for here, as everywhere else, the roads were blocked by refugees with no clear idea of where they were going, but fortunately the Germans were slow to follow up. At two points on the Bresle crossings the Germans were held up by British infantry companies. These were D Company of the 4th Border Regiment and A Company of the 1st/5th Sherwood Foresters, both of them line of communication troops of whom previously no one had had high expectations. As neither company had been informed that the general withdrawal was in process, they stayed where they were, though somewhat puzzled by the lack of communication from other members of their battalion, regiment, brigade or division. They held their position for six days, steadily throwing back all attempts by the Germans to cross the river at the points they were guarding. The only Germans who did manage to cross were promptly made prisoners. On 13 June, after a concentrated artillery and mortar barrage from the Germans, they learnt to their surprise that the remainder of 51st Division had now been taken prisoner at St Valéry-en-Caux and fighting had ceased altogether in that area.

But on 9 June there was still hope that pockets of 51st Division might reach Le Havre and be evacuated. There were, however, two main reasons why this would probably not occur: one was the distance and intervening obstacles, the other was the fact that Weygand was still ordering 9th Corps, which, of course, included 51st Division, to fall back to the upper Somme region. It did not appear to have entered Weygand's calculations that there were ten Panzer divisions across their route to the latter place.

As it was, it became impossible to reach Le Havre either. There were rivers to be crossed and German attacks to be fended off. And on the western side of St Valéry the Germans had already reached the coast and set up artillery positions on the cliffs. These, and their accompanying troops, would make it impossible for 51st to reach Le Havre, where shipping was now optimistically being assembled for their evacuation. They and various other units from 9th Corps therefore withdrew to St Valéry; by this time they had one day's food ration left.

On 11 June General Fortune received a message from the War Office reminding him that he was still under Weygand's orders and should comply with them strictly. To this, Fortune could only reply that it was absolutely impossible for him to comply with Weygand's orders. Having burnt his boats (metaphorically), he briefed his sub-commanders on the procedure for evacuation, which he hoped would be made possible by the arrival of ships from the Royal Navy. He pointed out that a successful evacuation would require the fullest co-operation by everyone, whatever his rank, that it might involve a walk of some five miles, that men would embark fully armed but that all vehicles would be rendered useless (as silently as possible) before that happened. He explained that the division might be attacked before the embarkation could take place and that any assault by the Germans must be defeated.

But time was not on General Fortune's side. The Germans, spurred and angered by the success of the Dunkirk evacuation, were determined that there would be no repeat performance at St Valéry. They had four divisions, one of which was 7th Panzer, for the attack on St Valéry itself and four more available for the back-up. Already they had guns on the cliffs overlooking the port.

They began shelling the town steadily even as Fortune was making his dispositions for the final evacuation. Second Seaforth, who were deployed on the western side at St Sylvain and Le Tot, came under heavy pressure from the tanks of 7th Panzer. Although the defence plan had assumed that the Seaforths would be supported by artillery and anti-tank guns, these had not reached them, having been delayed on the congested roads; the light infantry weapons carried by the Scots were no match for the German tanks, which broke through and occupied a commanding position on the western cliffs overlooking the harbour. This was an area which Fortune had needed to hold if the evacuation was to be possible, and now he had lost it. Too late, a French infantry regiment and some Royal Artillery arrived on the scene and tried to oust the Germans, who were now tightly established. Small groups of British infantry, some from the Kensingtons, Northumberland Fusiliers and Norfolks, tried to eject the Germans from various houses they were occupying in St Sylvain and Le Tot, but without success: they did, however, push the Germans back from the outskirts of St Valéry. The Seaforths were encircled in St Sylvain and Le Tot, but seven wrecked German tanks bore witness to the fight they had put up.

In the south of St Valéry the 1st Gordons managed to hold off a tank attack; the 7th Norfolks, who were a Pioneer battalion not intended for this sort of mauling warfare, showed enormous courage and tenacity, but were eventually overwhelmed by sheer weight of Panzer metal. On the east of the town the Duke of Wellington's and the Black Watch held out grimly. It was clear that the defending force, however gallant, could not long survive the weight of arms and numbers the Germans were now able to bring against them.

Although evacuation could not begin until the French admiral at Le Havre had given his permission, this was not long delayed. Unfortunately 51st Division's attempts to make contact with the Royal Navy ships, which they knew would be nearing the coast, proved unsuccessful. General Fortune did, however, contact both the C-in-C Portsmouth and the War Office and told them he considered that that night, 11 June, would be the last possible time for evacuation. In spite of the lack of communication with the ships which he hoped were approaching for the evacuation, Fortune was confident that they would arrive and that a large portion of his force would be rescued; the French did not share this view.

Meanwhile as the Germans continued to shell St Valéry, which was now full of burning buildings, the remainder of 51st Highland Division moved down through the dark and the drizzle, to the embarkation points; some units, such as the Seaforths, who were cut off from the harbour by German forces, continued to harass the enemy as vigorously as lay in their power. The Germans, anticipating Fortune to be at the point of surrender, sent in a captured French soldier with a message inviting him to do so. Fortune sent the man back with the message that no such thought had occurred to him.

General Ihler, commanding the remnants of the 31st Infantry Division, thought that further resistance was useless and could only prolong the agony, as the rescue ships would never arrive. He had already prepared a message to be sent to Weygand informing him he had no option but to surrender. Happily he had no means of transmitting it and requested Fortune to do so, as 51st Division still had working radios. Fortune put the telegram in his pocket and said he would think about it; it would not, however, be sent until there was absolutely no alternative to surrender.

The outlook gave no grounds for optimism. The 2nd Seaforths, 1st Gordons and 1st Black Watch were out of the battle, as they were surrounded in the positions they had held on to so doggedly and could not therefore come in for a last-ditch defence of St Valéry while the evacuation was proceeding. All the guns and vehicles which were essential to a successful defence had been destroyed in preparation for the evacuation of the night before, which had so disappointingly failed to materialize. The only infantry at Fortune's disposal were the remains of the 4th Cameronians, 5th Gordons, 4th Seaforths and about eighty Black Watch. Nothing could be expected from the French, for the Germans appeared to have worked through their positions already. However, for St Valéry to be held long enough for the ships to arrive it was essential that the cliffs on the west should be recaptured and the 2nd Seaforths relieved. Undaunted by the fact that their task was closely akin to hopeless, three Scottish battalions set off to eject the Germans who were now firmly established in their position.

Meanwhile General Ihler had made up his mind that, whether Weygand approved or not, surrender would now take place. With this in mind, French troops who had either surrendered, or wished to, marched across the front of the Scottish infantry carrying white flags. This move caused the Scots to hold their fire and the Germans were then able to slip in behind them. Fortune was in a difficult position in every sense of the word. He received a message from Ihler ordering a general ceasefire; it also notified him that the telegram informing Weygand of the fact should be transmitted forthwith. Fortune, knowing he was under French orders, though of equal rank to Ihler, made one last effort. He sent a message to the War Office saying that the French had surrendered and that he himself was under orders to do so, but would not until he was certain there was no possibility of evacuating the remainder of his troops. Then, observing that the French troops had all ceased fire and that white flags were everywhere, he realized that the position was hopeless and added a footnote: 'I have now ceased fire.'

It was not quite the end. Hardly had he sent off the message when he received one from the C-in-C Portsmouth. It ran: 'Regret fog prevented naval forces arriving earlier off St Valéry last night. Senior Naval Officer afloat will make every endeavour to get you off and additional ships are being sent to get you off tonight.'

Fog. If the weather had been on the side of the British at Dunkirk it had certainly turned against them at St Valéry. Looking at the situation philosophically in retrospect, it seems that the fact that fog made the evacuation of 51st Division impossible may well have prevented a bloodbath. On a clear night the ships and the beaches would have been perfectly visible to the German guns positioned along the cliffs, the harbour and beaches were within range of German machine-gun fire, which could not have failed to find many targets, and the Luftwaffe would have made a special effort to avenge its failure at Dunkirk. Even so, General Victor Fortune and the survivors of 51st Highland Division would have much preferred to take a desperate last gamble, rather than sit out the war in prisoner-of-war camps until 1945.

But all was not quite lost on 12 June 1940. Further along the coast at Veules les Roses, midway between St Valéry and Dieppe, ships came in that same night and took off 2137 British and 1184 French troops, as well as 34 seamen. More would perhaps have followed, but the Luftwaffe suddenly became aware of what was happening beneath its nose and sank some of the evacuation boats. Le Havre was another success story, if an evacuation can be counted as such. On 13 June 2222 British troops were evacuated to England, and 8837 were taken to Cherbourg to take part in the counter-offensive which would be launched, it was thought, from Cherbourg, Nantes and St Nazaire.

The battle for France was by no means finished. As the Panzers pressed relentlessly forward, they were pounded steadily by the RAF. The bombing continued all day on the 13th, through that night and then all through the following day. Nor was this the RAF's only contribution. They dropped mines in the Rhine, bombed army assembly points in Germany and attacked every marshalling yard they could reach. If Germany was going to win this battle, the RAF was going to make them fight every inch of the way.

On 12 June, the day of the surrender at St Valéry, General Alan Brooke took command of a second BEF – a forlorn hope if ever there was one. Even at this late stage attempts were made to preserve the appearance of Allied unity, for in Brooke's orders he was told that his force would be under overall French command, even to the extent of having to agree, if only temporarily, to the transfer of any of his own force to areas specifically under French command. Before Brooke set off, he was informed there had been discussions about forming a bridgehead in Brittany, although this plan would not be implemented while the French Army was still resisting. However, when Brooke met Weygand personally on 14 June, the French C-in-C told him that organized resistance by the French armies had already come to an end. Weygand added the surprising information that, although the Germans were already in Paris and the French government had moved to Bordeaux, 'the Allied governments' had taken a decision to organize a 'redoubt' in Brittany. Weygand himself expressed doubts about the feasibility of the proposal, as it would require at least fifteen divisions, and Brooke's reaction may be imagined; at best he might be able to have two at his disposal.

Very sensibly, Brooke acknowledged Weygand's order and enquired of General Dill, the CIGS, what the background was to this absurd decision. Dill informed him that there had been no *decision* by the Supreme War Council, but only a declared intention to study the Breton redoubt project. The fact that Brooke's original brief had given him the authority to withdraw British forces from French command, if the situation warranted it, now provided a dilemma. Weygand was saying that French resistance had come to an end, but one brigade of 52nd (Lowland) Division had already been landed in France as part of Brooke's Expeditionary Force, and was therefore under French command; if the other two brigades in the division followed suit, it could only result in the loss of an entire division.

Brooke now put all the British troops who had been under the command of the French 10th Army under the command of Lieutenant General J. H. Marshall-Cornwall and instructed him to withdraw them to Cherbourg. While withdrawing, they were to continue to assist the French Army whenever and wherever possible. The evacuation of British forces from Cherbourg had been ordered for 15 June.

Meanwhile 157th Brigade, from 52nd Lowland Division, had already seen action, first at Contes and then at Mortagne. They were now under the command of the French general, Altmayer, and on 16 June he ordered them to withdraw to Brittany with the rest of the French 10th Army. The absurdity of this last order, which would put a fifty-mile gap between the 10th and the other French armies, convinced Brooke that his only chance of saving the remaining British troops in France was to get them to Cherbourg as quickly as possible and put them on boats.

His decision was taken in the nick of time. The remainder of Beauman's Division had already left, 157th Brigade departed the same evening, 17 June, the troops from 1st Canadian Division had gone and the last troops of 1st Armoured Division departed after a desperate dash to reach the port; the Germans entered Cherbourg just as the last boats sailed out of the harbour. Brooke left from St Nazaire on an armed trawler, the *Cambridgeshire*, at midnight on 18 June and reached Southampton at 6 p.m. next day. The trawler was part of the escort of a slow convoy. He took the midnight train to London and reported the next morning to the War Office, where they asked why he had not saved more guns and vehicles.

In fact he had saved three hundred guns and, by his perspicacity and promptness, the lives of nearly two hundred thousand men – over half the number rescued from Dunkirk with considerably more resources and publicity. But the War Office is not noted for its sensitivity.

Under the watchful guardianship of the RAF 30,630 men were evacuated from Cherbourg, and another 21,474 from St Malo; 32,584 came out from Brest, after carrying out demolitions. Over sixty thousand were taken from Nantes, where the Luftwaffe succeeded in sinking the *Lancastria* with the loss of three thousand lives.

Other small groups were taken off from Bordeaux, Le Verdon, Bayonne and St Jean de Luz. Officially the evacuation had ended on 25 June by order of the French government, to conform with the terms of the Armistice, but in fact it continued unofficially until 14 August. The sum total evacuated from the area was 191,870: 144,171 were British, 18,246 French, 24,352 Polish, 4938 Czech and 163 Belgian.

20 The Final Moves

THE GERMANS, as might be expected, saw the battle of France in a very different light from the Allied view. Heinz Guderian considered that the campaign would have been completed much earlier if the German High Command had not repeatedly ordered his 19th Corps to stop. He stated that subsequently Hitler had told him that the order for the Panzers to halt outside Dunkirk had been given because the ground in Flanders, with its many ditches and canals, was not suitable for tanks. Guderian noted what Churchill had written in his history of *The Second World War* – that some German generals believed Hitler had stopped the tanks in order to give the British a chance to make a negotiated settlement. Guderian flatly denies this theory, but rather surprisingly says that the decision to stop the tanks was entirely Hitler's, not von Rundstedt's.

After the Dunkirk evacuation Guderian and his Panzers had been ordered south. By the time they had covered the necessary 210 miles, men and machines were showing signs of wear and tear. Both were restored after a few days' rest. Guderian visualized the next stage of the campaign as a dogged battle against seventy Allied divisions. The German Army was ready for this second phase of the battle by 9 June. Guderian then objected to the Group plan, that his Panzers should wait for the infantry to establish crossing points on the Aisne, but was over-ruled: the Panzers were to be reserved for the final thrust, he was told. However, when the infantry had great difficulty in advancing and managed to establish only one bridge-head, Guderian was able to obtain agreement for 1st Panzer to move

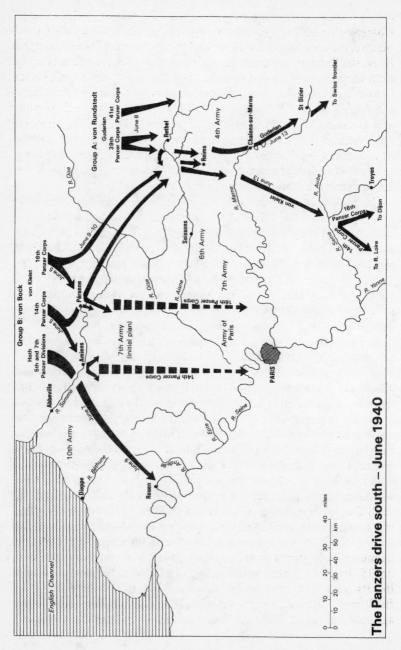

The Panzers drive south – June 1940

into it forthwith, without waiting for it to be extended. This was at Château-Porcien, and soon two other bridgeheads were established nearby, thus opening the way for 2nd Panzer as well. Once across the river, the Panzers' progress through the open countryside was rapid until they reached Juniville; there they had a two-hour tank battle before capturing the town. Guderian recorded that he personally tried to destroy a French Char-B tank with a captured 47-mm, and German 37-mm and 20-mm guns, but all the shells bounced off it harmlessly. In consequence of their inability to knock out the French tanks, the German suffered heavy casualties. In hindsight one can but wonder what would have happened in this campaign if the French tanks had been used properly throughout.

On 11 June, 1st Panzer was attacking La Neuville and found the going hard. Both 1st and 2nd Panzer were now being harassed and counter-attacked by the French. However, the Panzers were still moving forward on 12 June, the day St Valéry fell, and reached Chalons-sur-Marne. Reconnaissance troops from 2nd Panzer captured the bridge at Chalons intact, but were so confident of their own superiority that they failed to examine it for demolition charges: it blew up while German troops were crossing it and caused many casualties.

At this stage the Germans were beginning to create more obstacles to their own progress than the French could provide. The German infantry had force-marched in order to obtain a share of the action and were now hopelessly entangled with the armoured units. Guderian complained about infantry crossing his line of advance, but his voice went unheeded. Every day the Panzers received mutually contradicting orders: they would be told to attack specific targets, then given different ones. Guderian ignored most of the orders from Higher Command and simply kept his forces moving southwards.

On 13 June, 1st Panzer reached the Rhine-Marne Canal at Etrépy and established a bridgehead in spite of an order from the German 39th Corps not to do so. The division reached St Dizier on 14 June, when other Germans forces were entering Paris, and then advanced to Langres. By now the French whom they encountered were utterly exhausted and many prisoners were taken. Langres was captured on 15 June. Guderian was pleased, but also rather worried that the Panzers were now so far ahead of the infantry that their left flank was exposed to a French attack which was rumoured to be approaching from the east. Fortunately for Guderian, the 20th

(Motorized) Infantry Division soon arrived in Langres, giving him some comfort. On 16 June 1st Panzer, still in the lead, captured the Quitteur bridge over the Saône, but its joy was somewhat offset by the fact that their own side's planes came over and bombed a bridge which the Germans were building at Gray-sur-Saône. Guderian tried to contact the Luftwaffe for hours as they systematically destroyed the new bridge, but could not reach them.

On that same 16 June 39th Corps reached Besançon, and 41st Army Corps captured Port-sur-Saône, Vesoul and Bourbonne, taking thousands of prisoners, including some Poles. The following day 29th (Motorized) Infantry Division reached the Swiss frontier at Pontarlier.

But the campaign was not yet finished and the Panzers were still moving forward. Thirty-ninth Corps was now ordered to advance to the north-east and cut off all French forces in Alsace-Lorraine. (This, of course, included Hans Habe's 21st Foreign Volunteers Regiment, which still believed it had a chance of making a successful counter-attack.) The Panzers pressed on via Montbeliard to Belfort, which they reached on 18 June. Here, in spite of the disasters elsewhere, the French were still holding out in the forts and refused to surrender. The German division launched its attack on the forts one by one, using the 88-mm guns which would become renowned and dreaded later in the war.

Although the Germans were well aware that negotiations for an armistice had begun on 16 June, nothing was going to rob them of the opportunity to show how fast and far they could travel and how many prisoners they could take. By this time most of the French forces knew that the war was hopelessly lost and were easily taken prisoner, but there were still isolated detachments which were determined to fight to the end. Unfortunately, as Habe and his friends discovered, one small group of men can make little impact on an army which possesses superior firepower and has already surrounded them. For the Panzers the campaign had now become a tactical exercise, more like military manoeuvres than war.

On 19 June, 12th Army and 7th Army linked up north of Belfort. First and 2nd Panzer still maintained their position in the lead as the Germans advanced through the Vosges mountains, but here again there were acrimonious bickerings with the infantry, which wanted to share the credit of capturing well-known places. Guderian had no sympathy with the aspirations of the infantry and halted their formations on the grounds that they were cluttering up the roads and impeding the Panzers. In order to forestall the infantry from having their point of view supported, he sent an emissary to Army Group HQ stating his reasons for checking them. The infantry commanders realized they had been outwitted and could do nothing about it, but did not forget and waited their turn for revenge. There was nothing new in this situation: throughout the centuries various branches of any army have resented others obtaining the spoils and the credit, and have quietly rejoiced when some of their own comrades in rival formations have been cut up by the enemy.

On 20 June the Germans captured Cornimont, and the next day Bussang in the Vosges. There were now embittered arguments between the generals over whose units had captured the largest number of prisoners. Guderian's Panzers were allotted the largest share, a figure of 150,000. On 22 June it was announced that the French government had agreed to the terms which Hitler had dictated. This did not end the quarrelling over who had taken the most prisoners, but it did stop the Panzers from rushing hither and thither across the now defenceless countryside.

Guderian was not entirely happy with the Armistice terms when he heard them. He thought that the Germans should have occupied the whole of France, captured Malta by a parachute attack and immediately sent up to six Panzer divisions to North Africa. He was not confident that the Germans had the ability to invade and conquer England, but felt that if enough pressure was put on British possessions overseas Churchill would have to agree to a peace settlement.

According to Guderian, Hitler was so pleased with the success of the Panzers that he ordered their numbers to be doubled. In practice, this was mere juggling with figures; it did not produce an effective increase in strength, as the extra numbers were only achieved by halving the tank strength in each division.

Worse was to follow. During the winter of 1940, Guderian learnt that Hitler was contemplating an attack on Russia. This seemed the utmost folly, and Guderian expressed his views vehemently. His protests and arguments, mainly based on history, had no effect: the victories in France had filled his fellow generals with so much elation that 'they had eliminated the word impossible from their vocabulary'. A totally false impression of the invincibility of the Panzers had been given by the fall of France; easy victory had sown

227

the seeds of ultimate defeat. The French, who have an aptitude for expressing in words such psychological misjudgements, would, no doubt, have described it as *la folie de grandeur*.

Major General F. W. von Mellenthin, who subsequently wrote a book entitled *Panzer Battles*, pointed out in it that, although the Dunkirk evacuation had been a triumph for the Allies, it also represented a crushing defeat. The French Army had lost most of its motorized formations in Belgium, and the BEF had left behind all its guns, transport and tanks at Dunkirk. After these losses of material, there was little that British soldiers could do to help the French in the south, even if they did manage to make up a second BEF. Von Mellenthin's view was, of course, borne out by the failure of Alan Brooke's second BEF to achieve anything of real value. Von Mellenthin considered that the French inability to organize an effective defence in the southern sector was largely due to the bombing by the Luftwaffe, which prevented troops assembling at the points where they would be most valuable. Rather surprisingly, von Mellenthin felt that the Allied attacks on the bridgeheads over the Somme, notably at Abbeville, had been a mistake, for they had caused heavy losses among the Allied forces. But the losses were not very great; it was hardly to be expected that the Allies would allow the Germans to establish and keep bridgeheads over the Somme if that could be prevented; the Somme formed an excellent natural obstacle and the Allies were certain to try to use it. It was unfortunate that the Germans arrived there before they were expected. Von Mellenthin considered that the Allied defeat at St Valéry was due to the initiative and quick thinking of Rommel, who executed one of his later-to-be-famous hook movements and cut off 51st Division before the latter could reach Le Havre.

Further south, at Amiens and Péronne, the Germans under von Kleist had considerable difficulty in establishing bridgeheads, and sustained heavy losses. This reverse for von Kleist must have given great pleasure to Guderian, who would not have forgotten how von Kleist had earlier rebuked him for pressing on so fast. It has been said, unkindly and perhaps untruthfully, that Germany is the only nation in the world which has a word, *Schadenfreude*, to express pleasure at other people's misfortune. Guderian, no doubt, permitted himself a little *Schadenfreude* when he heard that the French counter-attack on von Kleist's troops had brought them to a halt and caused heavy losses. Guderian, of course, took many risks by trying to forge ahead well in advance of his supporting infantry. His armoured cavalry was able to sweep through open country, but left forest, woods, river crossings and other dangerous tasks to the infantry, hoping it would be available when needed.

The fall of Paris had no strategic effect on the campaign, though no doubt its influence on the morale of both sides was considerable. There was no army in Paris to threaten the flanks of the advancing Panzers, and the Germans had no objection to the French government declaring it an open city.

Von Mellenthin tended to be sympathetic to the infantry viewpoint because he was Chief of Staff in an infantry division during the campaign. It was his division, the 197th, which breached the Maginot Line. The fact that the French surrendered the position within a few hours is perhaps not surprising, because it was then 14 June and their morale had never been strong; what is remarkable is that, according to von Mellenthin, many of its strongpoints were much weaker than expected and crumbled under shells and bombs. The attack had gone in under cover of heavy artillery and aerial bombardment, which had included smoke shells to make the approach of the attackers almost invisible. Under cover of smoke, the German infantry was able to slip past the forts and use grenades and flame-throwers to attack from the rear. Von Mellenthin took a good look at the Maginot defences subsequently, and considered them poor, with badly sited guns and limited effectiveness. They compared unfavourably with the Siegfried Line, protecting the Rhine, and the Todt fortifications in the 'West Wall' along the French Atlantic coast. Von Mellenthin's view of the ineffectiveness of the Maginot Line has subsequently been challenged by military historians, who stress that the breakthrough took place in one part of the line only, and when France was on the brink of general defeat.

Nevertheless, however poor the morale of the defenders of the Maginot Line, there was nothing wrong with that of most of the other French units. Although, on occasion, the German infantry marched thirty-five miles a day when following up the Panzers through open country, they found the Vosges mountains a very different proposition when they reached them. The French had blocked the roads with trees, of which there was a plentiful supply, and had sited their machine-guns and snipers very effectively. On 22 June, 197th were doggedly fighting their way towards the summit of Donon, after having by-passed another German infantry division which had been stopped entirely. The ceasefire did not actually take effect until the morning of 23 June. The commander of the French 43rd Corps, which was opposing them with such tenacity, was General Lescanne, a man of sixty. 'The old man', remarked von Mellenthin, 'was clearly at the end of his tether, but he was polite – the terms of the surrender were quietly discussed as between officers and gentlemen. Lescanne and his officers were accorded full military honours.'

By the end of the war Germany would be using veterans who were older than sixty and unfit as well; they would also have mere boys in some of their youth battalions. But those days were years ahead and would have been inconceivable to von Mellenthin in 1940.

After the events of 1940 had faded from people's minds, obscured by the dramatic happenings which followed elsewhere, there grew up a belief that after Dunkirk the rest of the resistance to the Germans had collapsed entirely. But this was not so, astonishing though that fact may be in the light of the ineptitude of the French High Command. Something which certainly deserves recording was the spirited defence put up by the staff and cadets of the French military academy at Saumur. Saumur is a cavalry academy, but they fought as infantry and held up the Germans for three days; they did not cease fighting until their ammunition had run out.

Von Mellenthin considered that the campaign in France was a military masterpiece, superbly commanded and executed from the highest level to the lowest. In contrast, the Allied defence was unimaginative and rigid. Above all, the campaign highlighted the importance of surprise, mobility and leading from the front. He might have added that the German success was also due to a policy of ruthlessness, attacking neutral countries such as Belgium and Holland without warning, bombing and machine-gunning helpless refugees and using the terror tactics known as *Schrecklichkeit* which had earlier been demonstrated so effectively in Poland.

Part III

The
Results

21 Hindsight

NOT SURPRISINGLY, military historians began to discuss and analyse the battle of France almost as soon as it was over, and have continued to do so for the past fifty years. Jeffery A. Gunsburg, an American military historian whose researches among the papers of the combatant nations enabled him to analyse the campaign in his book *Divided and Conquered*, considered that the fall of France was the result of an *Allied* collapse and not, as is widely thought, a French collapse. If the British, French, Belgians and Dutch had used their resources properly, he argued, the Germans, even with an undeclared, surprise attack, would not have won. The British counter-attack at Arras showed how vulnerable the Germans were, morally and politically as well as militarily; but the moral initiative the Allies gained then was lost when Billotte was fatally injured. His death removed the last hope of a truly unified command. Gunsburg noted that the Dutch fought better than had been expected, and that Hitler commented on the fact in a letter to Mussolini on 25 May. Overall, Gunsburg commented, the higher direction of both the Belgian and the Dutch armies was poor, and faulty disposition often meant that second-grade and reserve Allied troops were set against the highest grade of German troops. The Dutch lost 3000 men in the short period during which they were fighting, and the Belgians, whose army was twice the size of the BEF, lost 7500. The French had 120,000 killed and 230,000 wounded. The British had 3500 killed in the Army and 1500 in the RAF. The Germans gave their losses as 27,000 killed, 111,000 wounded and 18,500 missing; presumably most of the 'missing' were killed, for the Allies cannot have retained many German prisoners. Most of the German losses were in the armoured units. The Luftwaffe losses were slightly higher than those of the RAF, the French air force slightly less.

Gunsburg considered the essential cause of France's defeat to be that Germany had double the population and three times the industry of France. However, this hardly explains the ineptitude shown by the French Higher Command – an ineptitude which astonished the Germans. This is not to say that the higher direction of the war would have been better if it had been in the hands of the British. There *were* far-sighted British generals at that time, such as Wavell, but they were some way removed from the corridors of power and not attracted by them.

But whatever one feels about the discrepancy in population and industry, the fact remains that in any military situation the attacker should have a numerical superiority of at least three to one if he is to have a reasonable chance of success. This is a time-honoured military formula which, although subject to occasional exceptions, has been created from experience. The Germans did not have superiority in manpower and they had an inferior number of tanks; what they did have was high morale and clear-cut plans – they knew what they wanted to do. In contrast the Allies, contemplating the evil, aggressive intentions of Hitler, hoped that, like a bad smell, he would fade away. When this showed no sign of happening, attempts were made to 'appease' him. When appeasement failed, it was hoped that passive, inert defence would cause his downfall, mainly because the German people, tired of the ranting demagogue's unfulfilled promises, would depose him and Europe would live happily ever after.

Having consulted numerous analyses of the campaign, Gunsburg concluded that 'the defeat of the West in 1940 can be largely explained in strategic and military terms with little recourse to ideology'. He stressed that one of its most dangerous effects was to convince many Germans, who up to that point distrusted both Nazism and Hitler himself, that Hitler was virtually infallible, and that his leadership would make Germany a great, invincible and stable nation. Three years later they were beginning to realize their mistake.

Colonel A. Goutard, French veteran and military historian, felt that many factors combined to cause the Allied defeat in 1940.

Among them he listed the political mistakes of the 1930s; the failure by the Allies to take the war to Germany while the German forces were already occupied in Poland; the ineptitude shown by the French in the Sedan area, not cutting through the Panzer columns when those had advanced ahead of their infantry; and, finally, the ultimate failure to retreat to North Africa and carry on the battle from there. 'Our defeat', he said, 'was due more to our conservatism of outlook and our unrealistic and preconceived ideas than to any military weakness inherent in our nation. It is when strategy parts company with common sense that we can expect disasters like Sedan and even Dien Bien Phu.'

Goutard recalled that there was much that France could remember with pride, even in defeat. He believed that the battle was not lost even after Dunkirk, although the collapse of Belgium and the evacuation of the BEF had placed a virtually insupportable burden on France. He reminded those who seemed to have forgotten that the French Army had suffered a similar defeat in the opening stages of the First World War, but recovered 'and in the next four years earned the admiration of the world. . . . We lost one and a half million men in the face of the enemy: a sacrifice three times as great as that of our British allies and twenty times that of our American allies.'

Although France had accepted Hitler's terms on 22 June, hostilities did not end in France until 25 June. Even at that late stage, French units were holding out doggedly in the south. The Germans were repulsed as they tried to cross the Isère at Voreppe, so tried a different approach via Les Echelles. Here the village was defended by two infantry companies, one from the 25th Sénégalles, the other from the 215th Infantry. These, a total of some two hundred, held out all day against vastly superior numbers but, when completely surrounded, had to surrender. The Germans were so impressed that they allowed them to fall back bearing arms. Other units showed comparable courage.

A day-by-day chronological account of the campaign was given by J. Benoist-Méchin in a book entitled *Sixty Days that Shook the West*. Although others might think the critical period lasted much less than sixty days, Benoist-Méchin considered that 11 July, when Pétain formed the Vichy government and broadcast to the French people, was an integral part of the fall of France. Pétain's broadcast promised a form of Utopia. His Cabinet included many of those who had voted against accepting Churchill's offer of an unconditional union with Britain, so the hostility to France's former allies was clearly foreshadowed.

Benoist-Méchin agreed with many others that Hitler had made a fatal mistake in halting the German armour outside Dunkirk, but felt that he had made an equally serious error in not permitting the German armoured divisions to continue their progress from southern France to North Africa and thence to Casablanca and Alexandria. Hitler's third, and perhaps greatest, failure of judgement was not to invade Britain immediately, whatever the cost.

What may be accepted as the official German view of the campaign in France was provided by Dr Hans-Adolf Jacobsen and Dr Jürgen Rohwehr in a book entitled *Decisive Battles of World War II: The German View*. Each section was by a different author, and Dr Jacobsen himself set out the received opinion on the French campaign. At the end of the Second World War, he himself was training to be an officer at the German Cadet Academy, but was taken prisoner by the Russians, who held him for four years. After release he studied at various German universities and worked with the Bundeswehr. He became Director of the Research Institute of the German Association for Foreign Policy at Bonn in 1960.

Jacobsen wrote that the 'irrevocable decision' to attack France and the Low Countries was communicated to the German generals on 23 November 1939. On that occasion Hitler announced that Russia 'need not be rated very highly as a military factor'. She was bound to Germany by a treaty – though, of course, they must remember that such agreements were kept for just so long as they remained useful and no longer. Britain was a dangerous opponent and must be 'forced to her knees by bomb and mine', but this could only be done by obtaining good bases in Holland and Belgium.

In fact the generals were already aware of Hitler's intentions, as he had announced them in mid-October (as Jacobsen pointed out), but they had little enthusiasm for them. Hitler had originally chosen 5 November as the date to launch an attack on the West, and had ignored Brauchitsch's advice to postpone it; however, bad weather had then showed it to be quite impossible. Brauchitsch, who was reprimanded by Hitler for opposing his strategic views, offered to resign his post as Commander-in-Chief of the Army, but was not allowed to do so. During the winter of 1939–40 the invasion of Belgium, Holland and France was arranged *twenty-nine* times but on each occasion was postponed, for a variety of reasons. Some of these plans included the invasion of Britain. Even as early as 25 October, Hitler had suggested that the Sedan area should receive the main German attack, but then had himself had doubts about it. In consequence, the plan to attack through Belgium and Holland remained in being until it was learnt that the Allies had obtained the German plans from the aircraft which had been brought down in Belgium in January 1940.

Jacobsen stressed that Gamelin and his staff should not have been surprised when the German Army crossed the Meuse because 'British military writers (for example, Captain Liddell-Hart) had already drawn attention to the possibility of a German attack through the Ardennes'.

For the attack on 10 May the German Army had mobilized within twenty-four hours, thus catching the Allies completely unaware. The Holland campaign was over in five days, although the Germans thought the Dutch had fought well. The bombing of Rotterdam was 'a tragic misfortune', caused by poor communication.

Despite the fact that the Allied military leaders were slow to recognize the threat represented by the German breakthrough at Sedan, von Rundstedt was constantly afraid that the Panzers would be cut off and encircled (as they should have been). When the Germans were closing in on Dunkirk, von Rundstedt and, soon, Hitler became very concerned about the possible danger to their southern flank. A major mistake in the north, they felt, could easily lose them the entire campaign. Hitler 'raved and bellowed' about the danger of ultimate defeat. The British counter-attack at Arras reinforced German doubts about ultimate victory: in view of Hitler's fears about the southern threat, halting the tanks appears to have been a sensible precautionary measure.

Goering's confidence in the ability of the Luftwaffe to destroy the Dunkirk evacuation had considerable influence on Hitler, who did not recognize it as a wish for self-aggrandizement rather than a sensible tactical plan. The Luftwaffe was much more closely linked to the Nazis than the Army was, but Hitler thought that if the Luftwaffe now won the campaign in the north, and the Army merely occupied the territory, this would be a salutary lesson for the latter. The Luftwaffe failed, and would fail again in the Battle of Britain, but this did not seem to affect the confidence of either Hitler or Goering in its war-winning potential.

They would subdue Russia first, then return and finish Britain later.

Jacobsen felt the worst aspect of the campaign in France to be that it convinced Hitler that he could over-ride his most senior commanders and dictate to them the strategy and tactics of success. His decisions, rash though they were, proved correct in France because of the ineptitude of the Allies who opposed him – but that fact proved disastrous for Germany. It confirmed his belief in his own invincibility and strengthened his ability to undermine the authority of those in the highest positions in his own armed forces. Although Jacobsen did not say so, the German catastrophe at Stalingrad in 1942–3 was almost entirely of Hitler's making, for he insisted on over-ruling the experienced commanders on the spot.

The hindsight German view of the results of their swift and comparatively easy victory in France therefore seems much the same as that of the British and French.

At the time of the fiftieth anniversary of the battle there is a fresh wave of speculations over the reason for halting the tanks on the Aa Canal on 24 May 1940. Among them are suggestions that Hitler, having conquered northern France, wished to make a friend and ally out of Britain who would then allow him a free hand in the rest of Europe. This, of course, would enable him to attack Russia without further harassment from the British Commonwealth, which contained formidable forces in Australia, Canada, New Zealand, South Africa and various colonies. British power in the Far East would act as a check on the Japanese until he himself was ready to take an active part in that theatre of operations. Hitler is said to have been encouraged by the allegedly pro-Nazi views of the Duke of Windsor, who might be replaced on his former throne at the head of a government staffed with appeasers such as Lord Halifax, Horace Wilson, R. A. Butler and Lord Beaverbrook. There were, of course, a number of German sympathizers in Britain, and they included Fascists such as Sir Oswald Mosley. Beaverbrook, while maintaining his friendship with Churchill, had established contact with Berlin, and was quite ready to betray his friend (for Churchill's own good, of course). Halifax had clearly lost confidence in Britain's ability to win the war, and was also maintaining his contacts with Berlin; this was simplicity itself when he went to Washington as Ambassador while America was still neutral.

However, examination of the relevant sources indicates that the order to halt the tanks was a purely military one and was taken with a view to subsequently annihilating the BEF, not saving it. It is notable that there was no corresponding order to save 51st Highland Division from extinction. Nevertheless the idea that Britain might be persuaded to accept peace terms seems to have been present in Germany long after the battle of France and may have influenced Hess to fly to Scotland on his abortive peace mission the following year.

The diaries of General Halder, Chief of the German Army General Staff in 1940, throw considerable light on this subject. These diaries were mostly in the form of notes, and contained some shorthand. Unknown to Hitler, Halder was anti-Nazi, and since 1937 had been actively opposing his Führer. In 1938 he had sent a secret emissary to Britain to warn the British government of Hitler's aggressive intentions. This had not, however, interfered with his own military task of planning the invasions of Czechoslovakia, Poland and France. However in 1942 Hitler deprived Halder of his military post and after the bungled assassination plot of 1944 had him imprisoned in Dachau on suspicion of complicity with the plotters. At the end of the war Halder appeared as a witness at the Nuremberg trials and was so helpful to the Allies that he was awarded the Meritorious Civilian Award – the highest civilian award which could be given by the US forces in Europe.

In his diary entry for 18 May 1940, Halder wrote:

The Führer unaccountably keeps worrying about the south flank. He rages and screams that we are on the best way to ruin the whole campaign and that we are leading up to a defeat. He won't have any part of continuing the operation in a westward direction, let alone to the south-west, and still clings to the plan of a north western drive.

This is the subject of a most unpleasant discussion at Führer HQ between the Führer on one side and Obdh [Commander-in-Chief] Colonel General von Brauchitsch and myself on the other.

On 24 May Halder wrote:

For the first time now, enemy air superiority has been reported by Kleist.

2000 Obdh returns from OKW [Supreme Command, in other words Hitler]:

Apparently a very unpleasant interview with the Führer. At 2020 a new order is issued cancelling yesterday's order and

239

directing encirclement to be effected in areas Dunkirk- Estaires-Lille-Roubaix-Ostend. The left wing, consisting of Armour and Motorized forces which has no enemy before it, will so be stopped dead in its tracks upon direct orders from the Führer. Finishing off the encircled army is to be left to the Air Force.

The following day he noted:

Battle plan ruined. Now political command [civilian, not military] has formed the fixed idea that the battle of decision must be fought not on Flemish soil but rather in northern France. To camouflage this political move the assertion is made that Flanders, criss-crossed by a multitude of waterways, is unsuited for tank warfare. Accordingly all tank and motor transport will have to be brought up short on reaching the line St Omer-Béthune.

He added: 'The Air Force, on which all hopes are pinned, is dependent on the weather.' He noted that Hitler was 'agitated', but that at 1330 on 26 May Hitler agreed the armour could move again.

Earlier in the diaries Halder had noted that the 'life' of a Panzer III tank was 1500–1800 kilometres. As they would have exceeded that already, it seemed good military sense to halt them and begin maintenance before throwing them into what promised to be a stern battle. However, he did not advance that point to excuse Hitler's order.

General Günther von Blumentritt, von Rundstedt's Infantry Chief of Staff, wrote a biography of von Rundstedt which was published in 1952. In it he staged categorically: 'The order was first of all issued to von Rundstedt on Hitler's instructions by the HQ Staff of the Army over the telephone, and later confirmed by telegram. Protests were useless. Hitler insisted. Panzer patrols were, however, allowed to go forward.' This version may, of course, be a means of disguising von Rundstedt's ineptitude by blaming the dead Hitler. But Hitler was prone to interfere at all times.

General (then Captain) Walter Warlimont, who was on Hitler's staff, believed that the order was yet another example of Hitler interfering and over-ruling field commanders. Field Marshal Keitel, who was present at the vital conference from which the order emanated, recalled that the risk from the southern flank was discussed and the generals left the decision to Hitler. Nevertheless, it seems more than probable that the version of events given earlier in the book is correct and that von Rundstedt's anxiety about the mechanical condition of his tanks and the weariness of the crews fitted in neatly with Hitler's apprehension about a massive French attack being launched on his southern flank.

There was, of course, never any possibility of that happening. Even before the order to halt the Panzers had been given General Billotte, soon to be involved in a fatal accident, had written of his total exhaustion and impotence against the enemy: '*Je suis crevé de fatigue, crevé de fatigue, et contre ces Panzers je ne peux rien faire.*'

22 The Invasion Which Might Have Been

As IS WIDELY KNOWN, the invasion and fall of France was quickly followed by apprehensions that a similar fate would befall Britain. It is generally thought that this threat did not begin until July 1940 and was removed by the Battle of Britain on 15 September of that year. In fact the danger was not entirely over until mid-October 1940, and even after that date an invasion was still regarded as a possibility. Furthermore, the aerial battle of 15 September was not the only one, nor the most critical. In earlier battles the RAF had inflicted great damage on the Luftwaffe, and the September battles were the last rounds, not the only ones. Unknown to the general public in Britain, there had been moments of great danger in what people were refusing to regard as a serious war, a '*drôle de guerre*' as the French called it, a 'phoney war', as it seemed to journalists with a knack of turning a neat, though not necessarily accurate, phrase.

An invasion of Britain had been contemplated as early as 31 October 1939, but ruled out as being too risky at that time. In the Norway campaign of April–May 1940 the Germans had captured enough British documents to know not merely the dispositions and quality of all British forces in the West but details of existing defences, road and harbour capacities, and nodal points in Britain as well as in France. In consequence on 10 May, even when the attack on Holland, Belgium and France was beginning, the Chiefs of Staff in Britain were already issuing directions for action against a possible German invasion. They had good reason. MI6 (secret service) and diplomatic sources all said that an invasion could begin at any moment. The fact that the Norwegian campaign had been launched and virtually completed without needing to take a single German soldier from his post in the army marked for the invasion of France gave support to this view. From his ringside seat on the German frontier Prince Bernhard of the Netherlands was aware that the Germans could launch an airborne invasion of Britain even while they were still conquering France, and warned the British government. MI6 reported that invasion barges were being made ready in German ports. The Hungarian Prime Minister was firmly convinced that German plans for invading Britain were well advanced, and told the Japanese Ambassador of his belief in a message that Britain intercepted.

The secrecy with which the Norwegian invasion had been carried out was particularly alarming. After it, the Chiefs of Staff estimated that if the Germans launched a raid with two hundred fast motor-boats, each carrying a hundred men, they could establish a foothold anywhere between Durham and Dover and then land a larger force into the area the raiders had captured. It was thought that this invasion would take place on a lonely shore and not be detected until it was well established.

In the circumstances there were doubts about sending further forces to France in May, as this would leave Britain denuded of troops and open to invasion herself. Germany was considered to have enough shipping for such an invasion, and there was a fear that she might have a substantial force of fifth columnists already planted in Britain, ready to move to key areas.

Although it was known that Germany had the idea of invasion in mind, British intelligence had no information about when or where it might take place. It was thought that raiders could set off from as far away as Norway, the Baltic or even the Gironde in western France, and land almost anywhere. Photographic reconnaissance was used to try to observe possible concentrations of shipping, but the Chiefs of Staff emphasized that negative reports did not mean that nothing was there: photographic reconnaissance had failed to warn of the Norwegian invasion. Bad weather made aerial or sea sightings improbable. When German U boats were withdrawn from patrol in July, that too was considered extremely ominous.

In late June, aerial reconnaissance reported that runways on French airfields were being extended, guns set up along the French coast where they might cover an invasion, and dive-bombers were now concentrated on the newly captured airfields. Dive-bombers were essentially aircraft for offensive operations.

Instead of dismissing the danger of seaborne invasion, the Royal Navy confirmed it. The Admiralty believed that a hundred thousand men could be put ashore in small craft, landing at widely dispersed points.

It was subsequently claimed that Hitler had doubts about destroying Britain and the British Empire, because he thought this might provoke even greater dangers from America, Russia and Japan. However, on 25 June the Wehrmacht operations staff sent a message to the Luftwaffe Chief of Staff, General Hans Jeschonnek, asking him for his comments on the Wehrmacht's invasion plans, which were shortly going to Hitler for his approval. Jeschonnek was at first unenthusiastic, but then had to give his support. It is noteworthy that the Luftwaffe then tried to destroy civilian morale, rather than ports and installations which would be useful to an invader. The Luftwaffe was also told that all fighter aircraft should be destroyed as quickly as possible, and that the best way to draw them into unequal combat would be to attack London. At that stage the Luftwaffe did not know that Britain had an efficient radar network. Had they known this they would have realized that the reason their bombers were always intercepted was British radar efficiency, not superior numbers of Spitfires and Hurricanes. As July moved on to August and Luftwaffe losses were high, Hitler, speaking through the German Higher Command, emphasized that air superiority must be gained prior to an invasion and that the Royal Air Force must be the prime target of all bombing.

On 16 July Hitler had issued what became known as Directive 16. It ordered a surprise invasion of Britain in the area between Ramsgate and the Isle of Wight, although both Cornwall and the Isle of Wight might also be occupied as preliminaries. Dive-bombers were to act as artillery and minefields must be cleared, but an invasion route off Dover must then be protected by mines laid by the Germans. Another sea lane was to be created between Alderney and Portland. There were many other provisos.

It was a comprehensive directive and the operation was to be called Seelöwe (Sealion). Fortunately it was never tried because the air superiority which Hitler had presented as a necessary preliminary was not achieved.

23 After the Fall

IN THE COURSE of this book reference has occasionally been made to the long-term effects of the events described. Although the fact that armed conflicts follow each other at regular intervals has made people declare that war never settles anything, that statement is manifestly untrue. Never was it more so than in the battle of France.

The decisive German victory of 1940 which led to a divided France and a German occupation lasting four years had irreversible outcomes which went beyond the immediate battlefield. Its first effect was to bring the war to Britain and to subject that country to a period of air warfare far worse than anything experienced by France. German bombers based on French airfields were able to pick their targets at will, and although Fighter Command made a magnificent effort in defence, it was inevitable that a certain number of bombers would get through. When they did, they devastated London, killing thousands, ruining vast numbers of homes and other buildings, and destroying much of the city's ancient heritage. Outside London many other towns and cities were mutilated in what became known as the Baedeker raids. Named after the nineteenth-century German publisher of guide books, they were aimed at places of great beauty or historical importance.

The first target to be attacked by German bombers was Coventry, an industrial city which happened to have a medieval cathedral. The destruction of Coventry in 1940 became such an emotional matter — largely because of newspaper pictures of the ruined cathedral — that the retaliatory raids later in the war were more ruthless than they would otherwise have been. Any remaining compunction about destroying Aachen and Dresden was banished by the words 'military necessity'.

Italy would probably have avoided the war altogether if the events of 1940 had taken a different course. Mussolini looked long and hard before he decided that Hitler was so clearly the victor that he too must declare war on stricken France. Later, Italy would suffer bombardment, occupation by the armies of both sides, and economic hardship.

The success of the German armies in France, which was followed by the failure to browbeat Britain into surrender, made Hitler determined to extend his conquests elsewhere and convinced that he could do so. His long-term plan was subdue Russia, but before attempting that vast task he decided he must eliminate any Allied threat which might come up from the Balkans. This, which Churchill described as 'the soft underbelly of Europe', meant Greece, Yugoslavia, Crete and other eastern Mediterranean islands. If his armies had been checked and held in France, Hitler would never have ventured on such a dangerous diversion. One of its most far-reaching effects was the setting up of Russian-backed partisan resistance, leading to the creation of post-war communist states in the Balkans.

If Germany had not attacked Russia with every prospect of beating her, the Japanese would have had doubts about becoming involved at that time. However, the combination of the French being eliminated and the British hard pressed in the Middle East presented an opportunity that might never occur again. The French fleet, which could have helped the Allies protect their colonies in the Far East, had been immobilized or sunk to keep it out of Axis hands. (Its absence from the Mediterranean had already allowed Mussolini's warships to move more freely than they would otherwise have dared to do.)

As a French colony, Vietnam was particularly influenced by what had happened to France. Falling under the influence of the Japanese in 1941, it provided bases from which the Japanese Air Force was able to bomb Malaya and sink the capital ships *Repulse* and *Prince of Wales* in December of that year. After 1945, when the French wished to resume control in what was then known as French Indo-China, they found that their defeat in 1940 had destroyed their credibility as a strong colonial power. They were now opposed by a communist guerrilla leader named Ho Chi Minh who, like Tito in Yugoslavia against the Germans, had been an active member of the resistance to the Japanese. Ho Chi Minh had become a communist some twenty years earlier in Paris, which he had visited when a cook on a French liner.

French efforts to re-establish themselves received little sympathy or support within France itself or from other European countries. After being decisively defeated by the rebels in 1954, at Dien Bien Phu, France gave up the struggle; the country was divided between a communist-dominated north and a US-supported democratic south. However, determined efforts by the communists to infiltrate and disrupt the south led to US intervention and the destructive war of 1965–73.

The rush to post-war independence of the former colonial possessions of the defeated European countries in 1940 – France, Belgium and Holland – led to many other political problems, civil wars and acts of violence. Elsewhere in Indo-China Cambodia had been a French protectorate since 1863, and in 1953 was granted full independence. Five years later the country became a battleground from which the communist Khmer Rouge, led by Pol Pot, emerged victorious and proceeded to massacre all of its former opponents, and many innocents, who had not managed to flee abroad. In 1978 Vietnam invaded and occupied it; however, the Vietnamese have now withdrawn, and the future of Cambodia looks uncertain. In the former Belgian colony of Rwanda, too, genocidal inter-tribal massacres have taken place on a scale of which the West prefers to remain unaware. It is arguable that the European protectors' inability to protect *themselves* in 1940 promptly robbed them of any authority and prestige they might have been able to exert in guiding their former colonies to a more stable and settled existence than they have subsequently known.

The defeat of France brought American troops by their thousands into Europe, providing many mutual benefits. After the war American money was invested in Europe, some of it as a gift, some as a loan, and in the process the USA rebuilt shattered economies. American investment also created modern Japan and eventually made her possibly the most prosperous country in the world – a development which the USA did not foresee and has not welcomed.

But the past cannot be altered: all we can do is to try to learn from it and not to repeat our mistaken. The greatest sufferers from the fall of France were the victors, for it caused them to embark on grandiose plans which led to their own eventual destruction. The devastating swiftness of the French campaign convinced Hitler that he was omnipotent and omniscient, and encouraged him to make his greatest mistake – the invasion of Russia. This and the conquest of eastern Europe *en route* enabled the Nazis to carry out their horrific programme of genocide, directed mostly against the Jews. Many of those who survived the holocaust subsequently went to the Middle East, where they helped build the new state of Israel. Modern Israel therefore also owes its existence partly to the fall of France.

Hitler's greatest mistake was also the one effect of the fall of France that was to have the greatest political significance in the post-war world. The USSR is said to have lost 50 million people in the Second World War; at the end of the war, however, it had under communist control half of Germany and all of Poland, Czechoslovakia, Albania, Yugoslavia, Bulgaria and Romania.

But that is not quite the end of the story. An even more awesome thought is what would have happened if France had *not* fallen in 1940. If by some failure of nerve on the part of Hitler or through a miraculous recovery by the Allies the war had settled into a stubborn, static affair, as had happened in 1914, a long, exhausting struggle could have ensued. Once more the German armies would have been tied down in France and, urged on by an increasingly desperate Hitler, would have battered away in a war of attrition. While this was happening, Russia, secure from attack by Hitler, but regarding the Nazi-Soviet pact with much the same cynicism as he did, would have waited patiently for the moment to strike.

That time might have come when the Allies and the Germans were both so exhausted that even in combination they would have been powerless to stop the Red Army's drive across Europe. The likely result would have confirmed the beliefs of the early twentieth-century 'geopoliticians' Halford Mackinder and Karl Haushofer, who invented respectively the concepts of the 'heartland' and the 'world island'. The controller of the heartland, in their view, would become the controller of the world. From the combined Russia-Europe, expansion into the Mediterranean and Africa would have been a simple matter. Then, with its vast conglomeration of power, it could easily have overwhelmed Japan, perhaps using man-power conscripted from Germany, France, Britain and many other countries. By this time the USA would be frantically arming and training her citizens, but would probably not have had the atomic bomb, which, when it was developed, had depended heavily on the European contribution.

Perhaps, by collapsing in 1940, France saved the world from an Orwellian nightmare future. Civilization may owe France a debt it can never hope to repay. By the same logic, the same debt is owed to Hitler himself, for the invasion!

Appendix: Forces Involved in the Battle of France

British Expeditionary Force

Commander-in-Chief

General The Viscount Gort

Chief of the General Staff	Lieutenant General H. R. Pownall
Adjutant General	Lieutenant General Sir W. D. S. Brownrigg
Quarter-Master General	Lieutenant General W. G. Lindsell

GHQ Troops

Royal Armoured Corps
1st Light Armoured Reconnaissance Brigade – Brigadier C. W. Norman
    1st Fife and Forfar Yeomanry
    1st East Riding Yeomanry

2nd Light Armoured Reconnaissance Brigade – Brigadier A. J. Clifton
    5th Royal Inniskilling Dragoon Guards
    15th/19th The King's Royal Hussars

1st Army Tank Brigade – Brigadier D. H. Pratt
    4th and 7th Battalions Royal Tank Regiment

Not brigaded

    4th/7th Royal Dragoon Guards
    12th Royal Lancers
    13th/18th Royal Hussars
    1st Lothians and Border Yeomanry

Royal Artillery
    1st and 2nd Regiments Royal Horse Artillery
    32nd, 98th, 115th, 139th Army Field Regiments
    1st, 2nd, 4th, 58th, 61st, 63rd, 65th, 69th Medium Regiments
    1st, 51st, 52nd Heavy Regiments
    1st, 2nd, 3rd Super Heavy Regiments

1st Anti-Aircraft Brigade – Brigadier E. D. Milligan
  1st, 6th, 85th Anti-Aircraft Regiments

2nd Anti-Aircraft Brigade – Brigadier E. W. Chadwick
  60th Anti-Aircraft Regiment
  51st, 58th Light Anti-Aircraft Regiments

4th Anti-Aircraft Brigade – Brigadier J. N. Slater
  4th Anti-Aircraft Regiment
  1st Light Anti-Aircraft Battery

5th Searchlight Brigade – Brigadier E. Rait-Kerr
  1st, 2nd, 3rd Searchlight Regiments

Royal Engineers
  100th, 101st, 216th Army Field Companies
  228th and 242nd Field Companies
  223rd Field Park Company
  19th Army Field Survey
  58th, 61st, 62nd Chemical Warfare Companies
  In addition there were thirty-eight General Construction companies; two Road Construction, one Excavator, four Tunnelling companies and one Workshop and Park company; one Field Survey depot; and two Water-Boring sections.

Infantry
  1st Battalion Welsh Guards
    Machine-Gun
  7th Battalion The Cheshire Regiment
  1st/8th Battalion The Middlesex Regiment
  4th Battalion The Gordon Highlanders
  6th Battalion The Argyll and Sutherland Highlanders
    Pioneer
  6th, 7th, 8th, 9th Battalions The King's Own Royal Regiment
  7th Battalion The Royal Norfolk Regiment
  6th Battalion The Royal Scots Fusiliers
  1st/6th Battalion The South Staffordshire Regiment
    Garrison
  9th Battalion The West Yorkshire Regiment

1st Corps

Lieutenant General M. G. H. Barker

1st Division
2nd Division
48th Division

Corps Troops

Royal Artillery
  27th and 140th Army Field Regiments
  3rd and 5th Medium Regiments

52nd Light Anti-Aircraft Regiment
2nd Light Anti-Aircraft Battery
1st Survey Regiment

Royal Engineers
102nd, 107th, 221st Army Field Companies
105th Corps Field Park Company
13th Corps Field Survey Company

Infantry – Machine-Gun
2nd and 4th Battalions The Cheshire Regiment
2nd Battalion The Manchester Regiment

2nd Corps

Lieutenant General A. F. Brooke

3rd Division
4th Division
5th Division*
50th Division

Corps Troops

Royal Artillery
60th and 88th Army Field Regiments
53rd and 59th Medium Regiments
53rd Light Anti-Aircraft Regiment
2nd Survey Regiment

Royal Engineers
222nd, 234th, 240th Army Field Companies
108th Corps Field Park Company
14th Corps Field Survey Company

Infantry – Machine-Gun
2nd Battalion The Royal Northumberland Fusiliers
2nd and 1st/7th Battalions The Middlesex Regiment

3rd Corps

Lieutenant General Sir R. F. Adam, Bt

42nd Division
44th Division

Corps Troops

Royal Artillery
5th Regiment Royal Horse Artillery
97th Army Field Regiment
51st and 56th Medium Regiments

*in GHQ reserve on 10 May

54th Light Anti-Aircraft Regiment
3rd Survey Regiment

Royal Engineers
213th, 214th, 217th Army Field Companies
293rd Corps Field Park Company
514th Corps Field Survey Company

Infantry – Machine-Gun
7th Battalion The Royal Northumberland Fusiliers
1st/9th Battalion The Manchester Regiment
1st Battalion Princess Louise's Kensington Regiment, The Middlesex Regiment

1st Division

Major General The Hon H. R. L. G. Alexander
1st Guards Brigade – Brigadier M. B. Beckwith-Smith
3rd Battalion Grenadier Guards
2nd Battalion Coldstream Guards
2nd Battalion The Hampshire Regiment

2nd Brigade – Brigadier C. E. Hudson
1st Battalion The Loyal Regiment
2nd Battalion The North Staffordshire Regiment
6th Battalion The Gordon Highlanders

3rd Brigade – Brigadier T. N. F. Wilson
1st Battalion The Duke of Wellington's Regiment
2nd Battalion The Sherwood Foresters
1st Battalion The King's Shropshire Light Infantry

Divisional Troops

Royal Artillery
2nd, 19th, 67th Field Regiments
21st Anti-Tank Regiment

Royal Engineers
23rd, 238th, 248th Field Companies
6th Field Park Company

2nd Division

Major General H. C. Loyd (to 16 May)
Brigadier F. H. N. Davidson (acting from 16 to 20 May)
Major General N. M. S. Irwin (from 20 May)

4th Brigade – Brigadier E. G. Warren
1st Battalion The Royal Scots
2nd Battalion The Royal Norfolk Regiment
1st/8th Battalion The Lancashire Fusiliers

5th Brigade – Brigadier G. I. Gartlan
2nd Battalion The Dorsetshire Regiment

1st Battalion The Queen's Own Cameron Highlanders
7th Battalion The Worcestershire Regiment

6th Brigade – Brigadier N. M. S. Irwin (to 20 May)
Brigadier D. W. Furlong (from 20 May)
    1st Battalion The Royal Welch Fusiliers
    1st Battalion The Royal Berkshire Regiment
    2nd Battalion The Durham Light Infantry

Divisional Troops

Royal Artillery
    10th, 16th, 99th Field Regiments
    13th Anti-Tank Regiment

Royal Engineers
    5th, 209th, 506th Field Companies
    21st Field Park Company

3rd Division

Major General B. L. Montgomery

7th Guards Brigade – Brigadier J. A. C. Whitaker
    1st and 2nd Battalion Grenadier Guards
    1st Battalion Coldstream Guards

8th Brigade – Brigadier C. G. Woolner
    1st Battalion The Suffolk Regiment
    2nd Battalion The East Yorkshire Regiment
    4th Battalion The Royal Berkshire Regiment

9th Brigade – Brigadier W. Robb
    2nd Battalion The Lincolnshire Regiment
    1st Battalion The King's Own Scottish Borderers
    2nd Battalion The Royal Ulster Rifles

Divisional Troops

Royal Artillery
    7th, 33rd, 76th Field Regiments
    20th Anti-Tank Regiment

Royal Engineers
    17th, 246th, 253rd Field Companies
    15th Field Park Company

4th Division

Major General D. G. Johnson

10th Brigade – Brigadier E. H. Barker
    2nd Battalion The Bedfordshire and Hertfordshire Regiment
    2nd Battalion The Duke of Cornwall's Light Infantry
    1st/6th Battalion The East Surrey Regiment

11th Brigade – Brigadier K. A. N. Anderson

2nd Battalion The Lancashire Fusiliers
1st Battalion The East Surrey Regiment
5th Battalion The Northamptonshire Regiment

12 Brigade – Brigadier J. L. I Hawkesworth
2nd Battalion The Royal Fusiliers
1st Battalion The South Lancashire Regiment
6th Battalion The Black Watch

Divisional Troops

Royal Artillery
22nd, 30th, 77th Field Regiments
14th Anti-Tank Regiment

Royal Engineers
7th, 59th, 225th Field Companies
18th Field Park Company

5th Division

Major General H. E. Franklyn

13th Brigade – Brigadier M. C. Dempsey
2nd Battalion The Cameronians
2nd Battalion The Royal Inniskilling Fusiliers
2nd Battalion The Wiltshire Regiment

17th Brigade – Brigadier M. G. N. Stopford
2nd Battalion The Royal Scots Fusiliers
2nd Battalion The Northamptonshire Regiment
6th Battalion The Seaforth Highlanders

Divisional Troops

Royal Artillery
9th, 91st, 92nd Field Regiments
52nd Anti-Tank Regiment

Royal Engineers
38th, 245th, 252nd Field Companies
254th Field Park Company

12th (Eastern) Division

Major General R. L. Petre

35th Brigade – Brigadier-Colonel A. F. F. Young (acting 10–12 May)
Brigadier V. L. de Cordova (from 13 May)
2nd/5th, 2nd/6th, 2nd/7th Battalions The Queen's Royal Regiment

36th Brigade – Brigadier G. R. P. Roupell
5th Battalion The Buffs
6th and 7th Battalions The Queen's Own Royal West Kent Regiment

37th Brigade – Brigadier R. J. P. Wyatt
2nd/6th Battalion The East Surrey Regiment

6th and 7th Battalion The Royal Sussex Regiment

Divisional Troops

Royal Engineers
    262nd, 263rd, 264th Field Companies
    265th Field Park Company

23rd (Northumbrian) Division
Major General A. E. Herbert

69th Brigade – Brigadier The Viscount Downe
    5th Battalion The East Yorkshire Regiment
    6th and 7th Battalions The Green Howards

70th Brigade – Brigadier P. Kirkup
    10th and 11th Battalions The Durham Light Infantry
    1st Battalion The Tyneside Scottish, The Black Watch

Divisional Troops

Royal Engineers
    233rd and 507th Field Companies
    508th Field Park Company

Infantry
    8th Battalion The Royal Northumberland Fusiliers (motorcycle);
    9th Battalion The Royal Northumberland Fusiliers (machine-gun)

42nd (East Lancashire) Division
Major General W. G. Holmes

125th Brigade – Brigadier G. W. Sutton
    1st Battalion The Border Regiment
    1st/5th and 1st/6th Battalions The Lancashire Fusiliers

126th Brigade – Brigadier E. G. Miles
    1st Battalion The East Lancashire Regiment
    5th Battalion The King's Own Royal Regiment
    5th Battalion The Border Regiment

127th Brigade – Brigadier J. G. Smyth
    1st Battalion The Highland Light Infantry
    4th Battalion The East Lancashire Regiment
    5th Battalion The Manchester Regiment

Divisional Troops

Royal Artillery
    52nd and 53rd Field Regiments
    56th Anti-Tank Regiment

Royal Engineers
    200th, 201st, 250th Field Companies
    208th Field Park Company

44th (Home Counties) Division

Major General E. A. Osborne

131st Brigade – Brigadier J. E. Utterson-Kelso
    2nd Battalion The Buffs
    1st/5th and 1st/6th Battalions The Queen's Royal Regiment

132nd Brigade – Brigadier J. S. Steele
    1st, 4th, 5th Battalions The Queen's Own Royal West Kent Regiment

133rd Brigade – Brigadier N. I. Whitty
    2nd, 4th, 5th Battalions The Royal Sussex Regiment

Divisional Troops

Royal Artillery
    57th, 58th, 65th Field Regiments
    57th Anti-Tank Regiment

Royal Engineers
    11th, 208th, 210th Field Companies
    211th Field Park Company

46th (North Midland and West Riding) Division

Major General H. O. Curtis

137th Brigade – Brigadier J. B. Gawthorpe
    2nd/5th Battalion The West Yorkshire Regiment
    2nd/6th and 2nd/7th Battalions The Duke of Wellington's Regiment

138th Brigade – Brigadier E. J. Grinling
    6th Battalion The Lincolnshire Regiment
    2nd/4th Battalion The King's Own Yorkshire Light Infantry
    6th Battalion The York and Lancaster Regiment

139th Brigade – Brigadier H. A. F. Crewdson (to 22 May)
Brigadier R. C. Chichester-Constable (from 22 May)
    2nd/5th Battalion The Leicestershire Regiment
    2nd/5th and 9th Battalions The Sherwood Foresters

Divisional Troops

Royal Engineers
    270th, 271st, 272nd Field Companies
    273rd Field Park Company

48th (South Midland) Division

Major General A. F. A. N. Thorne

143rd Brigade – Brigadier J. Muirhead
    1st Battalion The Oxfordshire and Buckinghamshire Light Infantry
    1st/7th and 8th Battalions The Royal Warwickshire Regiment

144th Brigade – Brigadier J. M. Hamilton

2nd Battalion The Royal Warwickshire Regiment
5th Battalion The Gloucestershire Regiment
8th Battalion The Worcestershire Regiment

145th Brigade – Brigadier A. C. Hughes (to 15 May)
Brigadier The Hon. N. F. Somerset (from 15 May)
    2nd Battalion The Gloucestershire Regiment
    4th Battalion The Oxfordshire and Buckinghamshire Light Infantry
    1st Buckinghamshire Battalion The Oxfordshire and Buckinghamshire
Light Infantry

Divisional Troops

Royal Artillery
    18th, 24th, 68th Field Regiments
    53rd Anti-Tank Regiment

Royal Engineers
    9th, 224th, 226th Field Companies
    227th Field Park Company

50th (Northumbrian) Division

Major General G. le Q. Martel

150th Brigade – Brigadier C. W. Haydon
    4th Battalion The East Yorkshire Regiment
    4th and 5th Battalions The Green Howards

151st Brigade – Brigadier J. A. Churchill
    6th, 8th, 9th Battalions The Durham Light Infantry

25th Brigade – Brigadier W. H. C. Ramsden
    2nd Battalion The Essex Regiment
    1st Battalion The Royal Irish Fusiliers
    1st/7th Battalion The Queen's Royal Regiment

Divisional Troops

Royal Artillery
    72nd and 74th Field Regiments
    65th Anti-Tank Regiment

Royal Engineers
    232nd and 505th Field Companies
    235th Field Park Company

Infantry
    4th Battalion The Royal Northumberland Fusiliers (motorcycle)

51st (Highland) Division

Major General V. M. Fortune

152nd Brigade – Brigadier H. W. V. Stewart
    2nd and 4th Battalions The Seaforth Highlanders
    4th Battalion The Queen's Own Cameron Highlanders

153rd Brigade – Brigadier G. T. Burney
    4th Battalion The Black Watch
    1st and 5th Battalions The Gordon Highlanders

154th Brigade – Brigadier A. C. L. Stanley-Clarke
    1st Battalion The Black Watch
    7th and 8th Battalions The Argyll and Sutherland Highlanders

Divisional Troops

Royal Artillery
    17th, 23rd, 75th Field Regiments
    51st Anti-Tank Regiment

Royal Engineers
    26th, 236th, 237th Field Companies
    239th Field Park Company

When the 51st Division moved to the Saar in April 1940, the following troops were attached to the division:

Royal Armoured Corps
    1st Lothians and Border Yeomanry*

Royal Artillery
    1st Regiment Royal Horse Artillery (less one battery)*
    97th Field Regiment (one battery)**
    51st Medium Regiment*

Royal Engineers
    213th Army Field Company**

Infantry
      Machine-Gun
    7th Battalion The Royal Northumberland Fusiliers**
    1st Battalion Princess Louise's Kensington Regiment, The Middlesex Regiment**
      Pioneer
    7th Battalion The Royal Norfolk Regiment*
    6th Battalion The Royal Scots Fusiliers*

Lines of Communication Troops

Major General P. de Fonblanque

Royal Artillery

3rd Anti-Aircraft Brigade – Brigadier W. R. Shilstone
    2nd, 8th, 79th Anti-Aircraft Regiments
    4th Light Anti-Aircraft Battery

Royal Engineers

*From GHQ Troops
**From 3rd Corps

104th, 106th, 110th, 212th, 218th Army Troops Companies
In addition there were four Road Construction companies, twelve Artisan Works companies, three General Construction companies, one Map depot, two Engineer Stores (Base) depots, Engineer Base Workshop, one section Forestry company, and lines of communication depot.

Infantry
4th Battalion The Buffs
14th Battalion The Royal Fusiliers
12th Battalion The Royal Warwickshire Regiment
4th Battalion The Border Regiment
1st/5th Battalion The Sherwood Foresters
In addition there were two infantry and two general base depots.

With the Advanced Air Striking Force

Royal Artillery

12th Anti-Aircraft Brigade – Brigadier W. T. O. Crewdson
53rd and 73rd Anti-Aircraft Regiments

The following arrived in France during May and June

1st Armoured Division

Major General R. Evans

2nd Armoured Brigade – Brigadier R. L. McCreery
The Queen's Bays
9th Queen's Royal Lancers
10th Royal Hussars

3rd Armoured Brigade – Brigadier J. G. Crocker
2nd and 5th Battalions Royal Tank Regiment
(The 3rd Battalion was detached and sent to Calais – see below)

1st Support Group – Brigadier F. E. Morgan
101st Light Anti-Aircraft and Anti-Tank Regiment
(The infantry battalions were detached and sent to Calais – see below)

Divisional Troops

Royal Engineers
1st Field Squadron
1st Field Park Squadron

52nd (Lowland) Division

Major General J. S. Drew

155th Brigade – Brigadier T. Grainger-Stewart
7th/9th Battalion The Royal Scots
4th and 5th Battalions The King's Own Scottish Borderers

156th Brigade – Brigadier J. S. N. Fitzgerald
4th/5th Battalion The Royal Scots Fusiliers

6th and 7th Battalions The Cameronians

157th Brigade – Brigadier Sir J. E. Laurie, Bt
5th and 6th Battalions The Highland Light Infantry
1st Battalion The Glasgow Highlanders, The Highland Light Infantry

Divisional Troops

Royal Artillery
70th, 71st, 78th Field Regiments
54th Anti-Tank Regiment

Royal Engineers
202nd, 241st, 554th Field Companies
243rd Field Park Company

Defence of Boulogne

20th Guards Brigade – Brigadier W. A. F. L. Fox-Pitt
2nd Battalion Irish Guards
2nd Battalion Welsh Guards

Royal Artillery
275th Anti-Tank Battery, less one troop
69th Anti-Tank Regiment

Defence of Calais

30th Brigade – Brigadier C. N. Nicholson
2nd Battalion The King's Royal Rifle Corps
1st Battalion The Rifle Brigade
3rd Battalion Royal Tank Regiment
(all the above from 1st Armoured Division)
1st Battalion Queen Victoria's Rifles
The King's Royal Rifle Corps (motorcycle)

Royal Artillery
229th Anti-Tank Battery, less one troop
58th Anti-Tank Regiment

Communication at all levels between all the above units was provided by Royal Signals.

Royal Air Force

British Air Forces in France

Air Officer Commanding in Chief
Air Marshal A. S. Barratt

Senior Air Staff Officer
Air Vice Marshal D. C. S. Evill

Headquarters – North: Group Captain S. C. Strafford
East: Squadron Leader R. Cleland

Air Component

Air Vice Marshal C. H. B. Blount

No. 14 Group – Group Captain P. F. Fullard

No. 60 (Fighter) Wing – Wing Commander J. A. Boret
Nos 85 and 87 Squadrons

No. 61 (Fighter) Wing – Wing Commander R. Y. Eccles
Nos 607 and 615 Squadrons

No. 70 (Bomber Reconnaissance) Wing – Wing Commander W. A. Opie
Nos 18 and 57 Squadrons

No. 52 (Bomber) Wing – Wing Commander A. F. Hutton
Nos 53 and 59 Squadrons

No. 50 (Army Co-operation) Wing – Group Commander A. R. Churchman
Nos 4, 13, 16 Squadrons

No. 51 (Army Co-operation) Wing – Wing Commander A. H. Flower
Nos 2 and 26 Squadrons
No. 81 (Communication) Squadron

Advanced Air Striking Force

Air Vice Marshal P. H. L. Playfair

No. 71 (Bomber) Wing – Air Commodore R. M. Field
Nos 105, 114, 139, 150 Squadrons

No. 75 (Bomber) Wing – Group Captain A. H. Wann
Nos 88, 103, 218 Squadrons

No. 76 (Bomber) Wing – Group Captain H. S. Kerby
Nos 12, 142, 226 Squadrons

No. 67 (Fighter) Wing – Wing Commander C. Walter
Nos 1 and 73 Squadrons
No. 212 (Photographic Reconnaissance) Squadron

Home Commands

Groups principally concerned in air fighting in France and Belgium

Fighter Command

Air Chief Marshal Sir Hugh Dowding

No. 11 Group – Air Vice-Marshal K. R. Park
Nos 3, 25, 32, 54, 56, 64, 65, 74, 79, 92, 111, 145, 151, 253, 501, 600, 601, 604, 609, 610 Squadrons

The following squadrons were also temporarily under operational command of No. 11 Group:

(From No. 12 Group) – Nos 17, 19, 66, 213, 222, 229, 264, 266, 504, 611 Squadrons

(From No. 13 Group) – Nos 41, 43, 72, 242, 245, 605, 616 Squadrons

Note Nos 3 and 79 Squadrons were sent to the Air Component and No. 501 Squadron to the Advanced Air Striking Force as reinforcements on 10 May; No. 504 Squadron reinforced the Air Component on 12 May; Nos 17 and 242 Squadrons joined the Advanced Air Striking Force as reinforcements on 8 June 1940.

Bomber Command

Air Marshal C. F. A. Portal

No. 2 Group – Air Vice Marshal J. M. Robb
  Nos 15, 21, 40, 52, 82, 107, 110 Squadrons

No. 3 Group – Air Vice Marshal J. E. A. Baldwin
  Nos 9, 31, 37, 38, 75, 99, 115, 149 Squadrons

No. 4 Group – Air Vice Marshal A. Coningham
  Nos 10, 51, 58, 71, 77, 102 Squadrons

No. 5 Group – Air Vice Marshal A. T. Harris
  Nos 44, 49, 50, 61, 83, 144 Squadrons

Coastal Command

Air Chief Marshal Sir Frederick Bowhill

No. 16 Group – Air Vice Marshal J. H. S. Tyssen
  Nos 22, 48, 206, 220, 235, 236, 500 Squadrons

  With the following temporarily under operational control:
  (From No. 17 Group) – No. 248 Squadron
  (From No. 18 Group) – No. 254 Squadron

  The following squadrons of the Fleet Air Arm were also temporarily under operational control of No. 16 Group:
  Nos 801, 812, 815, 816, 818, 819, 825, 826 Squadrons

German Armed Forces

Supreme Commander

Adolf Hitler

High Command of the Armed Forces
(Oberkommando der Wehrmacht [OKW])

Chief of OKW
Colonel General Keitel

Chief of Operations Staff
Major General Jodl

Commander-in-Chief German Navy   Grand Admiral Raeder
Head of Luftwaffe   Field Marshal Goering

Army High Command (Oberkommando des Heeres [OKH])
Commander-in-Chief Colonel General von Brauchitsch
Chief of Army General Staff General Halder

Army Group A	Army Group B	Army Group C

Army Group A consisted of Armoured Corps and contained 2nd, 4th, 12th and 16th Armies.

Fourth Army contained the Kleist and Hoth Groups. Kleist Group contained Guderian's 19th Corps and also 21st Corps. The Hoth Group contained 16th and 39th Corps. The other armies do not figure prominently so are omitted here.

Army Group B were all infantry corps and came under the command of Colonel General von Bock.

Army Group C was commanded by General von Leeb and was deployed against the Maginot Line.

The Waffen SS (Schutzstaffel) were administered by the Nazi party, but came under the command of the OKH in the field.

French Army Organization

Prior to January 1940 General Gamelin was Commander-in-Chief of the land forces in all theatres of war. He was assisted by General Georges, who was Deputy Commander for the North-East Front, which consisted of France itself. (The other fronts included the Alps and the North African Front.)

In January 1940 Georges became Commander of the North-East, leaving Gamelin in charge of co-ordinating operations and liaison with the Allies. Gamelin soon divested himself of the task of liaison with the Allies, a post which initially went to Georges but on 12 May was passed to General Billotte, without Gamelin being aware of the fact.

The French Army was in three groups. General Billotte commanded the forty divisions facing Belgium, General Prétalat commanded the twenty-six divisions in the Maginot Line, and General Besson commanded thirty-six divisions deployed against the Swiss frontier and Italy. There were thirty-two other divisions in reserve, but these did not contain a tank reserve.

Belgian and Dutch Armies

The Belgians had twenty divisions; the Dutch ten.

Select Bibliography

Anon, *Diary of a Staff Officer*, London 1940

Anon, *Infantry Officer*, London 1943

Balbaud, R., *Cette Drôle de Guerre*, Oxford 1941

Barlone, D., *A French Officer's Diary, August 1939–October 1940*, Cambridge 1942

Barnett, C., *The Audit of War*, London 1986

Bartlett, Captain Sir B., *My First War*, London 1940

Bauer, E., *Der Panzerkrieg*, Bonn 1965

Benoist-Méchin, J., *Sixty Days that Shook the West*, London 1956

Bloch, Marc, *Strange Defeat*, Oxford 1949

Bond, B., *France and Belgium 1939–40*, London 1975

Bucheit, Gert, *Der Deutsche Geheimdienst*, Munich 1966

Butler, J. R. M., *Grand Strategy, Vol. II (Official History)*, London 1959

Churchill, W. S., *The Second World War, Vols I and II*, London 1949

Colville, J., *The Fringes of Power: Downing Street Diaries, Vol. I 1939–1941*, London 1985

——, *Man of Valour, The Life of Field Marshal Viscount Gort*, London 1972

Ellis, Major L. F., *The War in France and Flanders 1939–40 (Official History)*, London 1953

Fraser, General Sir D., *Alanbrooke*, London 1982

——, *And We Shall Shock Them*, London 1983

Fuller, Major General J. F. C., *The Second World War 1939–45*, London 1954

Gamelin, General M., *Servir: Les Armées Françaises de 1940*, Paris 1946

Gardner, C., *A.A.S.F.*, London 1940

de Gaulle, General Charles, *War Memoirs, Vol. I 1940–42*, London 1955

Gorlitz, Walter, *The Memoirs of Field Marshal Keitel*, London 1958

Goutard, Colonel A., *The Battle of France 1940*, London 1958

Guderian, H., *Mit den Panzern in Ost und West*, Stuttgart 1942

——, *Panzer Leader*, London 1952

Gunsburg, J. *Divided and Conquered*, Connecticut 1979

Habe, Hans, *A Thousand Shall Fall*, London 1942

Hadley, P., *Third Class to Dunkirk*, London 1944

Halder, Franz, *Kriegstagebuch* (3 vols), Stuttgart 1962–4

Haupt, Werner, *Sieg ohne Lorbeer*, Holstein 1965

Hinsley, F. H., *British Intelligence in the Second World War, Vol. I (Official History)*, London 1979

Horne, A., *To Lose a Battle*, London 1969

Ironside, Field Marshal Lord, ed. R. Macleod and D. Kelly, *The Ironside Diaries 1937–40*, London 1962

Ismay, General The Lord, *Memoirs*, London 1960

Jackson, R., *The Fall of France, May–June 1940*, London 1975

Jacobsen, H. A. and J. Rohwehr, *Decisive Battles of World War II: The German View*, London 1965

Jacobsen, H. A. and A. L. Smith, *World War II: Policy and Strategy – Documents*, Santa Barbara, California 1979

de Jong, Louis, *The German Fifth Columns in the Second World War*, London 1956

Leverkucha, Paul, *German Military Intelligence*, London 1954

Liddell-Hart, B. H., *The Other Side of the Hill*, London 1948

——, *The Tanks 1939–45*, London 1959

——, *Memoirs*, London 1963

Lottman, H. R., *Pétain – Hero or Traitor*, London 1985

Macksey, K., *The Tank Pioneers*, London 1981

Macnab, R., *For Honour Alone: the Cadets of Saumur in the Defence of the Cavalry School, France, June 1940*, London 1988

von Manstein, Field Marshal, *Lost Victories*, London 1958

von Manteuffel, General Hasso, *Die 7 Panzerdivision im Zweiten Weltkrieg*, Cologne 1965 von Mellenthin, Major General F. W., *Panzer Battles 1939–45*, London 1955

Mengin, Robert, *No Laurels for de Gaulle*, London 1967

Mrazek, Colonel James C., *The Fall of Eben Emael*, n.d.

Namier, L. B., *Europe in Decay*, London 1950

Neave, A., *The Flames of Calais*, London 1972

Rommel, Field Marshal E., ed. B. H. Liddell-Hart, *The Rommel Papers*, London 1951

de Saint-Exupéry, A., *Flight to Arras*, London 1942

Shepherd, R., *A Class Divided*, London 1988

Shirer, W. L., *The Rise and Fall of the Third Reich*, London 1962

Spears, E. L., *Assignment to Catastrophe* (2 vols), London 1954

Stoves, Rolf, *I Panzer Division 1935–45*, Bad Nauheim 1962

Terraine, J., *The Right of the Line*, London 1985

Vilfroy, D., *War in the West*, Harrisburg, Pennsylvania 1942

Voisin, Pierre, *Ceux des Chars*, Lyon 1941

Waterfield, G., *What Happened to France*, London 1940

Weiss, Wilhelm, ed., *Der Krieg im Westen*, Munich 1941

Weygand, General M., *Recalled to Service*, London 1952

Woods, R., *A Talent to Survive*, London 1982

Index

Index